ALSO BY ED VIESTURS WITH DAVID ROBERTS

The Will to Climb

K2

No Shortcuts to the Top

THE
MOUNTAIN

My Time on Everest

▲ ▲ ▲

ED VIESTURS
WITH DAVID ROBERTS

A Touchstone Book
Published by Simon & Schuster
New York   London   Toronto   Sydney   New Delhi

Touchstone
A Division of Simon & Schuster, Inc.
1230 Avenue of the Americas
New York, NY 10020

First Touchstone hardcover edition October 2013

TOUCHSTONE and colophon are registered trademarks
of Simon & Schuster, Inc.

For information about special discounts for bulk purchases,
please contact Simon & Schuster Special Sales at
1-866-506-1949 or business@simonandschuster.com.

The Simon & Schuster Speakers Bureau can bring authors
to your live event. For more information or to book an event,
contact the Simon & Schuster Speakers Bureau at
866-248-3049 or visit our website at www.simonspeakers.com.

Designed by Akasha Archer

Manufactured in the United States of America

10   9   8   7   6   5   4   3

Library of Congress Cataloging-in-Publication Data

Viesturs, Ed.
    The mountain : my time on Everest / Ed Viesturs with David Roberts.
        pages   cm
    1. Viesturs, Ed.   2. Mountaineers—United States—Biography.
3. Mountaineering—Everest, Mount (China and Nepal)   4. Everest, Mount
(China and Nepal)—Description and travel.   I. Roberts, David, date.   II. Title.
    GV199.42.V54A3   2013
    796.522095496—dc23   2013010320
ISBN 978-1-4516-9473-4
ISBN 978-1-4516-9475-8 (ebook)

This book is dedicated to the many friends with whom I have had the pleasure of experiencing the challenge of Everest on my eleven expeditions. In so many ways they all contributed to my success and survival.

Eric Simonson
George Dunn
Greg Wilson
Craig Van Hoy
Andy Politz
Jim Whittaker
Robert Link
Steve Gall
Kurt Papenfus
Hall Wendel
Wong Chu Sherpa
Carolyn Gunn
Rob Hall
Scott Fischer
Paula Viesturs
Jan Arnold
David Breashears
Robert Schauer
Araceli Segarra
Jamling Norgay
Guy Cotter
Veikka Gustafsson
Dave Carter
Jimmy Chin
Peter Whittaker
Also with great thanks to the many Sherpas,
too numerous to list individually.
They are truly the unsung heroes of
Everest.

Contents

Introduction

Ed Viesturs is fond of twofers. No, not two burgers, but still two for the price of one. Ed's favored twofers are 8,000-meter peaks. A high altitude mountaineer has to have a big appetite just to savor one a season. But two? Well first, twofers nearly halve the cost. An even bigger advantage is being able to shuttle from peak one to peak two while already acclimatized and not too wasted from the first effort.

This book, *The Mountain*, offers other twofers. Though it speaks to us with Ed's first-person voice, it has two authors—Viesturs and Dave Roberts—two brains speaking through one mouth. Ed and Dave are friends. Both are climbers, though from different generations. Roberts's profession has been as a writer and as a teacher of writing at Hampshire College. Over the course of three prior collaborations they have achieved a symbiosis in which the whole is more than the sum of the parts.

Another twofer in *The Mountain:* first is a rich and introspective account of Ed's eleven Everest expeditions, integrated seamlessly within the broader context of his mountain journeys and of the rest of his life. The other part of this twofer is a concise, compelling account of the history of our human affair with the highest mountain on earth, from the discovery of Peak XV's height through early exploration to its first ascent in 1953 to the pioneering of new routes in new seasons and climbing in increasingly purer style.

Viesturs is best known as the first American to climb all fourteen of the 8,000-meter peaks. His quest was a tenacious sixteen-year commitment from Kangchenjunga in 1989 to Annapurna on his third attempt in 2005.

One cannot but wonder what enables a few determined human beings to accomplish such a feat. From the perspective both of a climber and a high altitude physiologist, I will speculate a bit on how Ed Viesturs and his select community of high-altitude wanderers manage to perform so well on 8,000-meter peaks without the use of supplemental oxygen. Are they a different beast from the average climber? In some ways, yes. In others, no.

One difference is evolution in style. A half-century ago, as members of the 1963 American Mount Everest Expedition, a few of us attempted a new route. Willi Unsoeld and I were indulging in brief bits of high-angle rock climbing on our summit day, with nearly forty pounds of oxygen cylinders as ballast in our Kelty packs. Our use of supplemental oxygen effectively lowered the physiologic altitude, which (presumably) more than offset the weight handicap. In his seminal essay "Games Climbers Play," Lito Tejada-Flores posited the need for uncertainty in climbing (and hence motivation, as Dick Emerson, our West Ridge sociologist teammate, opined). In 1963 there was plenty of uncertainty to keep us motivated, but each such element pushes back the boundaries of the unknown. To keep the outcome in doubt means ramping up the rules of the game. In mountaineering, that change has been toward a simpler, lighter, faster style. One example: Messner and Habeler's 1978 ascent of Everest without the use of supplemental oxygen represented a major paradigm shift in the style of high-altitude mountaineering. Of Ed's seven successful ascents of Everest, he topped out on three occasions just breathing the air around him. (When with clients,

Ed believes the guide should also use oxygen to optimize the well-being of the entire team.)

Another big change in climbing these high mountains is the amount of time and effort committed to the task. Our 1963 expedition was gone from home for nearly five months, more than twice the time involved in an Everest climb nowadays. I remember coming down from our traverse of Everest in1963 a tad tired and many pounds lighter. Part of the exhaustion was inherent in expedition-style climbing, which involved days and weeks of hanging out at high altitudes, humping loads, breaking trail, and putting in camps. In contrast, the current alpine style of light, fast ascents once one is acclimatized adds up to a lot less work and a lot less time spent physically and mentally deteriorating in the so-called Death Zone. Back then, mountain twofers were beyond imagination.

Are individuals like Ed Viesturs different physiologically from others? Perhaps. Over a decade ago, my colleague, Dr. Robert (Brownie) Schoene, a pulmonary and exercise doc at the University of Washington, put Viesturs through his paces on a treadmill, seeking an explanation for why Ed performs so well at extreme altitude. The findings? Ed's maximum work capacity is on par with that of an endurance athlete—his heart was able to deliver far more blood to exercising muscle than the average person's heart. But at extreme altitude, a person can only work at 20–25 percent of his or her sea-level maximum; the heart's ability to pump far exceeds the demands placed upon it. More intriguing was Dr. Schoene's observation that Ed was able to perform sustained work at 85 percent of his maximum (VO_2max); most mortals can manage only 55–60 percent of their maximum. Whether this difference in work capacity helps explain his exceptional high-altitude performance is an intriguing question that has yet to be investigated.

Another critical factor that may help explain better performance at high altitude (or any altitude, for that matter) is "efficiency," the ability to perform work at a lower oxygen cost. One can perceive this gift of efficiency in the seemingly effortless movement of the virtuoso long-distance runner. Studies to quantify the contribution of efficiency to performance are not easy to design, yet that capacity to get a bigger bang for the oxygen buck is likely one more factor that separates the Viesturs of the high mountain world from the average climber.

Although the physiology of exceptional human performance is intriguing, a lot of the story of such accomplishment comes from the mental side. Ed Viesturs began his high mountain quest one summit at a time. He found he was good at it, and his need for greater uncertainty morphed into his quest to climb all fourteen 8,000 meter peaks, and he wanted to do it without supplemental oxygen. His was not a unique goal. Reinhold Messner did it first, and Jerzy Kukuczka was not far behind. As I write, the 8,000-meter club is still pretty exclusive, numbering approximately 30 persons, only about half of whom, Ed among them, have climbed all fourteen without supplemental oxygen. In that, he emulated Messner's style, and, like Messner, he imposed his own personal limit on the amount of risk he was willing to accept.

By the very nature of their activity, climbers are anything but risk averse, but they differ greatly among themselves on just how much risk is palatable. At one extreme are the adrenaline junkies or stimulus addicts, who, if their life is not on the thin edge, come away feeling unfulfilled. That group has a high mortality. The majority of committed climbers aren't that extreme—from my perspective, Ed Viesturs had (and has) a lower tolerance than most for the prospect of dying on a mountain. To have the will to turn around a few hundred yards short of the summits of Everest and Shishapangma, or to part company with his climbing partners on Annapurna and descend because he didn't feel the conditions were right, bespeaks a perspective on life in which the climbing of a mountain is just a part. That's often forgotten in the intensity of the moment. Perhaps out of all that Ed Viesturs has done in his climbing life, it's this uncommon attribute that impresses me the most. If I examine my own past sins, Willi Unsoeld and I might well be accused of throwing caution to the winds on our West Ridge climb in 1963. True, back then, our feeling that this was a one-shot opportunity was part of the underpinning, but the tradeoff of a possibly shortened life simply did not intrude upon our thoughts. Ed seems different in the way he placed his passion into the context of life at large.

Several efforts to analyze the relationship between climbing experience (measured by numbers of expeditions) and expedition outcome (defined by success in summiting and death rate) have come to a common and curious conclusion. Analysis of the Elizabeth Hawley-Richard Salisbury database for all climbs on 8,000-meter peaks in Nepal has found that though the probability of reaching the summit increases appreciably with increasing experience, the likelihood of dying appears to be unrelated to the amount of experience. The reasons for this are unclear. Experience is not the same thing as one's willingness (or unwillingness) to accept risk. To my mind, Ed's thesis that the caution he has imposed upon his high-altitude sojourns has contributed to his long-term survival seems quite reasonable.

But I have to think that there's been another, ephemeral player in the game: *luck*. Luck is an unpredictable event that, like risk, can be bad or good, which happens *to* us, and is not something of our making. It's pervasive in all aspects of our lives, including wandering among high Himalayan hills. On our 1963 American Mount Everest Expedition, we had both extremes. Jake Breitenbach's death in the Icefall was our biggest bad luck. Though not to downplay the role of commitment, our success on a new route on Everest and our survival of an unintended bivouac above 28,000 feet were in no small part a consequence of good luck, with near-ideal conditions at critical moments. Looking again at Liz Hawley's database for about sixty attempts on our West Ridge route over the ensuing half century, a 10 percent success rate with deaths exceeding the number summiting gives a sense that we just happened to be in the right place at the right time. We were lucky. The word "luck" does not feature much in Ed's personal account, but it seems to me an inescapable complement to his approach to the world's highest places.

It's clear from Ed Viesturs's eleven journeys to Everest that this mountain holds a special place among his high-altitude wanderings. I hope you will be as entranced as I by his account of his affair with this thinnest of air.

Tom Hornbein
Estes Park, Colorado
May 2013

THE
MOUNTAIN

So Close, and Yet . . .

The first time I tried to climb Mount Everest was in the spring of 1987. It was a very different mountain then from the swarmed-over scene it's become today. By that spring, there had been only 209 successful ascents of the mountain by 191 different climbers. A single person, the Sherpa Sungdare, had reached the summit as many as four times.

It's become almost impossible nowadays to keep track of Everest statistics, but by the end of May 2012, the number of successful ascents was in the vicinity of 6,000, performed by about 3,500 climbers. Two indefatigable veterans, Apa Sherpa and Phurba Tashi Sherpa, have now reached the top of the world twenty-one times each.

In the spring of 2012 there were more than thirty different expeditions simultaneously trying to climb Everest via the South Col route, the line by which it was first ascended by Tenzing Norgay and Edmund Hillary in 1953. I saw photos on the Internet of as many as 150 climbers on the Lhotse Face, lined up like Depression jobseekers in a free-lunch queue, as they jumared their way up the fixed ropes. In contrast, on the north side of Everest in the spring of 1987, there were only three teams. Ours hoped to climb the Great Couloir from the head of the Central Rongbuk Glacier. A Swedish team had chosen the traditional route from the North Col up the northeast ridge. And a Canadian, Roger Marshall, was attempting a bold solo ascent via the Japanese and Hornbein couloirs—a route nicknamed the Super Direct.

In 1987, I myself was a different person from the mountaineer who, eighteen years later, would become the first American to get to the top of all fourteen peaks in the world higher than 8,000 meters (26,246 feet). I was twenty-seven years old, and though I'd climbed Denali in Alaska twice and had served for five years as a guide on Mount Rainier, this was my first expedition to an 8,000er. No matter how much I'd read about Everest, I was awed by the scale and majesty of the mountain, and not at all sure I was up to the challenge of scaling its north face by the Great Couloir.

The expedition was put together by Eric Simonson, a seasoned veteran who was also my fellow guide for Rainier Mountaineering, Inc. (RMI). Although Eric was only four years older than I, he had been guiding since 1973, and I looked up to him as a mentor. He'd already been to Everest in 1982, with a team led by our RMI boss, Lou Whittaker, that reached 27,500 feet on the same route—still 1,500 feet short of the summit. Eric had been hampered by a bad knee after a falling rock struck him high on this daunting face, and in 1987 he was determined to give it another shot.

Our expedition was a bit of a boondoggle, for a climber from Arkansas named Jack Allsup had approached Eric, offering to raise all the funds and pay all the expenses for five RMI guides, if we'd serve as glorified Sherpas for him and his buddies. The deal was that we guides would fix ropes, establish camps, and carry loads up the route, but not actually guide the Arkansas gang on their attempt—simply set them up so they could make their own independent push toward the summit. The official name of our team was the Arkansas Everest Expedition. Quite an irony: here I was, a guy who had escaped the flatlands of the Midwest to immerse myself in the rich Pacific Northwest climbing culture, only to be going on my first Everest expedition with a team based in the South!

I was grateful to be invited by Eric, who two years earlier had chosen me to serve as his assistant guide on a traverse of Denali with clients. For Everest, Eric also picked my fellow RMI guides Greg Wilson, George Dunn, and Craig Van Hoy. A free trip to Everest! Who wouldn't jump at that opportunity?

Once our team was assembled, all five us plunged into gear selection and packing, but Eric took on the brunt of the logistical work. A smart, analytical fellow, he's good at that sort of thing. JanSport jumped aboard as an expedition sponsor, supplying clothing, tents, and packs. They also offered to have our high-altitude suits custom-made by an experienced local seamstress.

I was pretty excited at the thought of getting a high-tech suit for an attempt on the summit. I imagined an extremely lightweight, trim-fitting down suit like the ones I'd seen Reinhold Messner and Peter Habeler wearing in photos from their pathbreaking climb of Everest without supplemental oxygen in 1978.

Only a day or two before we had to leave Seattle, Eric and I drove up to our seamstress's house to collect the suits. When I hefted mine, my jaw nearly hit the floor. The suits were filled with bulky synthetic insulation, and the outer fabric felt more like canvas than lightweight nylon. Unnecessary doo-dads such as stripes winding around the sleeves added another heavy layer to the already bloated suits. Rather than the sleek Maserati outfits I had fantasized about, we had no choice but to head off to Everest with these cumbersome monstrosities.

I was just finishing my doctorate in veterinary medicine at Washington State University in Pullman, out on the state's eastern plains. I envisioned a career as a vet, although climbing was my true passion. To leave for Everest in March, I had to rearrange my senior-year schedule so that I could graduate two months early. Fortunately, my classmates and teachers fully supported my "hobby," going so far as to buy expedition T-shirts. Still, in 1987 I could not have dreamed of making a living as a mountaineer. As it was, earning a modest income guiding on Rainier in the summers, but pouring that money into my tuition bills, I was living as cheaply as I could, renting a room in the Seattle home of my buddy Steve Swaim, who ran his own veterinary clinic. Just before the expedition, a woman I'd been involved with for two years abruptly broke off our relationship. I was hurt and baffled, but in another sense, comfortable with the freedom that gave me. I was fresh out of school, with no full-time job or major obligations, so taking off to Asia for an indeterminate length of time didn't bother me one bit. As I wrote in my diary at base camp, "I guess my life's pretty simple & uncomplicated at this point—yahoo!"

My Denali expeditions, the longest I'd been on so far, had each lasted about three weeks. But Everest in 1987 would turn into a three-month-long ordeal by logistics, weather, and high-altitude conditioning—literally eighty-eight days' round-trip from Kathmandu. Although I'd never been above 20,320 feet, I'd already made up my mind to try Everest without bottled oxygen. The example of great mountaineers such as Messner had instilled in me a purist aesthetic. I didn't want to "lower" the mountain to my level simply to reach the summit, but rather to take on Everest at its level. And the prospect of having to carry oxygen bottles and wear an oxygen mask on my face, in effect isolating me from the mountain, was unappealing.

Yet having made that decision, I approached the challenge with a lot of trepidation and self-doubt. As early as March 28, I wrote in my diary, "I still wonder what it's like up there without oxygen—have to see how I do as we go higher. It'd be great to do it without O_2—gotta be strong though 'cuz the summit day is gonna be an ass buster, especially coming down wasted. Hope I at least get a chance for the top."

Today, a truck road leads through Tibet from Nepal, and a spur leads straight to base camp on the north side of Everest. It's become a milk run—albeit a bureaucratically tangled one—for trekkers and climbers alike. But in 1987, the north side felt so isolated that Eric claimed it was "like going off to the Moon!" The Great Couloir route that we were going to attack is not the easiest or safest way to climb Everest from the north. In 1924, the third British expedition to the mountain reached the North Col at 23,000 feet via the East Rongbuk Glacier, a hidden tributary that the reconnaissance expedition of 1921 had completely overlooked. From the North Col, a shallow spur leads up to the high crest of the northeast ridge. It was on this route that George Leigh Mallory and Andrew Irvine went for the summit on June 8, 1924, and never returned, launching one of the great mysteries in mountaineering history.

Our team, however, made no use of the East Rongbuk approach. Instead, we established an advance base camp (ABC) at only 18,300 feet at the head of the Rongbuk Glacier proper. From there, the face sweeps up in a daunting rise of more than 10,000 feet to the distant summit. The face is also far more threatened by falling rocks and avalanches than the North Col/northeast ridge route pioneered in 1924. Although Greg Wilson, George Dunn, and Eric Simonson had all tried Everest before without success, and all three desperately wanted to get to the top, Eric chose the harder north face route because he wanted to finish the line that he and George had attempted in 1982.

On a three-month expedition, there are bound to be tensions among the climbers. We had a cordial but ambivalent relationship with the Swedish team. Although we shared some meals with them at base camp and benefited greatly from weather forecasts their team received from back home, we had an uneasy truce about the route itself. The Swedes planned to go up the East Rongbuk to the North Col and follow the Mallory-Irvine route along the northeast ridge. It was only late in the expedition that they changed their plans and decided to go diagonally across the north face and go for the top via the Great Couloir, thereby overlapping with our line on the upper half of the mountain. This worried us, because it meant the Swedes would depend on our fixed ropes, and their presence in the Great Couloir might create additional hazards by virtue of having too many climbers on the same part of the mountain at the same time.

As for the Arkansas gang, their sponsorship of our attempt was something of a mixed blessing. It's true that the five of us could not have afforded an Everest expedition on our own, and we were very grateful to have our way paid. But several of the Arkansas climbers were, frankly, too weak to have a chance on Everest, and the stronger ones were infected with a mild case of hubris, underestimating the difficulty of the route and overestimating their own strength and ability.

In addition, tensions developed among our group of five guides. It was almost inevitable that the weeks of strain as we slowly advanced the route should produce conflicts. For various reasons, not everyone was able to contribute equally to that effort. That's a given on big expeditions: good teamwork depends on everyone making the contribution he can muster. And sometimes your effort is diminished not by any unwillingness to pull your weight, but by illness or trouble acclimatizing. Eric had also hired five Sherpas, who helped carry loads, especially for the Arkansas team members, but we RMI guides accomplished all the leading and fixing.

Though a savvy expedition leader, Eric had a tendency to find fault with others if he thought they hadn't performed up to his own high standards. One of the roles of a leader, to be sure, is keeping the expedition rolling at a steady and consistent pace, even if it means "directing" the show from below. But on April 7, after George, Greg, and I put in a strenuous day getting gear up to Camp III, Eric called us over the radio from Camp I and voiced his disappointment that we hadn't moved faster. As I wrote in my diary that evening, "Geo called him an asshole—only half jokingly—over the radio." Since George had been on Everest with Eric in 1982, their close friendship allowed this kind of sharp repartee. I didn't say a word. I'd already long since formed my resolve in the face of criticism by someone who was my boss. As I wrote in my diary, "I'll just do my job and keep my mouth shut. Actions speak louder than words!"

As I would subsequently learn on my thirty-one expeditions to 8,000-meter peaks, I almost never suffer at altitude from any kind of illness. I'd get the occasional mild headache after a long, hot day of climbing to a new high point, or a touch of traveler's diarrhea, but nothing incapacitating. Part of this is attributable to the rigorous conditioning I always undertake before an expedition. A lot of it has to do with simply being smart and knowing how to take care of myself. But part of it's the luck of my genes, which have given me a physiology that functions well with little oxygen in my lungs. I've never suffered frostbite or been afflicted by pulmonary or cerebral edema, which has stricken even the strongest mountaineers, including Simone Moro and Jean-Christophe Lafaille, who would become my partners on later expeditions.

But on Everest in 1987, from breathing the cold, dry air, I developed a sore throat so painful that I could barely speak above a whisper. It lasted for weeks, and added to my doubts about getting to the top. On April 17, I wrote, "My throat feels like raw meat from breathing this dry air—really painful. The only way to alleviate it is to suck on hard candies." Two days later: "I'm losing my voice—it's rough and crackles and makes me cough. . . . At night my throat gets really dry and painful. Last night I sucked candy, drank some cough suppressants and finally had to take some Nuprin just so I could sleep. Augh!!"

At ABC one night, desperate to halt the coughing, ease the pain, and get some sleep, I took twice the normal dose of hydrocodone, a morphine-based drug that not only has pain-relieving properties but is also a powerful cough suppressant. Sure enough, the pain and the cough went away, but the morphine filled my head with paranoid thoughts about how completely isolated we were and how far from any hope of rescue. My drug-addled anxiety kept me awake all night and I couldn't wait for the sun to come up and the drug to wear off!

At one point or another, all five of us RMI guides developed dry, hacking coughs. That's a common ailment on Himalayan expeditions. Climbers have even been known to break their ribs from coughing so hard. That's exactly what had happened to Greg Wilson on a 1984 expedition to the north side of Everest, wiping out his hopes of getting to the top. But in 1987, the nonstop coughing that spread among us like a contagion didn't help our morale, which through April and early May veered wildly up and down.

Slowly, however, we advanced the route, fixing ropes on all the hardest passages. And gradually my sore throat healed, and I began to feel really fit. Those days were long and arduous, and sometimes we didn't get back to camp till sunset. The fixed rope came in huge spools. One of us would uncoil the spool while the other climber pulled the free end behind him as he moved upward, placing intermediate anchors along the way. Once they were in, the ropes allowed safe passage on each subsequent load carry, and we could zip down them, often using just arm rappels, as we descended.

After a long day of fixing rope and hauling loads, getting back to camp didn't exactly amount to rest and relaxation. Outside the tent, we had to remove all of our climbing gear—crampons, harness, packs, and hardware. The first person into the tent took off his boots and outerwear, then started the stove to begin the tedious process of turning snow and ice into water. After drinking as much as we could and filling our water bottles, we had to scrounge up a dinner out of whatever we found in our food bags. Altitude and fatigue played havoc with our appetites. Dinner might mean ramen noodles with tuna and freeze-dried peas, or dehydrated lasagna, or instant mashed potatoes with cheese. If we were too tired, we'd settle for a cup of soup and some crackers. Rehydrating was more important than eating well. After hours of kitchen duty, we could finally crawl into our sleeping bags, but it was a rare night when we got enough sleep.

On May 14, we established Camp IV at 26,800 feet, only 2,200 feet below the summit. That may not seem like such a great distance to overcome, but the Great Couloir stays technically serious all the way, and a summit push over such terrain can take everything you've got.

Because of our deal with the Arkansas members, we also had to step aside at some point and give them their shot. We agreed that once we guides had made our own summit bids, the Arkansans could make their attempt. We went first not because we were selfish, but because it was up to us to establish the camps and fix the ropes. Privately, the five of us had our doubts that our "patrons" would be up to such a challenge, and we all dreaded a scenario in which, as they gave it their best try, they'd get in trouble and we'd have to go to their rescue. As it turned out, though, they were wise enough to know when to turn back. In the end, none of the Arkansas team got above 25,000 feet, and none of them got in trouble.

My own mood, after almost two months on the mountain, was a mixture of excitement and apprehension. As I wrote in my diary, "After all this time & effort it's exciting to start goin' for the top of this mother!!! . . . I have my fears and doubts about the last 2000'. How will I do? Can I handle the lack of O_2? . . . If I summit, how difficult will it be to descend?"

We decided that on May 16, George Dunn and Greg Wilson would get the first try to go to the top. As the other three of us lingered in a lower camp, resting to build up strength for our own attempt, George and Greg pushed up the route over several days. On May 16, I wrote, "Waiting, watching, waiting! We paced around camp all day like expectant fathers at the maternity ward. We watched the upper mountain with binoculars all day."

Both George and Greg had suffered previous disappointments on the north side of Everest. In October 1984, both were members of another team led by Lou Whittaker making a postmonsoon autumn attempt via the North Col and a diagonal traverse into the

Great Couloir. Despite breaking his rib from coughing, Greg had set out with three teammates from Camp V at 24,900 feet. Strong winds forced them to turn back short of the couloir, then pinned them in their camp for two more days. After that, Greg generously agreed to act in a supporting role to give three teammates—Jim Wickwire, Phil Ershler, and John Roskelley—a last-ditch chance to summit.

Phil and Jim were planning to use supplementary oxygen, but John would go for the summit without. By 1984, Roskelley was widely considered to be the strongest American high-altitude climber, having spearheaded routes on Makalu and Nanda Devi, as well as making the first ascents of such technically difficult mountains as Uli Biaho, Middle Trango Tower, and Gaurishankar. In 1982, in fact, Reinhold Messner, then in his prime, had declared that he thought Roskelley a stronger mountaineer than he was.

On October 20, the three men woke early at Camp VI, pitched at 26,600 feet in the Great Couloir. Wickwire had decided during the night that he would opt out of the bid to reach the top. As he later wrote in the *American Alpine Journal*, "My drive to reach the summit, which had been untrammeled in 1982 . . . was now inexplicably diminished." His teammates knew, however, about the terrible string of fatal accidents in recent years of which Jim had had the misfortune to be an eyewitness. And they knew that he had lost part of a lung to surgery after making, with Roskelley and two others, the first American ascent of K2 in 1978. On the descent, he had barely survived a solo bivouac in the open just below 28,000 feet, then had nearly succumbed to pneumonia and pleurisy that forced his heli-evacuation from the Baltoro Glacier.

At 6:15 on the morning of October 20, Roskelley and Ershler left the tent. John led the difficult pitches through the Yellow Band.

But conditions were unusually severe, and no matter how hard he climbed, he felt his hands and feet growing numb, and he started shivering in the first stages of hypothermia. John knew that to go on would probably mean severe frostbite, perhaps even death, so at 28,000 feet he made the agonizing decision to turn around. Breathing bottled oxygen made all the difference for Phil, who pushed on alone over the last thousand feet and summitted at 3:45 p.m. It was a magnificent achievement, for Phil ended up as the sole member of the very strong 1984 team to claim victory.

George Dunn had also played an important role on that expedition. A pair of Australians who had reached the summit earlier that season had left their tent pitched at their high camp in the Great Couloir. The Americans were counting on using that tent for their own summit bid. The day before the traverse, thwarted by high winds that stopped Greg and his teammates, George and two others had succeeded in getting to the Great Couloir, but they couldn't find the tent. They had to endure a miserable bivouac in the open, sitting on unstable rocks on the edge of the couloir, before retreating all the way to Camp III the next morning. After that, George was pretty much out of commission in terms of summit attempts.

George had also been on the 1982 expedition via the Great Couloir, when he, Eric, and Larry Nielson had made the team's only serious try for the top. The men had set out from their Camp VI at 26,500 feet, but Eric and George turned around at 27,000. Larry pushed on alone, without supplemental oxygen, gaining another 500 feet, but wisely retreated, knowing he would be stretching his margin of safety too thin. Even so, he suffered frostbite during the attempt and subsequently lost part of a thumb to amputation. Undaunted, Larry came back to Everest the next year and climbed it successfully from the opposite side, via the "standard" South

Col route. He pulled off that feat without bottled oxygen, the first American to do so. By 1987, no other American had gotten to the top without bottled O's—a fact I was keenly aware of as I made my own attempt to duplicate Larry's achievement.

Earlier, the 1982 expedition had suffered a tragedy when Marty Hoey, the only female member of the team, was hanging from her jumar on the fixed rope at 26,100 feet in the Great Couloir. Suddenly she was falling free. Jim Wickwire, standing only a few yards away, yelled, "Grab the rope!" Marty was sliding headfirst, but she rolled on her side and made a valiant effort to seize the fixed line, only to fail. Jim saw her plunge out of sight, knowing that her fall wouldn't end for 6,000 feet. In disbelief, he stared at the intact fixed rope. Dangling from it were Marty's jumar and her waist harness. Somehow she must have failed to double back the belt through the buckle, and her weight had caused the belt to come loose, allowing her whole body to slip out of the harness. Marty had removed her leg loops from her harness to save weight. Had those loops still been attached, they might have saved her life.

That shocking accident, witnessed up close by Wickwire, would obviously contribute to Jim's ambivalence about going for the summit in 1984.

Lou Whittaker later organized a search for Marty's body at the base of the face, but concluded that she had been swallowed up by a massive bergschrund separating the Rongbuk Glacier from the wall. Like those of so many other Everest victims, Marty's body has never been found.

In a sense, then, by 1987 George Dunn had more Everest "baggage" than any of us on Eric's team. As he and Greg Wilson went for the top on May 16, it was George's third attempt to solve the puzzle of the Great Couloir.

Both men were climbing with bottled oxygen, but their progress was slowed by difficult climbing through the famous Yellow Band. They overcame that obstacle, fixing rope as they went, but Greg later said that the pitches he led were some of the hardest and most dangerous climbing he'd done anywhere in the world, at any altitude. The two men reached 27,500 feet before deciding they had to turn back. It was 500 feet higher than George had gotten in 1982, but to have to retreat again with the summit almost within their grasp was a huge disappointment for him.

On the descent, however, George and Greg had a nearly disastrous accident—the closest call of our whole expedition. As they rappelled the fixed ropes they had placed that day, George, descending first, got to the end of the lowest rope, He had a single knifeblade piton, which he pounded into what he called "manky" rock, making for a very insecure anchor. Below him, a steep fifty-foot pitch on which the two had left no fixed rope filled George with malaise—it looked very hard to downclimb unprotected, and the men had brought no climbing rope to belay each other, but only the heavy spool of thin fixed rope they had strung through the Yellow Band.

The last fifty feet above George had been easy going on soft snow, so when Greg rapped into sight, George stopped him with a command: "Cut the rope!"

"Whaa—?" Greg protested. But soon he understood. If the two men could retrieve the unnecessary lowest fifty feet of fixed rope, they could affix it to the knifeblade piton and make one last rappel over the short passage that gave George pause. Greg got out his knife, severed the line, and brought it down with him.

They strung the salvaged fifty feet of rope from the "manky" knifeblade anchor. Again George rapped first. At the end of the rope, he hollowed out a kind of butt stance in which he could sit. He had no hardware left to put in an anchor, but the going below looked easy. Providentially, George kept the jumar attached to his harness fastened to the end of the salvaged fixed line.

Greg got on rappel and weighted the thin cord. He was about halfway down when the knifeblade anchor popped loose. All of a sudden he was falling backwards, out of control.

As George later told me, "I thought about Marty Hoey. I said to myself, *Oh my God, this is it! We're going all the way!* Greg fell past me, then started bouncing. All I could do was sit there and wait for the sudden jerk of the rope."

Miraculously, George's butt stance and the jumar held, stopping Greg's fall after forty feet. "Are you okay?" George yelled down, sure that his partner must have been badly injured.

"I . . . I think so!" came back the quavering answer.

"We were stunned," George later said. "That's about as close as you can come to dying in the mountains and get away with it."

A few days later, Eric, Craig Van Hoy, and I got our chance. We began working our way back up the mountain for what felt like the nth time. After spending the night at Camp III, just above 25,000 feet, we faced the arduous task of climbing the steep couloir to Camp IV. Before leaving Camp III, we put on our monstrous custom-designed suits, in which we would live for the next few days. Although there was a long fixed rope strung up the couloir, it had been frozen under a windslab of hard snow. With every step we took, we had to pull the rope upward to cut it loose from the windslab. It was excruciating and frustrating work.

By 8:00 p.m. on May 20, the three of us had crammed ourselves into the two-man tent at Camp IV. Our plan was to wake up at 1:00 a.m. (assuming we'd get any sleep at all) and be off by 4:00 a.m. Eric is a tall guy, well over six feet, and he seemed to need more space than Craig and I did. Eric also had an oxygen bottle from which he was breathing during the night nestled between us. Packed in like sardines, wearing our bulky suits, we kept kicking and elbowing each other as we shifted position. It was a really claustrophobic setup: at one point, I was jammed into the corner of the tent, with the nylon fabric of the wall only an inch away from my face. Had I been afflicted with true claustrophobia, there's no way I could have gotten through the night. The space in the tent was so tight that I gave up trying to take off my boots and slept with them on, draping my sleeping bag over me like a blanket instead of crawling inside it, boots and all. So much for a restful night before what I knew would be one of the hardest days of my life!

Craig had had a hard time getting from Camp III to Camp IV, and it was clear that the summit push was going to be an ordeal for him. The camp was situated in a truly exposed niche in the Great Couloir, with a "front porch" of snow only about two feet wide by three feet long. Beyond that shelf, the slope dropped off into what felt like an infinite abyss. Only one of us could maneuver outside the tent at a time, and we stayed clipped in to the anchors guying the tent whenever we were outside. Inside the tent you could pee into a bottle, but taking a dump meant going outside and risking your life.

In the morning, Eric got off first. He'd slept all night breathing his supplementary oxygen, and now he loaded his pack with two fresh bottles weighing a total of 36 pounds. Because he had all that weight, he asked me to carry our 500 feet of fixed rope and a few pitons and carabiners. That didn't really seem fair—since I was climbing without bottled oxygen, I wanted to go as light as possible—but as is my penchant, I didn't protest. I just said, "Yeah, okay." I got moving about fifteen minutes behind Eric. It was still dark out, but it looked as though a good day was in the offing.

A bit later, Craig got ready to leave. As we found out later, he took one look at the couloir stretching above Camp IV and decided against going for the top. Like Wickwire in 1984, Craig lacked the heart for the final push. The ground leading up to the Yellow Band, which had no ropes fixed on it, looked to him too steep and intimidating. Instead, he spent the day carefully descending all the way to Camp II. Each of us has to make his own decision about acceptable risk. For Craig, I think, going down was the right call.

Because Eric was climbing with his oxygen tank cranked to about two liters a minute, while I was going without oxygen, he was faster and stayed a little way ahead of me through the early hours of the morning. Climbing alone, I felt that I was moving in some isolated capsule. Unroped, we had to focus all our concentration as we zigzagged our way upward within the steep confines of the couloir. Then something odd happened: both my left foot and my left hand kept falling asleep. I couldn't figure out why, but it seemed alarming. I knew it wasn't frostbite, but I wondered if I might be experiencing a minor stroke, induced by altitude. It was worrisome enough that I seriously contemplated turning around and going down. I thought about Roskelley in 1984, struggling to stay warm without supplemental oxygen, and finally deciding to call it quits. But after a while the tingling sensation wore off, so I continued upward.

Then something else odd happened. Out of nowhere, one of the Swedish climbers, Lasse Cronlund, came bombing up on my heels. He had apparently traversed from high on his northeast ridge route and entered the Great Couloir very near our highest camp. It was a last desperate attempt by the Swede to salvage his fizzling expedition. He must have rationalized that he could benefit from our fixed ropes and our support on his way to the summit. He was climbing so much faster than I was that I figured he must have his own oxygen set cranked to the max, about four liters to the minute. I let him pass me. Then we met up at the foot of the Yellow Band, where Eric was waiting.

We needed to relead the pitch on which Greg Wilson had pulled loose the fixed rope in his forty-foot fall on May 16. Cronlund offered to go first. It was a mistake. As I later wrote in my diary, "He was clumsy & flailed around, wasted time. . . . At one point he was directly above me, looked as if he was going to fall over backwards & take me along for the ride!"

At last, with a desperate scramble, Cronlund got to the top of the pitch, where he lay gasping for air. Eric and I came up on the rope, then Eric took the lead. By now we had reached the bottom of the ropes fixed by Greg and George, so all we had to do was clip our jumars to the lines and half-climb, half-pull on the jumar as we ascended. But now I discovered that Cronlund didn't have an ascender of any kind. I ended up tying a prusik knot—the simple substitute for a mechanical ascender, named after the Austrian climber who invented it way back in the 1930s—for him.

As we climbed on, the Swede started to slow down. It looked as though Cronlund was trying to crank his oxygen set even higher, but he'd obviously used up his supply. Then, almost without pausing to give it a serious thought, he turned around and started descending. Without the boost of bottled O's, he'd shot his wad. Once he passed out of sight below us, we didn't see Cronlund again the rest of the day. And as it turned out, none of the Swedish team made the summit.

Climbing through the Yellow Band was arduous and scary. Thank God, George and Greg had fixed ropes here. Even with the aid of the lines, however, I had to scratch for tiny footholds with the front points of my crampons. The rock of the Yellow Band had the texture of a roughly troweled concrete wall—mostly smooth with random irregularities. I felt nothing but admiration for George and Greg. I guessed now that the effort of putting in the route through the Yellow Band had cost them any chance of getting to the summit. But it had given Eric and me a great opportunity.

Above the Yellow Band there was more steep snow, which eventually led to another layer of exposed rock called the Grey Band. It was here that we fixed the 500 feet of rope that I had been carrying all day. Eric found a passage through this section by climbing up a narrow snow couloir to the right

Amazingly, there was no wind. Shortly after noon, I followed Eric as I kicked my front points up the last 60-degree slope of hard snow and emerged from the couloir. This stretch was rather desperate, so I had to move quickly and couldn't afford my normal high-altitude pace of fifteen breaths per step. As a result, I became hypoxic, flopping onto the relatively flat ground above, gasping for air like a fish out of water. Once I had recovered, I looked at the last section of the climb above me. It dawned on me like a revelation—we were going to reach the summit!

In the postmonsoon season of 1984, Phil Ershler had faced only packed snow on the summit pyramid, so he had been able to climb straight up it to the top. In May 1987, that same pyramid was reduced to bare rock with a few patches of ice and snow, so now Eric had to angle right, traversing the slope until he intersected the top of the West Ridge route pioneered by Tom Hornbein and Willi Unsoeld in their gutsy climb in 1963. We were only 300 feet below the summit.

But Eric, still slightly faster with his bottled oxygen, climbed a short distance above me and ran into a steep rock wall with almost no foot- or handholds. (We would later realize that it was here that Hornbein and Unsoeld had passed their point of no return, necessitating a traverse of Everest down the South Col route to have any chance of surviving.) We were out of rope and pitons. Eric spent a little time traversing right and left, looking for a way through that last rock band. Then we conferred. "Ed," he said, "I think we could get up this thing, but there's no way we could get back down without a rope."

I stared upward long and hard. Afternoon clouds had started to gather, portending a possible storm. But only 300 feet lay between us and the highest point on Earth! At last, however, reason prevailed. I said to Eric, "All right. I agree."

We turned around and started down. It started snowing lightly, making the down-climbing all the hairier. We reached our tent at 5:30 p.m. Eric was so exhausted that on arriving he vomited in the snow. We spent one more miserable night in that cramped and spooky site. I got back to Camp II the next day, and to ABC the day after. Eric followed a few hours behind me.

Once I was safe and sound, the turn of fate that had thwarted us only 300 feet short of the summit seemed all the crueler. If I'd been able to top out, it would have meant not merely that I'd climbed an 8,000er on my first try. I would have been only the second American to climb Everest without supplemental oxygen, after my friend and fellow RMI guide Larry Nielson.

But on May 22, as I ran into my teammates in the lower camps, I learned some shocking news. The same day that Eric and I had gone for the summit, Roger Marshall, the daring Canadian, had tried to solo the north face by the Super Direct. Once he got up the Japanese Couloir, he reached the bottom of the Hornbein Couloir, but then turned around. My teammates had watched through binoculars as Marshall descended with agonizing slowness. They wondered if he was suffering from cerebral edema, which had afflicted him twice before on Himalayan climbs.

At some point—my friends didn't see it happen—Marshall slipped and fell to his death.

It may sound like an exaggeration, but I literally thought about those last 300 feet every day for the next three years. I knew I'd have to come back to Everest and give it another shot.

But I never second-guessed the decision Eric and I made in the early afternoon of May 21. By 1987, I had already absorbed the lessons that other climbers more experienced than I had sadly left in their wake, when the pull of the summit proved irresistible. Having now felt the tug of war between ambition and common sense firsthand, I could see how in many cases ambition wins out. In 1979, the Swiss-born Alaskan Ray Genet—one of the three men who had pulled off the first winter ascent of Denali in 1967—reached the summit of Everest so exhausted that he collapsed and died shortly below the top on the way down. And the tough and courageous Brit Mick Burke, a stalwart on the trailblazing first ascent of Annapurna's south face in 1970, pushed on toward the top of Everest as part of another British team forging the first ascent of the southwest face in 1975. Two of his teammates, having topped out themselves, waited for Burke at the South Summit, just 300 feet below the top, but he never reappeared. To this day, no one knows what happened to Burke, but his partners were convinced he reached the summit. Burke was very near-sighted, and had complained about his glasses fogging up. It may be that, as the mist and fog swirled around him, he made a misstep and fell down the huge Kangshung Face. Like Marty Hoey's, Burke's body has never been found.

Later, there was another source of solace in our defeat. As it turned out, during both the spring and fall campaigns on Everest in 1987, not a single climber reached the top by any route. The mountain repelled all its suitors. And 1987 was the last year that Everest pulled off that kind of shutout.

Eric and I could probably have gotten to the summit on May 21. But I'm not sure I'd be here to tell about it today. For all the remorse that turning back so close to the top flooded me with in the months and years after our attempt, I can see in retrospect that it was one of the best decisions I've made in my life. It allowed me to pursue my dream on thirty subsequent Himalayan expeditions.

That near miss in 1987 was the first vivid demonstration of a moral I would come to live by as I pursued all fourteen 8,000ers: *Listen to the mountain. You can always come back. It will still be there.*

2

▲ ▲ ▲

Because It Was There

The Everest disaster of 1996, when eight climbers died, including five in a sudden storm on May 10–11, seems to have fixed for good in the public imagination a picture of what the scene on the world's highest mountain has become. That spring, as a member of the IMAX team led by David Breashears, I got caught up in the tragedy, and we played a role in shepherding the most injured survivor, Beck Weathers, down to advance base camp and safety. The leaders of the two big guiding outfits on the south side of Everest, Rob Hall and Scott Fischer, both perished in the storm. Rob and Scott were close friends and former partners of mine, and sixteen years later, I still miss them and feel an ache of sorrow about their untimely deaths.

Jon Krakauer's vivid account of the 1996 disaster, *Into Thin Air*, was a number-one bestseller in 1997, and has since become an enduring classic. The scenario, however, that too many readers have taken away from the book reveals a curious urge to view the "Everest circus" as a deplorable corruption of what mountaineering and adventure ought to be about. In that scenario, Everest is flooded every spring and fall by yuppies willing to fork over as much as $65,000 apiece to be guided up the mountain, making no decisions by themselves except to plod upward, one foot after the other, sliding their ascenders along the fixed ropes that have been strung from base camp to the summit. The scenario paints the clients as novices so clueless they can't even put on their own crampons. Sandy Pittman, with her espresso machine, becomes the cartoon narcissist and Manhattan socialite who threatened to sue the very guides who saved her life. Anatoli Boukreev, the strongest climber on the mountain that year, is lastingly tarred as the guide who cared more about setting records on 8,000ers than taking care of his clients.

This is a far cry from my understanding of what happened in 1996. I've never viewed clients attempting Everest—especially the ones I've personally guided—as "clueless yuppies." I wrote about the disaster at length in *No Shortcuts to the Top*, my memoir of becoming the first American to reach the summits of all fourteen 8,000ers, and the sixth climber worldwide to do so without supplementary oxygen. In this book, I won't repeat the account I laid out in 2006. There are aspects of *Into Thin Air* with which I disagree, but on the whole, I think Jon told the story of that catastrophic season accurately and impartially. The scenario outlined above is a caricature of what Jon actually wrote, for his book is far more nuanced and sympathetic than the two-dimensional takeaway the public seized upon. It's not Jon's fault that *Into Thin Air* was succeeded by Michael Kodas's bitter, even vengeful *High Crimes: The Fate of Everest in an Age of Greed* or by Tami Knight's hilarious parody, *Everest: The Ultimate Hump*—as well as by the media frenzy that condemned the inhumanity of some forty climbers who allegedly passed by a dying David Sharp in 2006 without stopping to help or even ask if he was all right.

It's true enough that every spring and fall nowadays, Everest is besieged by climbers, a good percentage of them paying clients. The traffic jam on the South Col route on a summit day in May is a spectacle to behold—and a mob scene to avoid, if you're on the mountain. On a single day in 2012, May 26, no fewer than 150 climbers got to the top. Not all of them stood on the summit at the same time, but still, I can imagine what that gathering must have been like at its peak—a cacophony of voices in different languages giving orders and advice to each other and screaming their joy over two-way radios and sat phones. In moments like that, Everest indeed is reduced to a circus.

On my last Everest expedition, in 2009, I ran into a mob scene on the South Col route, though one not quite so jam-packed as the crowd that thronged the mountain in 2012. Had I been climbing for purely personal reasons, rather than working for an equipment company, I would probably have turned around rather than risk getting stuck in some chaotic survival drama. Everest in 2009 was almost the polar opposite of the experience I had on the mountain back in 1987. It's dismaying that this situation has evolved, but it may be inevitable. For the government of Nepal, permits are a cash cow. The officials in the Ministry of Tourism could hardly care less about overcrowding on the slopes of their most famous peak. And who are we to tell one of the poorest countries in the world how to handle its business?

My foremost intention in this book, however, is to counter the sordid caricature of Everest as a circus for dilettantes. Between 1987 and 2009, I've gone on eleven expeditions to the peak, so I've seen it develop from a state of relative innocence (if a mountain can be innocent) to the standing-room-only theater of recent years. Yet, having guided clients on Everest four times myself, I've seen firsthand how helping a competent client fulfill the dream of a lifetime can be not only a morally admirable act, but one that verges on ennobling. My own Everest stories are for the most part extremely positive ones. As much as on Annapurna or K2, on Everest I've learned lessons that translated fruitfully into the rest of my life, and that I think I can pass on to others.

As I survey the history of Everest from its first reconnaissance in 1921 through the present, moreover, I'm struck not by the follies and fiascos sprinkled through its past, but by some of the most visionary deeds in the long chronicle of mountaineering. It's those deeds—Unsoeld and Hornbein on the West Ridge, Messner soloing the northeast ridge without bottled oxygen in only three days, the Poles in winter, the Kangshung Face, and the like—that I wish to celebrate here.

In *K2: Life and Death on the World's Most Dangerous Mountain* and *The Will to Climb*, I interspersed chapters evoking the most significant deeds and tragedies in the climbing histories of the two toughest 8,000ers, K2 and Annapurna, with my own expeditions to those peaks. I was lucky enough (and determined enough) to get up K2 in 1992 on my first try, but that complex adventure formed a turning point in my career, remains my closest brush with death, and taught me the most valuable of all the lessons I've learned in the mountains—to listen to my instincts rather than ignore them. Annapurna became my personal nemesis, the last of the 8,000ers whose summit I reached, and then only on my third try in 2005, after I'd begun to think there was no route or style of assault safe enough to justify attempting.

My eleven expeditions to Everest add up to eight more than I've undertaken to any other 8,000er. Everest in a real sense has spanned my entire career as a mountaineer. I won't pretend that I returned to the world's highest mountain so often because it intrigued me more than K2 or Annapurna did (or for that matter, Nanga Parbat or Makalu). My motives have shifted and changed over the years. At first I hoped simply to get to the top. Then I had my stab at going after a hazardous new route on the peak, as well as trying to climb it solo (my only solo expedition to an 8,000-meter peak). Later I returned to Everest as a guide, and still later to participate in filmmaking projects. The last time, in 2009, my ostensible motive was to help launch a brand of outerwear and equipment, called First Ascent by Eddie Bauer, that I had a hand in designing and testing myself. But I'd also come to think of Everest as an "old friend" I wanted to visit again, and, on the verge of turning fifty, I wanted to see if I was still up to its always stern challenge. It amazes me that because of the large number of climbers attempting Everest today, the general public seems to think that the mountain has gotten easier. It's still 29,035 feet high, and it was just as hard for me in 2009 as it was more than two decades earlier.

It's not surprising, then, that I learned a tremendous amount about climbing and myself on Everest, a mountain on which I've now spent a cumulative two years of my life. All the peaks I've climbed—including not only K2 and Annapurna, but Mount Rainier, whose summit I've now reached 210 times—were like master teachers who shaped the person I am today.

Moreover, no mountain in the world has a richer or more varied history than Everest. The follies and mob scenes of recent years are really only blips in that chronicle. Although other writers have written massive tomes devoted to that history—most notably Walt

Unsworth, in his comprehensive 789-page *Everest: The Mountaineering History*—very few authors have combed the accounts of the last nine decades to glean the nuggets of heroism and self-sacrifice—as well as, on the other hand, obsessive ambition and raw rivalry—that are sewn into the very cliffs and glaciers of that imposing mountain. And although a number of other climbers, most of them professional guides, have gone on even more Everest expeditions than I have, none of them has yet sat down and tried to write about what that wealth of experience meant for them.

It's only logical, then, to begin with the first three expeditions to approach and attempt that mountain, British teams that came in 1921, 1922, and 1924, and to focus on the driving force behind that drama, one of the most inspiring and enigmatic characters mountaineering has ever seen: George Leigh Mallory.

In 1852, the Great Trigonometrical Survey of India was busy mapping and surveying the virtually unknown wilderness of the Himalaya. It was one of those grand colonial British efforts dedicated to wringing every possible geographical truth out of the landscape. To measure the heights of towering mountains seen from great distances, the survey carried out an intricate series of triangulations by theodolite, starting from the shores of the Indian Ocean and leaping northward from one prominent point to the next.

As legend has it, a "computer"—a field worker charged with working out the numbers—rushed into the office of the surveyor general one day that year and announced that he had discovered the highest mountain in the world. This remarkable claim was the work of a Bengali man named Radhanath Sikhdar. Although he had been able to train his theodolite on the peak from a station no closer than a hundred miles away, and though he could see only the tiny upper pyramid of that mountain peeking over nearer ridges, Sikhdar had worked out a calculation of 29,002 feet above sea level. No previous measurement of any summit in the world approached such a height.

Sikhdar's calculation, and the network of readings that spider-webbed across India to buttress it, was a triumph of brilliant survey-ing. The official altitude of Everest today, worked out by Bradford Washburn in 1999, is 29,035 feet. Other surveys had wildly miscal-culated the heights of great peaks ranging from Pakistan to South America, but Sikhdar's measurement was off by a mere 33 feet.

Three years before that calculation, other members of the Great Trigonometrical Survey had pointed their own devices at the re-mote mountain and given it the prosaic name of Peak XV. That for centuries native Tibetans living to the north had admired the great mass of ice and rock and bestowed a worshipful name on it—Chomolungma, or "Goddess Mother of the World"—may have been known to the Brits, but struck them as irrelevant. Likewise for the Nepalis on the south, who called it Sagarmatha—"Goddess of the Sky" (or perhaps more literally, "The Head of the Great Blue Sky"). Ignoring local and traditional usage, in 1865 the survey changed the name from Peak XV to Mount Everest, in honor of Sir George Everest, the surveyor general who had preceded the func-tionary to whom Sikhdar announced his electrifying claim.

Having perfected their skills in the Alps in the second half of the nineteenth century, the best British and European climbers turned their sights to the Himalaya and the Karakoram in what is today Pakistan. Everest would have been the ultimate prize, but the first serious expedition to one of the highest mountains in the world was directed instead at Nanga Parbat, in 1895. The leader of that small

British team, the superb alpinist A. F. Mummery, vanished on the mountain with two Gurkha porters. K2, the world's second-highest peak, was attempted by an Anglo-German party in 1902 and by an Italian team in 1909. A Swiss expedition that went after Kangchenjunga, third-highest in the world, in 1905 ended in tragedy when four climbers were buried in an avalanche.

The reason no mountaineers attacked Everest during the first two decades of the twentieth century was that during those years both Nepal and Tibet remained adamantly closed to foreigners. With the end of World War I, the Royal Geographical Society (RGS) and the Alpine Club started lobbying energetically for permission to approach Mount Everest. Most of the diplomatic efforts were aimed at the government of India (under British rule, of course), which at its greatest extent, in 1909, included present-day Pakistan, Burma (or Myanmar), Bhutan, and Nepal. Yet fiercely insular Nepal remained resolutely opposed to foreign travelers. The small country was really a semiautonomous kingdom, with its own maharajah making the final decisions.

Further vexing the situation was that Everest lay smack on the border between Nepal and Tibet. Although Tibet had remained independent for centuries, the high, sparsely populated tableland was covetously eyed by British India, Russia, and China, each of which hoped to enfold it in its domain. Tibet was the ultimate prize in the Great Game for control of central Asia.

Bold explorers in the second decade of the twentieth century had reconnoitered *toward* Everest in the course of other expeditions. In 1913, John Noel, who would become the photographer and cinematographer on the British teams of the early 1920s, had reached a pass north of Kangchenjunga and watched as the clouds dispersed and the top thousand feet of Everest came into view.

Noel stood forty miles from the mountain—the closest any Westerner had yet gotten.

In 1920, an emissary named Charles Bell received permission to travel to Lhasa for an audience with the Dalai Lama. And to everyone's surprise, the spritual and political leader of Tibet decided to allow the British to travel across his country to try to climb Everest. In January 1921, the first Everest expedition was announced by the RGS, to be carried out that spring, summer, and early autumn.

All along, a debate had raged both within the RGS and the Alpine Club, as well as in the British media, as to whether it was humanly possible to climb to 29,002 feet. But in a sidebar to that debate, some skeptics wondered whether climbing Everest might rob the wilderness of some of its essential romance. There is an oddly twenty-first-century ring to these premonitions. A writer for the *Evening News* of London (quoted in Unsworth's book) dismissed Everest aspirants for attempting "a very foolish thing. . . . Some of the last mystery of the world will pass when the last secret place in it, the naked peak of Everest, shall be trodden by those trespassers."

In retrospect, the 1921 expedition to Everest can be viewed as both a colossal mess and a brilliant reconnaissance. The RGS and the Alpine Club convened a joint Everest Committee to sort out applicants. In the end, the committee made Lt. Col. Charles Kenneth Howard-Bury the leader of the expedition. The man had compiled a record of daring travel and vigorous big-game hunting in India, but he was not even a climber, and he would turn forty during the trip. Two other principals on the team, though competent climbers, were fifty-six and fifty-three years old, well past their prime. One of them, Alexander Kellas, would die suddenly of dysentery on the early stages of the approach march.

Rounding out the team, but assigned to distinctly secondary roles, were younger men. The only one who was a preeminent mountaineer, with first ascents in Britain and the Alps under his belt at age thirty-four, was George Mallory. He was probably the finest climber of his day in Britain, and one of the best in the world—legendary for his speed and grace. His mentor and partner Geoffrey Winthrop Young, the best British climber of the previous generation, described Mallory's catlike technique on rock:

> It contradicted all theory. He would set his foot high against any angle of smooth surface, fold his shoulder to his knee, and flow upward and upright again on an impetuous curve. . . . The look, and indeed, the result, were always the same—a continuous undulating movement so rapid and so powerful that one felt the rock either must yield, or disintegrate.

The makeup of the 1921 expedition set a pattern that, strangely, still crops up today on Himalayan expeditions. The leader, appointed by a committee of graybeards, is an older man whose own climbing credentials are either minimal or long in the past. The rationale is that only experienced veterans have the wisdom and judgment to organize expeditions, as they dictate which "troops" will be sent to the front line and when. Sometimes, if the man in charge is a tyrant, he ends up completely at odds with the best climbers on the team. One thinks of Ardito Desio, leader of the 1954 Italian expedition to K2, hanging its self-sacrificing hero, Walter Bonatti, out to dry. Or Karl Herrligkoffer, leader of the German-Austrian Nanga Parbat expedition in 1953, suing Hermann Buhl, the only member who reached the summit, for disobeying his orders.

Early in my own career, I found myself on a couple of expeditions run not by Herrligkoffers or Desios, but by men who had left their best mountaineering behind them to opt into the role of leading younger climbers and dictating their movements on the mountain. This situation can create a lot of stress and conflict. I've always admired guys such as David Breashears, who led our 1996 IMAX expedition from the front, rather than leaders who sit on chairs at lower camps, study the movements of climbers through binocs or telescopes, and give them orders over the radio.

The announced goal of the 1921 expedition was to try to climb Everest. But the graybeards on the committee also insisted that the team carry out various kinds of "research," from collecting rare botanical species to studying the region's geology and exploring unknown side valleys. We know today that that sort of divided agenda is a recipe for failure. The only way to make the first ascent of a high, difficult, and unknown mountain is to devote all the team's energy to that single purpose. Nearly all the early Himalayan expeditions underestimated their objectives. Mummery died on Nanga Parbat because he approached that 26,660-foot giant as though it were merely a slightly larger peak than Mont Blanc or the Matterhorn, at a slightly higher altitude, rather than a mountain embodying a whole new scale of alpine challenge.

In sheer logistical terms, just getting *to* Everest in 1921 was a major undertaking. At the beginning of May, the team set out from Darjeeling on horseback. Ahead of them lay a trek of more than three hundred miles north through Sikkim, over a series of high passes into Tibet, then west across the Tibetan plateau. The maps of the region were so erroneous that they proved nearly worthless. In lieu of known trails, the team members climbed various hills along the way, from which they tried to sort out the jumble of snow-capped ridges and peaks they saw in the distance.

Only weeks into the journey, the climbers were at serious odds with one another. Mallory had formed a strong antipathy to Howard-Bury and to the fifty-six-year-old deputy and climbing leader, Harold Raeburn. From the trail, he wrote to Geoffrey Winthrop Young, "Relations with Bury have not been easy. . . . He is a queer customer." And to his wife, Ruth: "I can't get over my dislike of [Howard-Bury] and have a sense of gêne [annoyance] when he is present." Mallory's poor opinion of Raeburn was solidified even before the team left Darjeeling: "Raeburn unfortunately was put in charge of the mountaineering section and is quite incompetent." The one member with whom Mallory got on well was Guy Bullock, a former classmate at Winchester School, with whom Mallory had climbed often in Britain. Bullock, to his credit, seemed to get along with everybody. The other saving grace for the expedition was a contingent of Sherpas (Mallory, in the diction of the day, called them "coolies") hired to carry loads and communicate with the locals.

Despite a string of logistical snafus and Kellas's death, the team arrived at Tingri Dzong, a trading village forty miles north of Everest, in late June, only a month after leaving Darjeeling. From that town the great mountain loomed majestically in plain sight to the south. By now, however, most of the team members, intimidated by the harshness of the landscape, were frittering away their energy collecting species and reconnoitering side valleys. They left Mallory and Bullock to form the two-man advance guard that would penetrate the great peak's defenses and reach the foot of Everest itself.

On June 25, the two arrived at the even more remote town of Chobuk. They had entered the lower reaches of the Rongbuk valley, and during the next few days, with their Sherpas, they plodded up the valley and onto the glacier. Mallory was both stunned and exhilarated by this first close approach by Westerners to the highest mountain on earth. And though it would take another year to realize it, he and Bullock had discovered the key to attacking Everest from the north.

What they failed to appreciate, however, was that a seemingly minor tributary of the Rongbuk Glacier on the east, which entered the main stream of ice two and a half miles above the terminus, was the crucial piece of the puzzle. For a full month, Mallory and Bullock wore themselves out exploring every nook of the Central Rongbuk. Crevasses, towering seracs, and towers shaped by the sun and called *nieves penitentes* thwarted their every stab. "The White Rabbit himself would have been bewildered here," Mallory later wrote.

No climber in the world had a keener route-finding eye than Mallory. Staring 10,000 feet above his camp on the Rongbuk, he recorded, "Last section of East arête should go"—thereby pinpointing the northeast ridge that he would be the first to explore three years later. And he recognized that a pass looming 4,000 feet above him on the left would be the vital way station from which to launch an assault on the summit ridge. He called that pass the Chang La, or North Col. But he and Bullock could see no way to climb to that col: the slopes leading directly up to it from the Rongbuk were too steep and too threatened by falling rock and ice. As for the true north face, the headwall rising above the end of the glacier—the very route we would attack in 1987—that seemed utterly impossible

Mallory would later castigate himself bitterly for missing the secret passage of the East Rongbuk tributary. Yet I can see how easy it must have been to overlook that V-shaped side canyon apparently leading nowhere. From the main body of the Rongbuk, the tributary looks like a minor streambed entering from the east. What you can't see from below is that the canyon opens up into a major eastern branch of the glacier, which serves as the key to the approach to the North Col.

During that month of butting their heads against the north side of the mountain, Mallory and Bullock did succeed in climbing to the Lho La, a low pass at 19,700 feet on the west ridge of Everest, separating it from the satellite peak of Lingtren. From the pass, the two men became the first Westerners to see the Khumbu Icefall and the basin just above it, which Mallory named the Western Cwm. (*Cwm*, pronounced "coom," is a Welsh word for just such a basin.) The 1,500-foot drop to the Khumbu, however, looked to Mallory like a "hopeless precipice," and the Khumbu Icefall appeared "terribly steep and broken." In any event, the question of approaching Everest via the Khumbu was moot, since all the terrain the two men beheld lay in Nepal, still off limits to foreigners. Yet with his uncanny route-finding eye, Mallory stared longingly at the southeast ridge and guessed that it would afford the best route up Everest. Thirty-two years later, Tenzing and Hillary would prove him right.

Another accidental discovery made by the 1921 expedition was that June, July, and August were the wrong months to attempt Mount Everest. Very little was known about the effects of the summer monsoon season on traveling in the high Himalaya, but now Mallory and Bullock blundered into its endless cycle of smothering clouds and falling snow. Nowadays, virtually all expeditions to the Himalaya confine their attempts to the spring and fall seasons, and each year the struggle in May to get to the top of Everest is a race against the inevitable arrival of the monsoon.

Disheartened but not ready to give up, Mallory and Bullock retreated to the lowlands to rendezvous with the rest of the team. The frosty relations between the two serious climbers and the team leaders had not improved during their monthlong separation. And here, Mallory made a devastating discovery. All through the reconnaissance of the Rongbuk, he had taken large-plate photographs of the ridges and faces of Everest, but now he learned that he had put the plates in the camera backwards. Every one was blank. This "hideous error," as Mallory later called it, compounded the frustration of finding no way to get to the North Col. Although he spent two days retracing his steps to expose a new set of photographs, he still failed to recognize the East Rongbuk as the key to the approach from the north.

Mallory would be the only climber to go on all three of the British Everest expeditions in the early 1920s, and on all three he was the driving force. But he was never the expedition leader, and there were, unfortunately, sound reasons for this. As brilliant as he was at climbing and route-finding, Mallory all his life would prove to be mechanically inept to a shocking degree, and extraordinarily absentminded as well. One of his later teammates would pithily characterize Mallory as "a great dear but forgets his boots on all occasions." Another remarked, "Mallory is a very good stout hearted baby, but quite unfit to be placed in charge of anything, including himself."

In the miserable monsoon weather, it would have been tempting to pack up and go home. But Mallory had sunk his teeth into the challenge and would not let go. In early August, he and Bullock, still supported by the Sherpas, set out from a village twenty-five miles to the east of Everest, as they ascended the Kharta Glacier. In this unknown region, the maps were utterly useless. The effort almost turned into a wild goose chase, as a Tibetan tribesman directed the team southward toward "Chomolungma," which he said lay five days' march away. Mallory soon guessed that the information was wrong. (It turns out that the Chomolungma to which the tribesman referred was actually Makalu, the world's fifth-highest mountain.)

The monsoon was now at its peak, with snow falling eight to ten hours a day. Buoyed, however, by the addition of two more young team members, Henry Morshead and Edward Wheeler, the party pushed steadily up the glacier. But when they reached a pass at its head, they were stunned by yet another setback. The Kharta headed not against Everest itself, as Mallory had hoped, but on a disconnected ridge still five miles east of the great mountain.

Yet from the Lhakpa La, as they named the pass, the men could see an easy route across the eastern branch of the Rongbuk Glacier, the tributary key to the puzzle that they had failed to notice from below months earlier, leading straight to Everest's North Col. By now, the Sherpas were on the verge of mutiny. But Mallory was frantic to close the gap. On September 24—almost five months since the team had left Darjeeling—Mallory, Bullock, Wheeler, and three Sherpas set out to close the gap. The going was easy but tedious, postholing in deep snow. Mallory cut five hundred steps in the ice leading up to the North Col, at 23,000 feet. They reached the top of the saddle at 11:30 a.m. At last Mallory had set his feet on the prize he had identified in early July as the key to the puzzle.

As soon as they stood on the col, however, the men were exposed to a fierce wind lashing their faces. Wheeler urged turning around at once; Bullock, though exhausted, agreed to push ahead a little ways. Mallory later said that he felt fit enough to have climbed another 2,000 feet. The six men stumbled only a short distance up the north ridge before even Mallory admitted the effort was doomed. They took shelter in the lee of the col and tried to warm their freezing feet. As Mallory later wrote, "The wind had settled the question."

All the way back to Darjeeling, Mallory was haunted by the conviction that he had failed. It took the exhortations of friends such as Geoffrey Winthrop Young to give him a bit of heart. "This end of the world is only using the word *success*," Young wrote to his protégé. Despite the divided ambitions of the team's leaders and other personnel, Young hailed Mallory's "colossal effort of lifting an entirely unsuitable party, on a single pair of shoulders, not only onto the right line but well up it."

Back in England, the Everest Committee was already talking up a 1922 expedition. Mallory argued that such a venture must take place in April and May, before the onset of the monsoon season, but pessimistically added, "It's barely worth while trying again . . . without eight first-rate climbers."

Privately, the man was not only deeply depressed by his "failure," but psychologically spent. As he wrote his sister, "I wouldn't go again next year . . . for all the gold in Arabia."

It wasn't Arabian gold that lured Mallory back to Everest, but writing the chapters of the expedition book, as he speculated just how men might strike out from the North Col, up the apparently straightforward slope of the north face, then along the ridge angling west toward the summit. And it was Mallory who persuaded the second British expedition to focus its efforts on April and May, before the monsoon arrived.

Once more, the Everest Committee chose older, less accomplished climbers to lead the campaign. General Charles Bruce had spent much of his long career as an army officer in India, but he was fifty-six years old and in mountaineering terms a virtual novice. The climber leader, Edward Strutt, forty-eight years old at the time, would later become a virulently reactionary president of the Alpine Club, in the 1930s decrying the German and Austrian attempts on the north face of the Eiger as suicidal lunacy devoted to glorifying the *Vaterland*.

Besides Mallory, only Henry Morshead returned from the 1921 team. But the party was rounded out by a number of strong and ambitious climbers, especially Howard Somervell, E. F. "Teddy" Norton, and George Finch. Born in Australia and educated in Switzerland, Finch had applied for the 1921 expedition, only to be rejected on spurious medical grounds. The real problem was that, in the staunchly patrician culture of British mountaineering, he was not quite the "right sort"—not only had he not graduated from Oxford or Cambridge, but he spoke English with a faintly German accent. As it would turn out, Finch had something of a chip on his shoulder, and stuck to his often contrarian views in the face of opposition by his teammates. But in 1922, he would prove the equal of Mallory as the strongest men on the mountain.

The plan was to arrive at the foot of the Rongbuk Glacier by the first of May and to reach the summit before the end of the month. Even by today's standards, that was a perilously narrow window of opportunity. Most expeditions approaching Everest from the north now arrive at base camp in early April, or even earlier, in late March, as we did in 1987. But Bruce's 1922 team realized that they need waste no further time exploring Everest's defenses—they would head straight for that half-hidden tributary of the East Rongbuk and charge up it to the North Col.

The central disagreement among the party had to do with the

idea of using bottled oxygen to aid in the ascent, a practice that had been sparingly employed on other high peaks and by pilots in the British air force. In the end, the committee approved the purchase of ten oxygen sets and several dozen bottles. The leading advocate for the use of bottled oxygen was Finch, and the vehement opponent was Mallory. It's fascinating to me to look back and recognize that Mallory's feelings about supplementary oxygen in 1922 were almost identical to mine from 1987 onward. As Mallory told his first biographer, David Pye, "When I think of mountaineering with four cylinders of oxygen on one's back and a mask over one's face, well, it loses its charm."

But Mallory's objections were also pragmatic: he didn't think bottled oxygen would work. A rack of three tanks and the frame to carry them in 1922 weighed 32 pounds, a burden that he thought would more than offset any gain obtained by breathing richer air. Mallory instead believed that a "deep-breathing" technique he had perfected in 1921 would suffice to cope with altitude. Artificial oxygen as an aid, Mallory declared, amounted to "a damnable heresy."

What's so ironic about this business is that on the 1922 expedition, Mallory would become a reluctant convert to Finch's viewpoint, and in 1924, bottled oxygen would be an integral part of the team's plan of attack. But in believing that a man could climb to 29,000 feet without supplemental oxygen and survive, Mallory was way ahead of his time. As late as 1978, many experts were still convinced that anyone trying such a feat would die or suffer severe brain damage, until Peter Habeler and Reinhold Messner proved the skeptics wrong.

The 1921 team had been splintered into factions from the start, but the 1922 party got along remarkably well. And at first, everything went like clockwork. Supported not only by Sherpas but by

Tibetan porters, the team reached the North Col on May 13, and by six days later had all the gear and food in place for two separate attempts on the summit. A good two weeks of decent weather before the monsoon promised to be in the cards.

On May 20, Mallory, Somervell, Norton, and Morshead set out from the North Col on the first attempt. Whenever we modern climbers look back at the photos from the British expeditions in the 1920s, we're amazed at the inadequacy of the clothing those tough, brave men wore as they tackled the mountain. There were, of course, no down jackets or sleeping bags in those days, no plastic double boots, not even balaclavas to cover the face and neck. Instead, Mallory and his teammates set out from the North Col wearing several layers of silk shirts and wool sweaters, topped with tight-woven cotton coats. They even wore knickers made of cotton, with long woolen socks. Instead of a proper hat to protect his face, Morshead simply wrapped a wool scarf around his neck. The men's single leather boots had metal hobnails attached to the soles, which, though they gave good purchase on ice, conducted the cold straight to the feet. Yet as they set off that day, Mallory claimed, "I feared no cold we were likely to meet."

Cold, however, was the party's brutal enemy. On a steep, icy slope, Mallory realized that he and his partners "sorely needed" their crampons, but they had left them at the North Col because they had already recognized that simply tightening the straps that bound crampon to boot would cut off circulation and inevitably lead to frostbitten feet. Somehow, the men pushed on to 25,000 feet, where they spent hours piling rocks to make level platforms for their tents. Even today, the necessity of a high camp on that spur, where there's no such thing as a natural level shelf, makes for one of the most unpleasant challenges of an ascent by the north face and northeast ridge. Over the years, teams have piled stones and gravel to craft platforms that subsequent parties reuse. Adding to the discomfort are the incessant gales blowing from the west, battering bodies and searing faces with windburn.

After an all but sleepless night, the four men started out at 8:00 a.m. on May 21. Almost at once, Morshead, who was already feeling the onset of frostbite in his fingers and toes, turned back. The other three plugged on. In the first several decades of attempts on 8,000-meter peaks, virtually no team ever set off before sunrise. It was simply too cold. In addition, since headlamps had yet to be invented, those early climbers had to carry handheld flashlights, which would have made for awkward and dangerous movement in the dark.

But the key to getting up a mountain like Everest today is to set out from your highest camp in the middle of the night. I've even left camp as early as 11:00 p.m., just to get a jump on the deterioration in the day's weather that usually starts in early afternoon, to build in slack time for unexpected delays, and to ensure that I'll reach the summit before 2:00 p.m., my personal and inflexible turnaround time.

In light of these circumstances, I'm impressed that Mallory, Norton, and Somervell gave themselves a 2:15 deadline to reach the summit or turn back. By 2:15, they had reached an altitude that Mallory calculated with his barometer as 26,895 feet. If his reading was correct, the summit lay only 2,140 feet above. It must have been tempting to push on, for the weather was holding fine, but Mallory had measured their progress so far at only 400 vertical feet per hour. As he would later write, "We were prepared to leave it to braver men to climb Mount Everest by night."

Still, it was an extraordinary performance. No one else had ever been so high on the surface of the earth. The men ate a quick lunch of Kendal mint cake, chocolate, raisins, and prunes, sipped from a pocket flask of brandy, and started down.

It was then that a catastrophe came close to wiping out the team of four. They were all roped together, with Mallory in the lead, cutting steps for purchase (always an awkward business going downhill). Norton was the anchor, last on the rope. Suddenly Morshead, third on the rope, slipped and fell. He pulled Norton off his stance, and as the two men slid downward, they plucked Somervell off his feet.

Anticipating the disaster, Mallory performed the only thing he could do, driving the pick of his ice axe into the slope and belaying the rope over it. As he later wrote, "In ninety-nine cases out of a hundred either the belay will give or the rope will break." (The ropes of the 1920s, made of hemp, manila, or cotton, had a far lower breaking strength than the nylon ropes that first came into use two decades later.) Mallory clung to the head of his axe with all his strength, watching as the rope "gripped the metal like a hawser on a bollard." It was fortunate that the jerks came piecemeal, as each falling man in turn came to the end of his stretch of rope. Mallory's belay stopped them all.

This heroic act deserves to be better known than it is. It's reminiscent of Pete Schoening's "miracle belay" on K2 in 1953, when in a similar situation one man held the interlinked falls of five of his teammates with a rope looped around the shaft of his ice axe. But Mallory was so modest about his brilliant deed that in the official expedition book, he did not even name the climber whose slip had launched the near-disaster or the man who saved four lives. The protagonists were identified only as "the third man," "the leader," and so on.

Badly shaken, the four men limped down to the North Col. An exhausted Morshead saw his fingers swell with frostbite and start to turn black. He would later suffer the amputation of one toe and six fingertips. Somervell was so dehydrated that on reaching camp, he promptly drank seventeen cups of tea, one after the other.

Two days later, Finch set out on the second attempt, using bottled oxygen. His only partner was Geoffrey Bruce, Charles Bruce's nephew, who, though fit and willing, had never before climbed a real mountain. Nonetheless, Finch had so much faith in the oxygen apparatus that he was sure the two men would make the first ascent of Everest. At Camp V, they endured a sleepless night, holding on to the tent poles as a gale threatened to rip their shelter from the mountain. Undaunted, they got off at 6:30 a.m. on May 25.

By late morning the two men had passed the high point their teammates had reached three days earlier. They pushed on for another 500 vertical feet. Despite his passion and his optimism, Finch had to give in to the inevitable. Bruce was already suffering badly from frostbitten feet. He would later have to be sledged partway down from the North Col. At about 27,400 feet, the men turned around. Finch later wrote, "I knew that if we were to persist in climbing on, even if only for another 500 feet, we should not both get back alive."

So the 1922 expedition tasted defeat. Yet theirs had been a brilliant thrust into an unknown world, where Finch and Bruce had set a new altitude record. The team believed they had paved the way for the first ascent of the apex of the globe. By all rights, they should have returned to Britain to a heroes' welcome. But fate had a cruel trump in store for them.

During the first days of June, the monsoon continued to hold off. Mallory convinced his teammates to rally together for one more last-ditch attempt. From a low camp, four men set off with fourteen Sherpas to reestablish the depot and camp on the North Col. Finch gave it his all, but the effort of May 25 had worn him out, so he threw in the towel at Camp I. That left only Mallory, Somervell, and a young teammate, Colin Crawford, to push the attack.

On June 7, with the Sherpas in tow, Mallory led the way up the steep slopes beneath the North Col. An abundance of new snow had fallen during the previous week, but Mallory, delighted at the firmness the surface gave him for step-kicking, surged upward. Just below the col, Somervell took over the lead.

Ninety-one years later, it is impossible to judge whether Mallory and Somervell ignored evident signs of avalanche danger that the new snow had created. In 1922, no science of avalanche prediction had yet been developed. As we now know, however, the prevailing west-to-east wind piles up heavy loads of snow on the lee side of the North Col, which form windslabs—lighter snow layered over the older, firmer surface beneath. All it takes is a trigger—a falling rock or the footsteps of a climber—to break loose the slabs, unleashing massive avalanches.

Suddenly the men heard a sound, as Mallory later put it, "like an explosion of untamped gunpowder." From a hundred yards above Somervell, a huge slab of snow had broken loose. It engulfed the three Englishmen and the lead Sherpas, but their ride was short and they managed to dig themselves out of the debris. Not so the Sherpas following lower in the line of kicked steps. They were hurtled over an ice cliff at least forty feet high. By the time their would-be rescuers reached them, six Sherpas lay dead, killed apparently by the impact of the fall rather than smothered in the avalanche. The body of a seventh Sherpa was never found.

So the party retreated from Everest not with a gallant attempt in their wake, but burdened by a terrible tragedy. It was the first time any Sherpas had been killed serving Western climbers in the Himalaya, and though their surviving comrades bore the loss stoically, the impact of the disaster on the close-knit Sherpa culture can hardly be reckoned today.

Mallory and Somervell bore the heaviest guilt. On the hike out, Somervell agonized, "Why, oh, why, could not one of us Britishers have shared their fate?" Mallory never ducked his responsibility in putting the Sherpas in the path of fatal harm. Tom Longstaff, a respected veteran who had left the party earlier, wrote censoriously to a friend, "To attempt such a passage in the Himalaya after new snow is idiotic." Back home, Mallory wrote to his mentor, Geoffrey Winthrop Young, "And I'm to blame. . . . Do you know that sickening feeling that one can't go back and have it undone?"

For the rest of his short life, the catastrophe hung over Mallory's spirit like a black cloud. And in a perverse way, it contributed to his determination to go back to Everest once more and settle the score.

It would take almost two years for the Everest Committee to launch a third expedition. Thanks to massive debts racked up by the first two ventures, Mallory and others had to go on tour lecturing about the great adventure. In early 1923, Mallory launched a long and dispiriting circuit of the United States, appearing often before half-packed houses and apathetic audiences. To conduct the tour, he not only had to take a leave from his job teaching at the Cambridge University extension school, he had to spend months away from his beloved wife, Ruth, and his three equally beloved children.

It was during this tour that Mallory uttered the four-word phrase that has became the most famous quotation in mountaineering history. In New York City in March, a reporter asked him why anyone would want to climb Everest. "Because it is there," Mallory shot back.

Ever since, mountaineers have treasured that answer as embodying a profound and mystical truth, with all the riddling paradox of a Zen koan. Yet some who knew Mallory well, including his biographer David Pye, heard it as a throwaway dismissal of a clueless journalist, uttered by a man exasperated by audiences that could not grasp the stirring magnitude of the quest for Everest. In either case, the quip has won its immortality.

In early March 1924, the team sailed for India. Back from the 1922 expedition were not only Mallory, but Norton, Somervell, and Geoffrey Bruce. Rounding out the roster were seven other climbers, two of whom—Noel Odell and Andrew Irvine—would play pivotal roles in the assault. Once more, General Charles Bruce was the elderly expedition leader, but when he contracted malaria on the hike in, he was replaced by Norton, as Mallory took over Norton's role as climbing leader.

During the months of lecture touring and brooding upon the previous failures and the tragedy of the seven Sherpa deaths, Mallory gradually became obsessed with Everest. In my book about Annapurna, *The Will to Climb*, I tried to distinguish between commitment and obsession in mountaineering. Over the years, I've come to see that it would be simplistic to regard commitment as a good and necessary thing, obsession as its evil mirror image. They're really points along a continuum. But even when Annapurna came to haunt my thoughts every day, as I wondered if I could ever get to the summit of my last 8,000er, I never allowed myself to become obsessed with the mountain.

Nor will I flat-out declare that obsession is always a mistake in climbing. Jean-Christophe Lafaille, the most gifted partner I ever roped up with, had become obsessed with Annapurna after it killed his mentor, Pierre Béghin, in 1992, and nearly killed him. That's why J.-C. pushed on along the east ridge in 2002, while I turned back. He had always been willing to cut the margin of safety thinner than I was, and technically, he was a better climber than I was (or than almost anyone in the world on 8,000-meter peaks). When J.-C. disappeared on a solo attempt on Makalu in 2006, it was not obsession per se that killed him. Although his actual fate has never been learned, I've always thought it most likely that he fell into a crevasse. J.-C. was climbing toward the summit, alone and therefore unroped on glacial terrain. No amount of skill can save you from breaking through a snow bridge and dying in the depths of a crevasse.

As he set off for Everest in the spring of 1924, Mallory's thoughts were contradictory. One side of him was brimming with optimism. From a village on the hike in, he wrote to Ruth, "I can't see myself coming down defeated." And to his former teammate, Tom Longstaff—the same partner who had criticized Mallory's decision to climb back up to the North Col in bad avalanche conditions— "We're going to sail to the top this time, and God with us—or stamp to the top with our teeth in the wind."

The other side of Mallory was almost fatalistic. To his friend Geoffrey Keynes, before even leaving England, he wrote, "This is going to be more like war than mountaineering. I don't expect to come back." (There's more than a whiff of obsession in that enigmatic statement.)

In his 2011 book, *Into the Silence*, Wade Davis makes an interesting connection between war and climbing. Virtually all the members of the 1924 expedition had served on the front in World

War I, and, like all their fellow soldiers, had been shattered by the experience. (Mallory's mentor, Geoffrey Winthrop Young, lost a leg in the war, but continued to climb for decades thereafter.) Davis's argument is that in the wake of the horrors of the war, from friends killed in the trenches to comrades felled by mustard gas, Everest came to figure for the British as "a symbol of national redemption and hope."

Mallory's own experience in the war was both scarifying and disappointing. On the front in France in 1916 and 1917, he had his share of close calls and saw friends shot to death beside him. But in May 1917, with the battlefield at its most intense, he was invalided home, on account of a bad ankle that had never healed after a climbing accident suffered eight years earlier. Although he never said so, Mallory may have felt a lasting guilt about not serving through the end of the war, when some of his closest friends (including the poet Rupert Brooke) gave their lives in doing so. And that, in turn, may have fueled his obsession with Everest.

On April 29, the team reached its base camp at the foot of the Rongbuk Glacier. All during the hike in, the members had been suffused with confidence. Norton wrote, "I doubt if so strong a party will ever again be got together to climb Mount Everest."

But at the Rongbuk Monastery, the team received a stunning psychological blow. The head lama, pleading illness, declined to perform the *puja*—the ceremony blessing the climbers about to attack the mountain, intended to ensure their protection by the gods. Even today, almost ninety years later, a *puja* is required before we set foot on Everest. For the Sherpas, the ceremony means that they are "preblessed" in the event that tragedy befalls them during the climb. For me, it feels as though we Westerners are giving respect to the mountain and showing our humility. And the *puja* sets a good tone for approaching the mountain cautiously.

At the Rongbuk Monastery in 1924, moreover, any hope that the disaster of 1922 had been forgiven was dashed. There the climbers saw a freshly painted mural depicting the Sherpas' deaths. In the words of one member, the mural depicted "the party being pitch-forked down the mountain-side by hoofed devils and sent spinning into the colder hell."

As they started up the East Rongbuk Glacier, it was obvious to the climbers that the loyal Sherpas were badly spooked. One of them, Angtarkay, had been dug out of the debris in 1922. Now he suffered something like a mental breakdown on the approach march, and never set foot on the glacier.

The Buddhist maledictions of the monastery seemed to come to fruition in one setback after another. Storm followed storm, the temperatures were unfathomably low, and the snow conditions were atrocious. Stronger than the 1922 team this party of eleven Britons certainly was, but the weakness of Sherpa support clogged the logistics, and the campaign was soon drastically behind schedule.

Mallory had planned May 17 as the summit day. But with all the snafus, it was not until May 20 that he and three partners first struggled through to reach the North Col. More storms followed, in one of which four Tibetan porters got stranded overnight. It was not until June 1 that enough gear and food had been carried to Camp IV on the col to allow the first party to head upward. The monsoon might arrive any day.

So far, Noel Odell had proven himself to be, along with Mallory and Norton, one of the three strongest climbers. The wild card was Odell's twenty-two-year-old protégé, Andrew "Sandy" Irvine, still an Oxford undergraduate. Though he was a champion oarsman for the university eight, Irvine had precious little mountaineering experience of any kind. His great talent, however, was as a tinkerer with gear, in which capacity he was something of a genius. That skill, most observers have concluded, was what made Mallory choose Irvine rather than Odell as partner for his own summit attempt. By now, completely won over to the use of oxygen apparatus, Mallory, with his mechanical ineptitude, needed an Irvine to solve all the glitches the complicated and ill-designed tanks and respirators posed.

On June 1, Mallory and Geoffrey Bruce led eight Sherpas up the slopes from the North Col, hoping to establish a Camp V somewhere on the down-sloping shelves at 25,300 feet. Only Mallory and four of the Sherpas completed the vital trip, as Bruce, who had "strained his heart," led the other four back to the col. After that push, Bruce was finished for the expedition.

On June 2, Norton and Somervell, with the six gamest Sherpas, set out on a three-day attempt to reach the top, predicated on establishing a Camp VI higher on the slope. The Sherpas, unwilling to continue, were sent down at various stages, but by the evening of June 3, Norton and Somervell were ensconced in a shakily pitched tent at 26,800 feet.

They got off at 6:40 a.m. on June 4. Remarkably, both men were climbing without bottled oxygen. For several days, Somervell had been afflicted by coughing fits—much like the ones we experienced in 1987, but, as it would turn out, far more serious in Somervell's case. Norton took the lead all day. At 27,000 feet, they reached the foot of the Yellow Band. Here, instead of climbing to the crest of the northeast ridge, Norton chose to move diagonally rightward toward a couloir he saw in the distance (the Great or Norton Couloir, as it would come to be named). The going was dicey, across slippery, downward-sloping plates of rock interspersed with hard snow.

At noon, Somervell could go no farther. He waited as Norton forged on, traversing at the very top of the Yellow Band. Crossing increasingly treacherous ground, Norton reached the near edge of the couloir, but he knew that was his limit. Just as they had with Mallory in 1922, Norton and Somervell had imposed upon themselves a sane turnaround deadline of 2:00 p.m.

The team would later calculate Norton's high point as 28,126 feet, only 909 feet below the summit. No one will ever be able to say for sure, but it is possible that Norton reached an altitude higher than anyone else would climb for the next twenty-eight years. Without bottled oxygen, his was a magnificent achievement.

On the way back to the North Col, Somervell suffered his worst coughing fit of the whole expedition. It ended, to his horror, when he coughed up an explosion of blood and mucus that he later learned was the lining of his larynx.

The 1924 expedition might well have ended now, with a new world altitude record and no loss of life. But still the monsoon held off. On June 6, Mallory started up from the North Col with Sandy Irvine, using bottled oxygen, accompanied by eight lightly burdened Sherpas. The next day, Noel Odell and a Sherpa climbed to Camp V, crossing paths with the Sherpas headed down. One of them handed Odell a note from Mallory, written at Camp VI at 26,800 feet. Its jaunty tone camouflaged the dire news that he and Irvine had lost their cook stove when it "rolled down the slope." Without the stove, it would be impossible to melt snow for drinking water, making the summit push all the more arduous.

Odell spent the night alone at Camp V, while the Sherpas descended on their own to the North Col. The sunset and night were sublimely beautiful, "an ineffable transcendent experience," he later wrote, "that can never fade from memory." As he set out on the morning of June 8 to push on solo to Camp VI, Odell had "no qualms for Mallory and Irvine's progress upward." The sky had been clear at dawn, but now clouds rolled in.

Remarkably acclimatized and in his solitary element, Odell, a geologist by profession, wandered from ledge to ledge, marveling at rock bands in which he found ancient fossils. At 12:50 p.m., he surmounted a "little crag." The clouds briefly cleared. On the ridge stretching above him, he spotted two tiny figures, one following the other, as they climbed a snow slope leading to "what seemed to me to be the last step but one from the final pyramid. . . . I could see that they were moving expeditiously as if endeavouring to make up for lost time."

Then the clouds closed in. Odell's is one of the most legendary last sightings in exploration history.

The man reached Camp VI by mid-afternoon. In the tent, he was disturbed to find pieces of oxygen apparatus strewn about, as if Irvine had attempted desperate last-minute adjustments to the balky gear. And he found a flashlight that the perpetually absent-minded Mallory had accidentally left behind. Odell scrambled 200 feet above camp, whistling and yodeling in hopes of an answer from his friends. Then he descended all the way to the North Col.

By now, all the other members of the expedition were out of commission in terms of supporting the summit pair. Ever hopeful, in an incredible performance, Odell climbed once again back up to Camp V on June 9, then to Camp VI on the tenth. But there, his worst fears were confirmed. The tent was just as he had left it two days before. Mallory and Irvine could not still be alive. They had vanished into the mists of Everest, and of history.

With a heavy heart, Odell laid two sleeping bags out on the snow in the shape of a T—the prearranged signal to his teammates watching from below through a telescope that the worst had happened.

The great question in everybody's minds, not only in 1924 but for decades afterward, was whether Mallory and Irvine might have reached the summit before perishing. Odell believed they could have. In 1933, on the first expedition to Everest after the 1924 venture, Percy Wyn Harris found an ice axe lying on a slab of rock some 250 feet short of what climbers have come to call the First Step on the northeast ridge—thus considerably below where Odell last spotted Mallory and Irvine. Obviously the axe belonged to one of the two men, but what was it doing there? Had Mallory or Irvine laid it down momentarily to attend to some other task, just before disaster struck, or had one of them somehow dropped it during a fall? And if so, on the way up the mountain, or on the descent?

On May 29, 1953, when Edmund Hillary set foot on the summit of Everest to notch its first verifiable ascent, the first thing he did was to peer down the opposite, north side of the mountain to look for any signs of Mallory and Irvine. He found none, but twenty-nine years had intervened.

In 1999, twelve years after he and I had come so agonizingly close to summitting on Everest, Eric Simonson led a team to the mountain to search the upper zone of the eastern part of the north face for any signs of the climbers who had vanished seventy-five years before. And on May 1, Conrad Anker made one of the most stunning discoveries of twentieth-century exploration, as he found Mallory's body in a shallow basin just below 27,000 feet. The corpse, miraculously preserved by the cold and dry air, lay facedown. Mallory's fingers were still planted into the slope, as if he had tried to arrest his fall with his bare hands. His right leg was badly fractured, and in his dying moments Mallory had laid his other leg on top of it, as if to protect it from further damage. A braided cotton rope was tied to Mallory's waist, but the line had severed about ten feet from the body.

My co-author, David Roberts, wrote a book with Conrad about the discovery and about Mallory. In *The Lost Explorer*, Conrad meticulously examined the question of whether the two men might have reached the summit on June 8, 1924. His conclusion: almost certainly not.

Conrad's argument was a model of careful, sound reasoning. The body lay at a point on the face almost directly below where Harris had found the ice axe in 1933, suggesting a scenario in which, roped together, one of the men fell, the other dropped his axe to belay, both were pulled off the mountain, and the rope broke in the fall. (A tantalizing sidebar to the whole scenario is that a Chinese climber, Wang Hangbao, may have discovered Irvine's body in 1975, only twenty minutes from his expedition's Camp VI, near 27,000 feet. Wang himself was killed in an avalanche before he could guide Western investigators to the "old English dead," as he described the body. Subsequent searches in the area have come up empty.)

The clincher for Conrad, though, was the notorious Second Step, a ninety-foot-high cliff at 28,240 feet on the northeast ridge that Mallory himself had recognized as the most serious obstacle on the route he hoped to follow to the top. (By traversing into the

Great Couloir on June 4, 1924, Norton was avoiding coming to grips with the Second Step.)

In 1999, sixteen days after finding Mallory's body, Conrad Anker and Dave Hahn climbed the northeast ridge to the summit. Since 1975, when a Chinese expedition had bolted a ladder in place on the crux stretch of the Second Step, all climbers on that route have climbed the ladder rather than the rock and ice beneath it. On May 17, Conrad tried to free-climb the Step without using the ladder. It took a desperate effort, and he felt that he had compromised his "experiment" by having to step on one rung of the ladder to get his crampon-shod foot onto a wrinkle of rock beside it. Conrad rated the pitch at 5.10—harder, probably, than anything Mallory (or any other Brit) had climbed even on the crags of Great Britain by 1924.

In 2007, Conrad returned to Everest as the lead climber playing the role of Mallory in a film called *The Wildest Dream*, which had been inspired by *The Lost Explorer*. This time Conrad got permission from the Chinese authorities to remove the ladder temporarily while the film crew shot him attempting a genuine free ascent of the Second Step. Again it took a monumental effort, including a slip that Conrad caught by grabbing a cam he had placed in a crack. He got up the Step, to the cheers of his teammates and the film crew. And again, he rated the pitch as 5.10.

In *The Lost Explorer*, Conrad allowed the possibility that Mallory, climbing at his most brilliant or perhaps finding the Second Step unusually clogged with snow, making it easier, might have led the pitch free. But the clincher in Conrad's argument was that, had Mallory and Irvine climbed the Second Step, they would have had to descend it on the way back, to reach the point from which Mallory fell off the northeast ridge. It would have been impossible to down-climb such a pitch (let alone in the dark, without the flashlight Mallory had left in the tent). Instead, the men would have had to rappel the cliff. But there is no good place to fix an anchor above the Step, and no trace of any rappel gear from 1924 has ever been found in the vicinity.

Reluctantly, Conrad concluded that all the evidence argued against any chance of Mallory and Irvine having made the first ascent of Everest.

Time and again over the years, people have asked me whether I think Mallory and Irvine made it to the summit on June 8, 1924. The answer I give shocks most of them. But it's firmly rooted in the philosophy that I've adhered to throughout my mountaineering career.

My answer is this: *It doesn't matter whether Mallory and Irvine got to the summit. It's irrelevant. They didn't make it back down.*

That may seem a harsh judgment, even a dogmatic one. But the cardinal motto of all my climbing—a motto that readers of my previous books have told me strikes a sympathetic chord—is this: *Reaching the summit is optional. Getting down is mandatory.*

I admire Mallory tremendously, both as a climber and as a visionary explorer. Almost single-handedly, he figured out the puzzle of Everest. But at some point in his quest, he succumbed, I believe, to a deadly obsession with the mountain. In 1922, he had wisely turned back from his summit attempt at 2:15 p.m. If Odell saw him and Irvine still headed upward at 12:50 p.m. on June 8, 1924, then, given the place where his body came to rest, Mallory almost certainly ignored a turnaround deadline on his third expedition. He may well have climbed into the night without a flashlight.

We'll never know exactly what happened to cause the fatal fall off the northeast ridge. We may never find Irvine's body. We know that Mallory carried a small Kodak camera with him, and for decades observers hoped that finding the camera and exposing the film might solve the question once and for all. To the 1999 team's great disappointment, the camera was not with Mallory's body, though various scraps of paper and other objects were found in his pockets. It may be that Mallory gave Irvine the camera to carry. By 2013, so thoroughly has the north side of Everest been combed for clues, it seems likely that the camera will never be found.

Meanwhile, I'm sticking to my guns. An ascent doesn't really count unless you come back alive.

Yet ever since I first read about the early expeditions to Everest as a teenager, the saga of those gallant efforts on the world's highest mountain has stirred my blood. They're the stuff of myth. And Mallory, for all his flaws, remains the tragic hero of that myth.

3

▲ ▲ ▲

My Way

Just fifteen months after coming so close to the summit with Eric Simonson, I went back to Mount Everest. Once more, because there was no way I could raise the funds myself to pay for such a trip, I was content to piggyback along on someone else's expedition. The invitation came through my close friend and fellow RMI guide Andy Politz. The spark was a chance meeting in the Whittaker bunkhouse at the foot of Mount Rainier, as several climbers overheard Andy recounting his epic two-man ascent of the south face of Mount Saint Elias on the Alaska-Canada border in 1984. They introduced themselves to Andy and asked if he wanted to join an Everest expedition they were planning.

Four of the five guys were from Georgia; the other was a doctor from Aspen. They were strong technical climbers on rock and ice, but lacked high-altitude experience in the great ranges. That was something, they guessed, that Andy could supply in spades. And they wondered if Andy could bring along another mountaineer with Himalayan experience. So Andy asked me.

The trip was planned not for the spring of 1988, but for the autumnal postmonsoon season, though we'd start our hike in in mid-August, with the monsoon still in full force. By that summer, I was already signed up for a 1989 expedition to Kangchenjunga, the world's third-highest mountain, to be led by my RMI boss, Lou Whittaker. When Andy invited me to join the crew from Georgia, I tussled for weeks with the pros and cons of accepting the offer. The cons mostly had to do with taking another protracted leave from my career as a veterinarian, which, though barely launched, was already in danger of being sabotaged by my passion for mountaineering. The pros were simple: How could I turn down another chance at Everest that somebody else would pay for?

I recognized the irony. In 1987, I was a hired gun on the officially named Arkansas Everest Expedition. In 1988, our team of seven became the official Georgia Mount Everest Expedition. What was behind this strange linkage between me and the South?

Andy's and my friendship went back to 1982, when I'd first landed a job as an RMI guide. Though Andy was the same age as me, he'd worked for RMI since 1979. Still, we gravitated toward each other from the start. We often rode our bikes together to work, up the eighteen-mile road from our summer lodging in Ashford to the Paradise trailhead, gaining some 3,000 feet along the way. In a playful, competitive vein, Andy and I invented what we called the "load wars." On Rainier, the junior guides were regularly charged with carrying the food and gear for a trip with clients up the grueling four-and-a-half-mile trail from Paradise at 5,400 feet to Camp Muir at 10,000. This was the first leg of our usual two-day ascent of Rainier, and although the hike was physically demanding for the clients, it became routine for us guides. Most of the guys would try to carry as little as possible, but Andy and I took on the challenge of cramming our backpacks as full as we could, just to get in another tough workout. We'd carry loads of as much as 90 pounds. At Muir, we'd ostentatiously unload our stuff, one item at a time, piling it all on the floor—blocks of cheese, frozen steaks, cartons of eggs, heads of lettuce, giant cans of beans. Eyeing the piles, the other guides would vote on which of us had won the "load war." Another trick Andy and I played on each other was to sneak a heavy rock into the other guy's pack for the even more grueling ascent from Muir to the summit. Only on top would we disclose the subterfuge. Sometimes we'd say nothing at all, and the victim would find the hidden rock only when he got home and emptied his pack. I think we nailed each other about equally with this sadistic little trick.

By 1988, Andy had a lot more big-range experience than I did. Besides the new route on Saint Elias and an ascent of the massive Wickersham Wall on Denali, he'd already been on two Everest expeditions and an attempt on K2. In 1985, Andy had been one of the strongest members of a big American team trying the West Ridge of Everest, the line that Willi Unsoeld and Tom Hornbein had so boldly pioneered in 1963. Despite the abundance of talent in that party, they were thwarted by weather and snow conditions, and the summit pair had to turn back at 28,200 feet, just 800 feet short of the top.

The next year, Andy joined an even more ambitious team trying to make the first ascent of the south-southwest ridge of K2, the route called the "Magic Line" by Reinhold Messner. I'd been invited on that expedition, but had to decline because of vet school. After only three weeks on the mountain, with fixed ropes strung up the lower part of the route and caches of gear laid, John Smolich and Alan Pennington started up the approach gully. The early sun striking the upper face melted out a precariously placed boulder that plunged down the wall. The rock in turn triggered a massive avalanche. Smolich and Pennington never had a chance. Their teammates found Pennington's body, but not Smolich's. With their morale shattered, the party closed up shop and went home.

A fellow RMI guide, Smolich was a good friend of mine. I admired him because he was always training—he'd wear ankle weights during the hike up to Camp Muir. But John was even closer to Andy. After such a shocking tragedy, you'd think that Andy would ponder long and hard before going on another expedition to an 8,000-meter peak. But only two months after the K2 disaster, he returned to Everest for an attempt by the traditional North Col–northeast ridge route. This team, too, failed to summit.

Decades later, Andy told me why he'd gone to Everest so soon after losing one of his best friends on K2. "It wasn't cathartic," he said. "I just felt more relaxed on a big mountain than at home. If we hadn't made any mistakes on K2, and John and Alan were killed, I think I would have quit climbing. But we made a big mistake on K2. We should have waited at least another day before heading up the route. There was this herd mentality on K2 that year. All the big boys were there."

By the "big boys," Andy meant such famous climbers as Jerzy Kukuczka, Renato Casarotto, Alan Rouse, Wanda Rutkiewicz, and Benoît Chamoux. Indeed, nothing like such an all-star cast had ever before assembled on K2, or for that matter, on any 8,000er. There's no question but that the sense of rivalry contributed to one of the most catastrophic seasons on a single peak in mountaineering history. As I recounted in detail in *K2: Life and Death on the World's Most Dangerous Mountain*, by the end of the summer of 1986, thirteen climbers had lost their lives on K2.

Two years later, despite their lack of big-range experience, the

Georgia gang had gotten a permit not for the traditional South Col or north-face routes on Everest, but for the massive Kangshung Face on the east—the last of Everest's three major faces to be climbed. A Herculean effort by some of the best American climbers in 1981 and 1983 had culminated in the first ascent of the Kangshung, with six climbers reaching the top. And in the spring of 1988, just three months before we started our hike in, a four-man team had put up a new route on the left side of the face. That turned into an epic, as only one climber, the Englishman Steven Venables, pushed on to the summit, nearly dying in the process. The American Ed Webster would probably have topped out, too, but on his summit day, he briefly took off his mittens to shoot a photograph, and in a matter of seconds suffered such severe frostbite that he would later lose several fingertips to amputation.

The Georgia crew wanted to try a variant on the Venables-Webster route, even farther to the left. If Andy and I were taken aback by the ambition of our teammates, I don't recall it. I was just eager to get back to Everest, and seeing another whole side of the mountain had its own appeal. Privately, I gave us a 50-50 chance of success. But I thought that making an attempt on such a formidable route could only make me a better climber. On the approach, we rationalized to ourselves that all the technical difficulties of the route lay in the initial 2,000-foot-high buttress of mixed rock, ice, and snow. We thought the Georgians' technical skills would help us surmount that barrier. From the top of the buttress, it looked like straightforward climbing on moderately steep snow and ice, another 7,000 feet to the South Col. Then from the South Col to the summit, we'd be following the "standard" route first climbed by Hilllary and Tenzing in 1953.

What we didn't have the experience to weigh properly beforehand was the difference between the Kangshung Face in the spring and in the fall, postmonsoon. Before heading to Everest, in fact, we didn't even consult any of the Americans who had been on the face. For my part, that omission was natural. In 1988, I was still a newbie, a nobody. Who was I to talk to a famous climber like Ed Webster? But Andy had been on the West Ridge with Ed. It may be curious in retrospect that Andy didn't bother to consult Ed about the face, but it didn't seem so at the time. Even if we had talked to some of the Kangshung veterans, I'm not sure that it would have altered our approach. We pretty much had to have a go of our own to see how things would pan out.

After a lengthy overland journey by truck, we started the hike in from the remote village of Kharta on August 17. Full of optimism, we had no inklings of just how thoroughly Everest would smack us flat.

I'd turned twenty-nine two months before the trek. I was still single, without a serious relationship in my life. But it surprised me to learn early on during the trip that I was the only guy on the expedition who wasn't married. Andy was not only married, but six months earlier, his wife, Lisa, had given birth to their first child. Named Jonathan, he was nicknamed Bam Bam, because he was already pretty big and almost hyperactive. He took after Andy in that respect. My RMI buddy was built like a gorilla. As far as I knew, he'd never lifted weights in his life, but without his shirt on, he looked like he worked out every day. I surprised myself by managing to stay even with Andy in our load wars.

All during the expedition, Andy talked about his wife and kid. It was clear that fatherhood had profoundly changed his feelings about risk in the mountains. (I would find out the same thing for myself nine years later.) Andy clearly missed Bam Bam, and he'd told me that this was going to be his last expedition—how wrong a prediction that would turn out to be!

Because of our various schedules, the Georgia crew hiked in to base camp before we did. They traveled through Tibet to get to the mountain, while Andy and I came in from Nepal, bringing high-altitude tents and other supplies that we had bought in Kathmandu. That journey was fairly epic in its own right, as the roads in Nepal had been washed out by the monsoon rains. Unable to drive all the way to the border, we had to hike for several days through torrential downpours made more miserable by leeches and sweltering heat. Low on cash, we lived in squalor as we overnighted in the cheapest roadside inns we could find. And because the Georgians' budget was so tight, we couldn't hire enough porters to haul all our loads, so Andy and I had to make the soggy trudge burdened with 60-pound packs ourselves.

Andy had met the guys on Rainier, of course, and he'd made a trip to Georgia before the expedition to work out logistics, but my teammates were complete strangers to me before we met at base camp. We'd decided not to hire Sherpas for the climb, but a team of yak herders carried all our gear from Kharta to the foot of the mountain. The herders came across on the surface as friendly and helpful, only to rob us blind of rope and other essentials behind our backs. We spent lots of time and energy guarding our gear. I'm always happy to trade or give away valuable equipment to porters and Sherpas after a climb, but having it vanish before the climb added to the stress of our ambitious objective.

By starting the expedition in mid-August, we were confronting the tail end of the monsoon at its most sodden. We figured that we could endure any amount of rain in the lowlands, then be ready to roll in September on the Kangshung Face. But the hike in proved tougher and scarier than I'd expected, with hairy river crossings on makeshift bridges. And the rain became a daily tribulation. As I wrote in my diary on August 23, "Will it ever stop raining?? Everything is wet! Gore-Tex is wet, shoes & socks are wet, the inside of the tent is wet—give me a break! Not even an hour's worth of sunshine to dry stuff out. Yak shit everywhere you step."

The next day we reached base camp, where I met the five members of the Georgia team. They seemed like nice guys, and from the start it was evident that they were going to be stronger climbers than our Arkansas partners the year before. They fully expected to play equal roles with Andy and me in fixing ropes through that formidable buttress at the bottom of the face. A good thing, since we could see at once how much more serious the Kangshung Face was than the north face rising above the Central Rongbuk.

The east face of Everest looks nothing like the other two better-known faces of the great mountain. Essentially, the Kangshung unfolds as a massive, uninterrupted precipice spilling almost 12,000 feet from the summit to the glacier. The upper slopes, though festooned with crevasses and seracs, lie back at a reasonable angle, and are made entirely of snow and ice. It's the lowest part of the face, where the angle radically steepens, baring a series of fiendishly technical rock-and-ice buttresses, that makes the Kangshung so formidable. And there's no line anywhere on the massive wall that you can count on to be free of avalanches and falling rocks. The big snowslides that spill from the massive slopes high above the buttress seem fairly predictable, triggered by certain patterns of snowfall and wind direction. But what worried us most were the cliffs of ice that were poised above us, like so many swords of Damocles. They could calve loose at any time, and when one of those monsters came down, there was nowhere to run, no place to hide.

I have to admit that I was daunted as I first walked the glacier below the wall, no matter how many photos of it I had perused. So was Andy, and so were the Georgia climbers. Still, each of us tended to internalize his fears, and we kept up a brave, positive front when we talked about the route. Since we planned to attack a line at the far southern or left-hand edge of the face, we spent the first twelve days relaying loads to an advance base camp and then to Camp I, on a rocky moraine at 17,300 feet directly below our buttress—but far enough away from it that we could be sure (or so we hoped) that no avalanches would engulf our tents. With the first days of September, the monsoon at last started to peter out, and we had a number of beautiful mornings when the whole face gleamed under intense sunlight. Our morale soared with the sun's rays.

As I wrote in my diary on September 3, "The route really looks good/doable! But that's with binoculars." Our optimism extended to style, as well. That day, Andy announced that he was going to climb without bottled oxygen. I'd already made the same decision myself. As I told my diary, "I'd rather fail without O_2 than make the summit with O_2." The Georgia crew had no such compunctions. They figured the route was going to be tough enough that any aid with altitude would be welcome.

On September 4, two of the Georgians, Jan Schwartzberg and Richard Tyrrell, started up our route. It was not a promising beginning. Fixing rope as they climbed, in two days they got only 1,200 feet of lines in place, even though the initial couloir was quite easy. As I wrote in my diary, "We could walk <u>around</u> what they fixed." Even so, while they were on the face, a big avalanche came off Lhotse, just left of our route, and "dusted" the buttress the guys were climbing. "I'm sure Richard & Jan got quite a scare—I would have," I wrote in my diary. When they rejoined us in camp, they were worn out and voicing second thoughts about our route.

As were Andy and I. Already we were pondering a whole new approach to the Kangshung, which I outlined in my diary. "I'm starting to get mixed feelings about our route," I wrote. "We've got to climb <u>very</u> early in the morning & <u>fast</u> to be safe. Maybe it's too risky to try to fix the route and carry loads? Maybe Andy & I should try to flash the route alpine style? We'd be hangin' it out but would only have to go up & down once."

Looking back twenty-five years later, I'd have to say that the idea of blitzing up the buttress without fixed ropes and going alpine-style all the way to the summit verged on the grandiose. At the time, however, speed seemed to Andy and me the only rational response to constant exposure to avalanche risk. Yet we knew that the really strong team that had made the first ascent of the Kangshung Face in 1983 had laboriously built up fixed ropes through their buttress, despite being vulnerable for weeks on end to snow slides and rock falls. Only after they'd gotten massive loads up to a camp on the easier terrain above the buttress did they prepare for a push to the top, and to do so, they established yet another camp at 25,800 feet. It was from that high refuge that the six climbers who summitted finally set out.

For Andy and me to go alpine-style all the way from Camp I to the top would not only have been hanging it out—it would have been a feat that no one before us had pulled off on Everest. By 1988, other climbers, including Messner and Habeler and Erhard Loretan and Jean Troillet, had made fast, light, oxygenless ascents of Everest, but only by routes that other climbers had previously pioneered. Even by 2013, no party has ever completed a new route on Everest in true alpine style.

In the end, all our plans for a blitzkrieg of the Kangshung proved moot. The turning point came when Andy and I first went into the lead on the buttress. We started up on September 10, leaving our tent at Camp I at 2:45 a.m. It was a cold, starry night, and in pitch darkness, we jumared up the ropes Jan and Richard had fixed a few days before. It was eerie moving up a steep snow gully with only a tunnellike cone of light from our headlamps to indicate the way.

We'd been on the route for only fifteen minutes when an avalanche came down from somewhere far above—we could hear it, but saw nothing. Terrified, we hung from our jumars, the front points of our crampons planted in the slope, and hugged the wall. As I wrote that evening in my diary, "All I could see was powder rushing past my light beam as I gripped my jumar and tried to breathe without choking on the spindrift—scary! Finally it stopped. We both started getting the heebie-jeebies."

So much for an early start as the solution to the hazards of the route! If an avalanche could cut loose at 3:00 a.m., it could strike at any time. Still, Andy and I pushed upward for a while longer, until we found a section where the avalanche debris had actually buried the fixed ropes. That was enough for us. We rapped off the route and trudged back to camp. It was still before sunrise as we crawled into our sleeping bags, but twenty minutes later an even bigger avalanche tore loose from somewhere up on Lhotse. Our tent was blasted with ice pellets and wind driven ahead of the debris. Andy and I were so freaked out that we decided to abandon Camp I and head down to advance base, where we knew we'd be out of any firing lines. Later that day I confessed my thoughts to my diary: "One more episode like that and I'm gonna seriously consider calling it quits. It's just not worth it. Too many avalanches, too dangerous, too scary."

Yet at the same time, both Andy and I wondered whether we were being wimps. After all, the Americans on the Kangshung in 1981 and 1983 had faced the very same hazards, with lots of close calls, yet persevered on the second expedition to push the route all the way to the summit. There was a consolation of sorts, however, in the example set by John Roskelley. Although we both lived in Washington State—Roskelley in Spokane, I in Seattle—and though we would become partners the next year on Kangchenjunga, by 1988 I had met John only briefly as we crossed paths on Rainier. I knew him better by his stellar reputation.

Outside magazine had anointed Roskelley as the leading American high-altitude mountaineer. But John arrived at base camp under the Kangshung Face in 1981, spent one day on the route, rapped off, and promptly told his teammates that the whole face was unjustifiably dangerous. Then he tried to convince the team to abandon the Kangshung and move their expedition to the conventional North Col route, and when that appeal failed, he left the team and headed home.

I had rationalized going to Everest in autumn, after the monsoon, with the premise that the abundant summer snowfall ought to decrease the technical difficulty of the route (snow being easier to climb than rock). I knew that the trade-off was that more snow on the face meant more avalanches. I believed, however, that serac collapses—as great a hazard as snow slides on the Kangshung—should come with equally random frequency in the spring or fall. Seracs cut loose whenever they want to.

On the trip, however, Andy came to a different conclusion. September in the Himalaya, he argued, is a warmer month than April, and higher temperatures made it more likely not only that avalanches would be triggered but that towers and blocks of ice would melt out and go crashing down the face. "It's a dumb time to be here," Andy bluntly remarked halfway through the expedition.

Whoever was right, that Kangshung adventure started to fix in my mind a preference for the spring season over the fall on 8,000ers. In Pakistan, where five of the world's fourteen highest peaks are located, the monsoon isn't an issue, and nearly all the expeditions take place in summer. But in Nepal and Tibet, where the other nine highest peaks are found, the monsoon is the crucial factor in the yearly round. After 1988, I would go on twenty-two more expeditions to 8,000ers in the Himalaya proper (as opposed to Pakistan's Karakoram). Only three of them would take place in autumn—two on Cho Oyu, where avalanche danger isn't as extreme as on the other peaks, and the ascent route becomes easier with new snow covering loose rock.

Not all mountaineers agree with me. Some of the greatest, including Jerzy Kukuczka and Erhard Loretan, have pulled off brilliant ascents on 8,000ers in September or October. But in my book, the technically easier snow-covered ridges and faces are counterbalanced by the increase in avalanche danger. And there's another key consideration. If you go to an 8,000er in the spring, you're likely to spend April on the lower part of the peak, then May, with longer days and warmer temperatures, up high. In the fall, it's just the opposite. You spend September getting camps and supplies in place, but by the time you go for the summit, in mid- or late October, the days are short, the first winter winds have arrived, and the temperatures are brutally cold.

• • •

Meanwhile, the Georgia Mount Everest Expedition was in something like disarray. Privately, I struggled with my mixed emotions. Part of me had already decided I wouldn't risk another day on the buttress, but the loyal teammate in me felt that I couldn't crap out and let down my partners. I didn't say much, but my diary became a record of quivering ambivalence. On September 11, several of us hiked back up to Camp I to check out the route. On a bright sunny day, slides were spilling off the great face with alarming regularity, and through binoculars, we could see that avalanche debris had covered even more of our fixed ropes. "Now I'm back in the 'no-go' mode," I wrote. "What to do, what to do? Should I look at the evidence and trust my gut feelings? But, then again, no major feats have been done without a bit of daring."

Yet by dinner time, I'd agreed to go up with Andy the next day and try to retrieve the fixed ropes, so that we could use them on another line to the right of Jan and Richard's couloir, a route that looked safer. I'd come up with yet another rationalization—that since the slopes had already avalanched over our route, there wasn't enough loaded snow left above it to slide again.

In the middle of dinner, a huge avalanche came down right over our route. So much for my rationalization! That settled it for me—I wasn't going up there on September 12. Andy still couldn't make up his mind. We spent the rest of the evening hashing out the pros and cons. And we both slept poorly, sitting bolt upright in the middle of the night each time we heard the roar of a new slide out there in the darkness.

The next day, despite all those warning signs, Andy, Jan, and Donnie Mims went up to clear the ropes. I watched them for hours through the binoculars, my heart sometimes in my throat. I saw Donnie turn around and descend; when he got back to camp, he said he was feeling ill but also spooked by the route. Jan and Andy were back by 10:30 a.m. Their retrieval effort had been jinxed, as they found some of the fixed ropes severed by crashing debris, others stretched as tight as guitar strings. That discovery clinched the case against the route Jan and Richard had first attacked. But it didn't settle the question of whether there was another line to the right that might be safer.

We spent the next week in this miserably anxious and uncertain state. Camped under our buttress, Andy and I invented a nickname for a prominent ice cliff looming above us. "Old Blue," we called it, in homage to Yellowstone's Old Faithful, because some part of the cliff collapsed every day at 10:00 p.m. The jaunty nickname, however, was a kind of gallows humor meant to defuse the anxiety with which the whole Kangshung Face had infected us.

We kept shuttling between advance base and Camp I, building up loads for an assault we doubted we had the nerve to launch. In my diary, I started second-guessing the whole enterprise. "Why did Joe [Dinnen, leader of the Georgia team] go for the east face anyway? Slim chance right off the bat! We shoulda gone to the north side from the beginning."

The tension was taking its toll on Andy's and my friendship, as well. We started bickering over all kinds of trivial issues. On September 13, Andy's emotions overflowed. On a short walk away from camp, he suddenly put his arms around me. He had tears in his eyes. He said that I shouldn't let anybody else influence my personal decision about the route, and that I was probably the smartest guy of all if I chose not to go back up on the buttress. Andy kept thinking about Lisa and Bam Bam. Yet he felt committed to a last try. Still, he openly voiced the fear that "the big one" might come down while he was on the face and that he wouldn't come back alive. He had resolved that this was to be his last major expedition, and he didn't want to throw in his cards without a fight.

The clincher came on September 21. After several days at advance base, six of us hiked back up to Camp I to check things out. My diary recorded the shock of our arrival: "An avalanche air blast had destroyed both tents and ravens did a number on all of our food—about 50 days worth. All that was left was tea, cocoa, & nutritional supplements—no *meals*, no lunch food! How depressing! We cleaned things up and carried some wet gear down to ABC."

It's a testament to our commitment, I suppose—or perhaps to our pigheaded denial—that Andy, Richard, and I clung to the hope of one last blitzkrieg shot at the route. By now, the other four Georgians had thrown in the towel. On September 26, the three of us hiked back to Camp I with heavy packs, hoping to make an alpine-style stab the next day. But high cirrus was starting to form over the mountain, and I knew that those kinds of clouds usually presaged really bad weather.

Andy wanted to go up on the buttress just to retrieve two racks of expensive cams we had hung from our highest anchor. (Camming devices for protection had recently come on the market, and they were not only expensive, but they seemed like the most precious piece of gear we could arm ourselves with in the mountains.) I tried to talk him out of it. "It wasn't worth risking my life just to go up for that [gear] so I headed to camp," I wrote in my diary. "Soon afterward, Richard and Andy arrived, saying I was right and it wasn't worth the risk." More than two decades later, Andy still rued the loss of those cams.

So ended the 1988 Georgia Mount Everest Expedition. On that scary buttress, which is still unclimbed today, we got to only 19,000 feet—a monumental 10,000 feet short of the summit. As

I headed back to the States, I couldn't help toting up my Everest record to date. O for two—two tries, two failures. But my deeper feelings were captured in the last line of my expedition diary: "All I can say is—thank God I'm <u>alive</u> and goin' home!!"

Only five months after coming back from the Kangshung Face, I was off to Nepal again, on the expedition to Kangchenjunga that Lou Whittaker had organized. At last I'd had to face the choice that would become the turning point in my life—whether to pursue a vocation as a veterinarian or somehow become a full-time mountaineer. Before heading off to Kangchenjunga, I'd reluctantly resigned from the two jobs I held at vet clinics run by friends. It was a scary decision: after all, I'd spent four grueling years at Washington State University earning my doctorate, on top of four previous years at the University of Washington pursuing a degree in zoology just to get *into* vet school. To throw away a potentially lucrative and stable career just to go gallivanting on the world's highest mountains seemed perilously close to shooting myself in the foot. By 1989, there were still virtually no Americans making a living from climbing alone, as opposed to serving as tech reps for gear companies, working as mountain guides, or being instructors at Outward Bound and NOLS. A true professional climber has to earn his living by attending trade shows, endorsing and helping design products, letting his picture be used for advertising, going on the road to do slide shows, and proclaiming the virtues of the company that is sending him out there. One sponsor alone seldom provides enough cash to live a normal life and pay for expeditions to boot. In general, it's harder work hustling sponsors than climbing the toughest mountains.

Kangchenjunga was a long, arduous expedition, but on May 18, 1989, I stood on the summit of the world's third-highest mountain with my teammates Phil Ershler and Craig Van Hoy. At last I'd succeeded on an 8,000-meter peak. From the top of Kangchenjunga, I could see Everest eighty miles to the east, and the sight renewed my longing to tackle the 300 feet that had stood between me and the summit in 1987. No sooner had I returned to base camp than Lou told me that his twin brother, Jim—lastingly famous as the first American to reach the world's highest point, in 1963—was organizing a massive, multinational trip to Everest for 1990, and that Jim wanted me on the team.

The concept behind the Everest International Peace Climb, as Jim called it, was both ambitious and political. As he later outlined the plan in the *American Alpine Journal*,

> *Our goal was to place three climbers, one from each country, on the top of the world. They would demonstrate that through friendship and cooperation high goals can be reached. We chose our enemies to climb with—the Soviets and the Chinese. This was before glasnost, before perestroika, before the Reagan-Gorbachev summit, before Gorbachev went to Beijing. We would hold the summit of all summit meetings, enemies becoming friends.*

After 1963, Jim Whittaker had become a household name. For decades he remained by far the best-known American climber. And his celebrity nudged him into political realms, starting in 1965, when the National Geographic Society asked him to lead an expedition to the newly named Mount Kennedy in the Yukon, just east of the Alaska border. The peak had been discovered by Brad Washburn's team in the winter and spring of 1935, as they made a monumental traverse of the unmapped Saint Elias Range. They had named the peak East Hubbard, as it was a slightly lower satellite of another mountain named by a surveyor back in 1891. Washburn saw at once that though East Hubbard boasted a spectacular north ridge angling 6,000 feet from glacier to summit, it would be an easy walk-up from the south. After President Kennedy's assassination in 1963, Washburn and the NGS engineered the renaming of East Hubbard to Mount Kennedy. The peak was so remote that by 1965, it remained unclimbed. The publicity coup would be to persuade Bobby Kennedy to join a team making the first ascent.

Although he had never climbed a mountain of any size before, Bobby was in good shape. With all kinds of help from a supporting cast of "real climbers," he slogged with Whittaker to the top, unfurled several flags, and left some of his brother's prized memorabilia in a snow pocket on the summit.

The trip sparked a lasting friendship between the Whittaker and Kennedy families, resulting in shared vacations at Hyannis Port and on Puget Sound. Jim threw himself into campaigning for Bobby during the 1968 presidential race, and after Bobby's assassination in Los Angeles, Jim toyed with the idea of running for the U.S. Senate himself.

Though that never happened, by 1989 Jim had an extensive network of contacts in high places all across the globe. And to put together the Peace Climb, he would have to pull out all kinds of logistical and political stops, at the cost of very big bucks.

In early 1989, at the age of twenty-nine, I was a pretty apolitical animal myself. Promoting cooperation among China, the Soviet Union, and the United States appealed to me less than getting another chance to go after Mount Everest, but at the same time, I realized that the Peace Climb might help me attract attention and sponsors in the future. The third time on Everest, I hoped, would be my charm. As it turned out, and as even Jim had to admit, the expedition would produce as much cross-cultural tension as it did friendship. Long-drawn-out expeditions composed of good friends can be stressful enough. Putting together climbers from three different cultures with three different climbing styles amounted to a built-in recipe for conflict.

Jim ended up making multiple trips to Moscow and Beijing just to persuade the Soviets and the Chinese to join the expedition. For years, Soviets had not been allowed into China, and thawing that hostility presented Jim with one of his toughest hurdles. But once the rosters of climbers were in place, everybody got together for shakedowns on Mount Rainier and in the Caucasus.

On Rainier during the summer of 1989, we set up a massive base camp on the Nisqually Glacier, not far from the Paradise trailhead. From there, the climbers assaulted various routes on the peak. The Russians expressed surprise that we had such a significant mountain right in our backyard. But here, during these "practice" climbs, it became evident to everyone that the Chinese climbers weren't up to the standards of the Soviets and the Americans. To save face, the Chinese Mountaineering Association (CMA) eventually substituted Tibetans for Chinese on Everest.

Throughout the expedition, I relished the bitter irony behind this switch. Since 1959, when the Chinese invaded Tibet, forcing the Dalai Lama to flee, the Beijing government had relentlessly oppressed the Tibetan people. But now, the CMA decided that it had to be Tibetan climbers who represented China in the eyes of the world. Those Tibetans had plenty of high-altitude experience, and they were tough as nails. I befriended a couple of them and was delighted to run into my former partners on later expeditions in the Himalaya.

The Caucasus shakedown was an unexpected treat for me. I'd been to the Pamirs twice, but never to this impressive range between the Black and Caspian seas. Instead of hunkering in tents, we were housed in training-camp dorms and fed hearty meals enlivened by endless toasts infused with gallons of vodka. Several of us climbed Mount Elbrus, at 18,510 feet the highest peak in Europe, but little more than a long snow slog. More challenging was the north face of Jhantugan, a steep, technical snow-and-ice route that Robert Link, Steve Gall, and I teamed up to climb.

On the other hand—perhaps as penance for a free vacation in the Caucasus—Whittaker enlisted several of us in Seattle to pack food and gear for the whole expedition. Yes, it was a voluntary chore, but the clear expectation was that if you lived in the area, you'd pitch in with the packing. That's an onerous job even for, say, a six-man team of friends. But Jim had decided that all the food for all the climbers would be bought and packaged by the Americans— although in the end, both the Soviets and the Tibetans supplemented our rations with some of their favorite indigenous foods. In the fall and early winter of 1989, we spent numerous weekends and evenings in an industrial warehouse south of Seattle performing this drudgery. Jim insisted on individual man-day food packs, so we had to sort out hundreds of tiny boxes of crackers and raisins, as well as soup packs, tea and coffee packs, cookies, candies, and God knows what else, stuffing them all into ziplock bags and then into bigger bags, each labeled for a specific camp. I tried to argue, to no avail, that this was a waste of time, since a lot of this stuff would never get eaten, as climbers sorted out what they craved and left the rest behind before carrying these hefty bags up the mountain. Some nights after packing I'd go home and dream of conveyor belts loaded with food speeding by. The one side benefit was that I got to keep some of the leftovers. For months afterward, I had a supply of corn nuts, beef jerky, and Grandma's Cookies stored in my basement apartment.

We also sorted out individual boxes of gear for each member—everything from boots and socks to gaiters, mittens, and sunglasses, not to mention long johns, shell jackets and pants, down parkas, ice axes, harnesses, sunscreen, and water bottles. The job seemed endless.

By the time we assembled in Lhasa on March 1, 1990, our team comprised twenty-one climbers listed on the official permit, as well as team leaders, doctors, and base camp staff, several of whom eventually made their own bids for the summit. Our entourage was rounded out by interpreters, a base camp manager, two American cooks, and, eventually, eighty-two yaks, with a Tibetan driver for every four beasts of burden. Our gear and food added up to an ungodly twenty tons. And the expedition budget had finally peaked at $1,100,000—still to this day by far the most expensive expedition I've ever been part of. The Peace Climb would also be the largest expedition team I ever joined, and even Whittaker said that he'd never been on so big and complex an operation (and that includes the fairly massive 1963 American Everest expedition when he was the first to reach the summit).

It took us five days to drive by truck to the foot of the Rongbuk Glacier, where we set up base camp, on the very same site where we'd established our 1987 base. Here we unloaded the mountain of boxes that we had meticulously packed in Seattle. We used some of the boxes to build an enclosure sheltered from the constant wind, which we called "the beach," complete with lawn chairs.

Jim had deliberately planned an early arrival at the foot of the mountain, anticipating the logistical snafus that such a complicated trip would spawn. And so they did, right from the start. We'd paid the Soviets handsomely to supply 150 lightweight titanium oxygen bottles. Now, when we unpacked the crates, we discovered that the bottles had arrived in good shape, but minus the masks and regulators, which had been left in Moscow!

To add to the confusion, our satellite phone, with which we could have sent out urgent pleas to get the missing gear on the way to Everest, wasn't working. In the end, our deputy leader, Warren Thompson, had to drive back to Lhasa to phone the United States to get the wheels rolling. Even so, Jim had to rely on his friendship with Teddy Kennedy to get the senator's aides to unsnarl the red tape that was keeping the masks and regulators in Moscow.

The Tibetans had their own snafu, when the special boots we'd ordered for them failed to arrive at base camp. It was only on March 23 that the boots got trucked to base camp, allowing the "Chinese" contingent to contribute to our load-carrying.

Personally, I got off to a bad start on the expedition. At base camp, I had a persistent neck ache that made it hard to sleep, as well as a nagging sore throat not unlike the one that had afflicted me in 1987. I could attribute the sore throat to sleeping in the cold, damp hotels of Tibet, but the neck problem had started mysteriously many months earlier in Seattle. Now it turned into a neck spasm that radiated pain down my right arm and that would not go away. Fearful that I wouldn't pull my weight on our team, I actually considered telling Jim about my ailment and bowing out of the expedition. "I'm depressed 'cause I'm not my usual 100% self and it irritates me!" I wrote in my diary. Also: "What a cold, windy base camp this is. I'm spoiled by Kangch. The group size of this trip gets to me also."

The snafu with the oxygen masks and regulators, however, had no bearing on my own agenda for Everest. Even before leaving the States, I'd resolved again to try to get to the summit without bottled oxygen. Not that the prospect didn't daunt me. In Beijing, on the way to Lhasa, I'd dwelt on the obstacles of the northeast ridge route our party would tackle. "The last bit of ridge just below the summit is quite steep!" I wrote. "Also the Second Step looks difficult. I'd have to say right now that this route is gonna be a bitch to do without O's."

The yaks and drivers arrived on March 15, and soon we had an orderly flow of supplies heading up the East Rongbuk Glacier, with three camps along the way. The highest, at 21,500 feet, served as our advance base camp. On my first carry up the glacier, I anxiously hoisted my pack, only to discover that my neck spasm had completely vanished. The anxiety evaporated at once. On March 20, despite still feeling less than shipshape because of my sore throat, I roped up with Steve Gall as, followed by three Soviets, we forged the route up to the North Col at 23,500 feet. I led all day, putting in five fixed ropes to complete the safety line up the steep slope from the glacier to the col. Gasping for air, I cheered out loud as I crossed a last bergschrund and stood on the pass at which we had all stared from below three years earlier. This, despite the fact that other parties in previous years had left the col a mess; the place, as I wrote in my diary, "was a pit—old tents, trash, shit, etc."

Jim was holding our huge team together through sheer managerial acumen. Not an easy task, for each contingent had its own leader, Vladimir Shatayev for the Soviets, Losang Dawa for the Tibetans, Jim for us Americans. The Soviets, in particular, tended to march to their own drummer. Carrying far lighter loads from camp to camp than we Americans did, the Soviets bombed into the lead, then criticized us for being slow. They seemed to be caught up in an internal competition to prove who could move from camp to camp the fastest, whereas we Americans understood the need to supply the camps properly. One of the Soviets went so far as to carry no water on a long day's climb; then, during rest breaks, he would ask us to hand over our water bottles so he could hydrate!

All of us Americans started to resent the Soviet style. In my diary on March 20, I griped, "The Soviets think they're studs. They don't drink all day; they climb when they're ill. It's some macho thing they need to prove. As Steve [Gall] says, 'They're vying for the Lenin Award'!"

We'd planned to establish Camp IV on the North Col, but on March 21, a fierce blizzard swept across the mountain, forcing all of us back down to base camp. And on that day, a crisis struck that could have wrecked the whole expedition.

Despite having turned sixty-one just before the expedition, Jim was determined to pull his own weight as a team member. He had carried a load up to Camp III on the nineteenth, even though the effort exhausted him. Then, on the long descent to base camp in the blizzard two days later, stumbling in whiteout conditions, Jim felt a sharp pain in his calf muscle. During the next few days, the calf swelled with inflammation. The team doctor examined Jim and concluded that he probably had thrombophlebitis, a blood clot in the calf that, if it migrated to the heart or lungs, could kill him.

All climbers know the tragic story of Art Gilkey, who was stricken with thrombophlebitis in a high camp during the 1953 American

K2 expedition. Gilkey was convinced at first that he suffered from nothing worse than a "charley horse," but Charles Houston, the team leader and doctor, made a careful examination and diagnosed the potentially fatal blood clot. Soon Gilkey could no longer walk. In a desperate effort to lower their comrade in a makeshift litter, the whole team nearly came to grief in a series of linked falls, saved only by Pete Schoening's "miracle belay." Then fate gave the men a gruesome reprieve, in the form of an avalanche that swept Gilkey off the Abruzzi Spur. Freed from the impossible task of lowering the litter on steep technical slopes, the others staggered back to base camp alive.

There was nothing for Jim to do now but leave the expedition and seek a thorough diagnosis at a hospital. Stymied by delays and red tape, he was driven three hundred miles to Kathmandu, where, in an emergency room, he was put on heparin, an anticoagulant. When Jim's condition failed to improve and the supply of heparin ran out, he had to fly to Bangkok, the nearest city with doctors competent to give him a genuinely expert diagnosis.

In his absence, Warren Thompson, our deputy leader, was put in charge, but Thompson was a less forceful leader than Jim, and the discipline of the whole expedition began to fall apart. The Soviets scarcely heeded the orders of Shatayev, their own official leader, while they blithely ignored Thompson's advice and instructions.

Communication among our three teams presented another tedious obstacle. Each night, we'd have long radio calls from camp to camp. The interpreters had to translate our comments from Russian to Tibetan to English, through all the necessary permutations. Higher on the mountain, we had no resort to interpreters. Some of the Russians spoke a passable English, but none of the Tibetans did, and we linguistically challenged Americans could hardly fathom a word of the other two languages. We made do with a lot of gesturing and sign language. Somehow our high-altitude version of charades often got the message across.

In Bangkok, Jim was examined by a specialist, who concluded that he didn't have thrombophlebitis after all, but only a torn calf muscle. The whole trip out to a pair of hospitals had been unnecessary, but you can't blame the expedition doctor for being overcautious. It took Jim six more days to get back to base camp. As he later wrote,

> *Completely wasted and no longer acclimatized, I crawled out of the jeep and limped into the waiting arms of my teammates. My heart was pounding erratically; I couldn't just feel it, I could hear it. But when they sat me down to a sumptuous dinner, preceded by vodka and caviar, I felt like a king.*

With Jim back at the helm, our snafu-ridden machine began to operate more smoothly. To maximize the chances of success, Jim had planned not only the usual Camps V and VI above the North Col, but a Camp VII way up on the northeast ridge, at around 28,000 feet. No expedition had ever camped so high on the route, but from tents pitched there, on summit day climbers would have to gain only a thousand feet of altitude. Jim's rationale was based on the observation that before 1990, no climber had ever gone from Camp VI to the top and back without completing his descent after nightfall.

Members from all three countries contributed to the effort to place Camp V at 25,600 feet, but as usual, we Americans bore the brunt of the work. On April 12, in extremely high winds, I carried a load to within 200 feet of the Camp V site, but the whole day un- nerved me. As I wrote in my diary,

> *Physically and mentally exhausting. Ridiculously dangerous. . . .*
> *After snow ends, climbing is on blocks and scree "trail." Very windy.*
> *I was going really slow on the scree. Finally dumped my load because*
> *of wind/exhaustion. Going down was frightening. . . . The wind*
> *nearly took me off on the ridge. I had doubts about getting down to*
> *Camp IV!*

It wasn't until the end of April that we got Camp VI established at 26,900 feet. The site was to the right of the north spur proper and below the northeast ridge. It was a marginal place for a camp, with makeshift tent platforms built by previous expeditions out of rocks and gravel. Those platforms were covered with the remnants of old shattered tents. We pitched our own tents right on top of the debris, anchoring them with ice screws and as many large stones as we could find.

I made my first carry to Camp VI on the twenty-fourth. At last I was starting to feel really fit, as my sore throat had finally gone away. From the site, I assessed the climbing above. "Summit looks close but deceptive," I wrote in my diary. A few days later, we had tents and gear in place at Camp VI. The plan was for the first sum- mit party to carry everything they needed up to 28,000 feet, where they would establish Camp VII. They would sleep there, then go to the summit the next day.

Back at base camp, Jim was now deliberating about which climbers to send up on the first summit attempt. To make the ideal statement about international cooperation, he intended to select two Americans, two Soviets, and two Chinese for that team. But to maximize the chances of success and to ensure that all members reached the summit together, he insisted that those climbers use supplemental oxygen.

I'd worked my ass off for almost two months on the expedition, and it had paid off not only in terms of getting into great shape, but in winning Jim's confidence. On April 25, he told me he wanted me to be on the first summit team, along with Robert Link, my buddy from RMI. Years later, in his autobiography, *A Life on the Edge*, Jim wrote, "Among the Americans, Ed Viesturs was unnaturally strong. In miserable conditions that drove others back down, he made carry after carry to the high camps, without supplemental oxygen. But that was the problem; he wanted to summit without oxygen."

All of us had gone all the way down to base camp to rest up for our summit attempts in the relatively rich air of 17,000 feet. There, Jim took me aside and told me he really wanted me on the first team, but if I were to be chosen, I'd have to agree to use bottled oxygen.

"Sorry, Jim, but I'm not climbing with oxygen," I said. "It's fine with me if you choose somebody else."

"Go to bed and sleep on it," Jim answered.

"Jim—I'm not going to change my mind."

Jim may have thought I was just being stubborn, but I learned later that he respected my decision. I was fully aware of the sacrifice I was making. There was no guarantee there would even *be* a second summit team. But having decided on both my previous Everest attempts and on Kangchenjunga the year before not to use bottled O's, I was resolute. As in the Frank Sinatra song, I wanted to be able to look back decades later and say, "I did it my way."

In the end, Jim chose Robert Link and Steve Gall for the first attempt. Joining them were the Tibetans Da Cheme and Gyal Bu and the Soviets Sergei Arsentiev and Grigori Luniakov. On May 2, they started up the mountain. They were stalled for a day in a blizzard at Camp V, then reached Camp VI on May 5. The next day dawned clear and calm. They pushed on up the northeast ridge, pitched tents at 28,000 feet as they established Camp VII, and got an early start on May 7.

Within that team of six, however, fierce antagonisms had already broken out. It turns out that Sergei and Grigori had never intended to use bottled oxygen. They were strong, highly motivated climbers, having been principals on the massive Soviet team that had pulled off a traverse of Kanchenjunga's five summits the year before. Now, to save their places on the first team, they lied both to their own leader, Vladimir Shatayev, and to Jim, agreeing to use supplemental oxygen. There were suspicions among the rest of us that the Soviets might try to pull off this ruse: we knew they wanted to get to the top without oxygen. But nobody ratted them out to Shatayev or Jim.

In the end, Sergei and Grigori, climbing without bottled O's more slowly than Steve and Robert and the two Tibetans, jeopardized the whole climb. On the summit, the Tibetans and the Americans had to wait for forty-five minutes before the Soviets arrived. That vigil meant risking hypothermia and frostbite.

When they learned what had happened, both Shatayev and Jim were royally pissed off. An embarrassed Shatayev vowed, "Don't worry, Jim. It will be taken care of when they get back to Moscow, I promise you." But if Sergei and Grigori were ever reprimanded or punished back home, we never heard about it.

For the second team, Jim paired me with Ian Wade, our climbing leader, and the Soviets Mstislav ("Slava") Gorbenko and Andrei Tselinshchev. We set off from base camp the day after the first team. I'd already decided not to spend a night at Camp VII, but to go from Camp VI all the way to the top in one push. That would mean, I knew, getting a really early start on summit day, sometime around 1:00 a.m. I calculated that if I could climb only 200 vertical feet an hour above 27,000 feet, it should take me ten hours to get to the top. If so, I'd be well within my 2:00 p.m. turnaround deadline.

Not only Jim, however, but many of my teammates were dubious about my plan, as they argued that no one had pulled off such a round-trip summit day without having to bivouac. I thought that was simply because other climbers hadn't left Camp VI early enough. After endless discussions over the radio, I was allowed to try the climb the way I wanted to. Andrei and Slava also decided to make the attempt from Camp VI. Ian opted to add a night at Camp VII and go for the summit the day after us, with four of the Tibetans.

On the eve of my attempt, I was really keyed up and anxious. On May 1, I wrote, "Spent rest of day fidgeting & restless—can't relax."

I got to Camp IV on the North Col without any trouble, but was stranded there for two days in high winds followed by heavy snow. I'd been under constant tension for weeks, and now it exploded in a single diary outburst:

I'm slowly going wiggo!! . . . We've been fighting this bullshit for 2 months. Spent the whole day vegging in the tent, snoozing and dreaming of sun, warmth, beaches and beautiful women. I'm so tired of this bullshit weather and bullshit politics. All I want is 3 good days to climb this thing, then let's get the fuck outta here. I'm nearly @ wit's end.

Finally, as the weather cleared on May 6, I climbed from Camp IV to Camp V. Even though Slava and Ian were using bottled oxygen, I broke trail all the way. I felt terrific. Our loads were heavy, but we'd catch a break higher, as we'd arranged to use the sleeping bags left by the guys coming down from the successful first attempt. On May 7, it took me only three and a half hours to climb to Camp VI. There I crossed paths with Robert and Steve on their way down. Their pairing up was truly fortuitous, since they'd become very close friends during our training climbs and on the expedition itself. I congratulated them heartily, even though I felt wildly envious that they'd already made the top. My qualms were ratcheted up a notch when they told me that they doubted that I could go all the way from Camp VI to the top and back without bottled oxygen. After we parted, I stood there and watched them descend toward warmth, safety, and comfort, all too aware of the huge challenge I still faced before I could relax.

On May 8, just as I'd planned, we got started at 1:30 a.m. I carried only essentials in my pockets—two water bottles, some energy bars, spare mittens, and a camera. Anything else would have only slowed me down. It was a beautiful night with a full moon. Right off the bat, Andrei, who was also climbing without bottled O's, complained about the cold, but I felt warm and cozy in my full down suit and face mask. Once more, I took the lead. Climbing at different speeds, we were soon separated from one another in the dark. But just below Camp VII, a strange thing happened. I lost the packed trail of the route, veering too far to the right, where I found myself tiptoeing along on scary downsloping plates of rock. Fortunately, I recognized the error, climbed up and left, and found the steps again. Despite my "detour," I reached Camp VII at 4:45.

Only a thousand vertical feet still to go, and nine hours till my turnaround deadline.

In the four-man tent at Camp VII, we found Sergei and Grigori, resting after their descent from the top. Andrei and I crawled in, hoping to brew up drinks and escape the cold, but then Slava arrived, and the shelter felt claustrophobic. Unable to breathe, I left the big tent and crawled into a smaller one, where I waited alone for the sun to rise.

With first light at 7:45, I started upward again, in advance of the Soviets. Nowadays, on ascents of the northeast ridge, the crest is strung with fixed ropes, and all you have to do is slide your jumar up the lines. But in 1990, there were no ropes fixed so high, so I was solo climbing on a wildly exposed ridge. The track clung to a path slightly below the crest on the right. It was nasty, scary going on downsloping ledges. At one point I seriously thought about turning around. There was a wide gap in the rock face that required an awkward step across, and I had my doubts about whether I could reverse the move on my way down. "One slip and I'd be history, tumbling down the face," I later wrote in my diary. But I'd come too far and put in too much effort to give up now. Instead, I moved as cautiously as I could, checking each footstep before I committed my weight to it.

All through the expedition, I'd agonized over the Second Step, the last real obstacle on the route, where a 90-foot nearly vertical cliff interrupts the ridge. As mentioned in chapter two, in 1975 a Chinese expedition had bolted an aluminum ladder to the 40-foot crux at the top of the cliff, and ever since, every climber had surmounted the ladder rather than the underlying rock. When I got to the Step on May 8, however, I was gratified to find not only the ladder but some old fixed ropes in place, to which I clipped my jumar for added protection.

As I climbed the ladder, I was stunned at the thought that someone had hauled this heavy contraption all the way up to here in 1975. With a large enough team, I supposed, almost any feat could be accomplished, but the guys who took turns carrying the ladder to 28,240 feet and attaching it to the cliff had no doubt sacrificed their own chances of reaching the summit.

Climbing the vertical ladder took a tremendous effort. On top, I lay in the snow, panting like a fish out of water. Recovering from a burst of anaerobic exercise at sea level takes only a few seconds of breathing. But here, with only one-third as much oxygen in the air, I needed desperate minutes of sucking in huge volumes of air to recover. Climbing at extreme altitude, I had learned to pace myself so that I was always just on the verge of going hypoxic: not too fast, but also not too slow, or I'd never get anywhere. Usually this meant taking as many as a dozen or so breaths for every step. But on the ladder, resting and pacing were not possible, so that my ability to keep myself oxygenated was taxed to the limit. Along with the physical ordeal, I felt a surge of anxiety and claustrophobia.

The slope just above the Step led to the base of the final summit pyramid. Here the snow was as bad as I'd ever experienced anywhere—dry, with no consistency, like loose sand. Each step forward also meant slipping backward half a step. I had taught myself to break an ascent into smaller, more manageable chunks, with intermediate goals along the way—a boulder twenty yards higher, then a ridge in the snow a bit farther along. I could see, however, that the rock of the final summit pyramid would provide more solid footing. Getting to those rocks became one of my goals. The summit itself was still too far away to think about.

All at once, Slava came up behind me and passed me, since he was breathing a rich mixture of oxygen from his tank. We exchanged only nods of encouragement, but with Slava now breaking trail in the sandlike snow, I felt a huge relief. Then Andrei also passed me, even though he was climbing without bottled oxygen. I had to admit, he was one strong mother! The gap between me and them lengthened.

Suddenly, a strange feeling came over me. I felt extremely sleepy, and with it, a heightened sense of dread. I couldn't shake the drowsiness. The fact that it was warm and windless may have added to my lethargy. Some rational part of my brain called out, *This is it! Time to turn around.* But the weather was still so good, and I was so close. I pushed on, but whenever I paused to catch my breath, I dozed off for a few seconds. What was happening? Was I suffering the effects of the last few nights of anxious anticipation without solid rest, or something more ominous? Again a voice told me, *You should turn around now, or you'll die on the descent.*

But I was only 200 feet below the summit—even closer than Eric and I had gotten in 1987, on easier terrain. I ran through everything in my head. The weather was good and it was early in the day, but still I told myself, *You could turn around. You could come back another time. The mountain will still be here.* Yet the thought of having to put in all this effort a fourth time just to climb the last 200 feet was hard to face.

I pushed on. At last I reached the summit pyramid. Now I could start climbing rock gullies instead of crappy snow. This took more concentration, but it was more interesting, and suddenly I snapped out of my mysterious sleepy stupor. As I worked my way up the gullies, I kept looking down to memorize the route, so as not to lose my way on the descent.

After a while, Andrei and Slava appeared—they'd reached the top and were on their way down. Since we were unroped, I carefully stepped to the side to let them go past me. I congratulated them. They said, "Summit not far."

I trudged onward and finally emerged onto the final summit ridge. I felt fine. But I was moving so slowly—fifteen breaths for each step. The highest point of snow ahead of me looked like the summit, but I knew there might be a higher point beyond that, so I kept my hopes in check and plodded on.

Then, all at once, I realized there was nowhere higher to go. I'd reached the summit of Mount Everest. A sense of incredulity washed over me. I was alone in the universe. At that moment, there was no one on Earth who stood higher than I did.

I felt tears freezing to my cheeks. I took out my camera and shot several self-portraits. This was no easy task, as I needed to use my ice axe stuck into the snow as a monopod. Balancing my camera on top of the axe, I set the auto-timer and got myself into position, hoping to appear somewhere in the frame. I took several shots to make sure I got one good one. Believing that I would never again stand on the highest point on the planet, I wanted the moment to last and last. But I also sensed the urgency of starting back down. After less than half an hour on top, at 12:30 p.m. I began the descent. As I took the first steps, following my own tracks, I warned myself, *Be careful. Don't let up now.*

It took several hours for me to get back to Camp VI, but I arrived well before dark. The typical afternoon clouds had drifted in during my descent, and visibility was marginal by the time I arrived at the tent. It was too late and I was too tired to descend any farther. Slava and Andrei had already headed down to a lower camp, so I had the tent to myself. I was perfectly content to be alone for a night at Camp VI, after having spent most of the day climbing alone. Not having had to share my moments on the summit with anyone else seemed perfect, too.

I was overjoyed and relieved, yet extremely tired. Even though I had eaten only a couple of energy bars during the last seventeen hours, I had no appetite. I knew, however, that I had to rehydrate. I spent several hours melting snow for drinks and filling my bottles, dozing off again and again as the stove purred away. Finally, fearing that I might burn the tent down, I turned off the stove and collapsed into my sleeping bag. My last thought before sleep was, *After three long attempts, I've done it. I've climbed Mount Everest.*

The next day, May 9, as I began my descent, with the weather still holding good, Ian Wade, who'd overnighted at Camp VII, made it to the top. So did four Tibetans, including their only female team member, Gui Sang. And on May 10, Mark Tucker, the fifth American in our team; four Soviets, including their only woman, Yekaterina Ivanova; and one more Tibetan all topped out. All told, twenty of our climbers had reached the summit, a new record.

Jim Whittaker could not have been more proud of our team's effort. Ignoring all the rancor and dissension that had marred our two and a half months on the mountain, he summed up the Peace Climb for the *American Alpine Journal*:

> *We took some of the strongest mountain climbers in the world and had the most successful climb in Everest's history. What if we took the best scientists, engineers, agriculturists—regardless of nationality— and sat them down with interpreters to solve the problems of global warming, acid rain, starvation? We could save the planet!*

Such utopian musings were far from my mind as, during three exhausting days, I made my way down the mountain, passing through seven camps before I got back to our base on the Rongbuk Glacier. The overwhelming feeling for me was relief. Pride and joy would come later.

The last entry in my diary, reflecting on my determination to try Everest without supplemental oxygen, was "I proved to myself that I could do it. Now I can think of other goals."

During those last days of May, a return to Everest in the future seemed like the least likely event on my horizon. But I knew that those other goals would include high mountains. I'd reached the top of the first- and third-highest peaks in the world. What about the second—the formidable K2? And what about my career? Had I turned my back for good on being a veterinarian? Had Everest turned me into a full-time mountaineer? And if so, how could I possibly make ends meet doing what mattered most to me in life?

4

▲ ▲ ▲

Fast and Light?

After the mysterious disappearance of Mallory and Irvine in June 1924, nine years passed before Everest was again attempted. Between 1933 and 1938, four expeditions—all of them British, and all attacking the northeast ridge pioneered by the 1922 and 1924 teams—tried to climb the world's highest mountain. It was on May 30, 1933, that Percy Wyn Harris found the ice axe lying on a slab at about 28,000 feet, short of the First Step on the final ridge, a discovery that only deepened the mystery of 1924.

That same day, Harris and Lawrence Wager, climbing without bottled oxygen, surmounted the First Step and pushed on. Recognizing from a distance the formidable obstacle that the Second Step posed, they opted to traverse below the crest, angling westward along slabs at the top of the Yellow Band, just as Somervell and Norton had in 1924. They found the going terrifying: loose powder snow covering downward-tilting slabs of unstable gray rock. Though they were roped up, the men knew that a fall by one would almost surely spell death for both of them.

At 12:30 p.m., on the near edge of the Great Couloir, they called a halt at 28,200 feet. The summit still loomed 800 feet above. Harris and Wager recognized that to push for the top would inevitably mean descending in the dark, a risk they wisely declined to take. With disappointment tempered by relief, they turned around.

Theirs had been a superb achievement. They had exactly matched Norton's high point from 1924—the highest place on earth yet reached by human beings, unless Mallory and Irvine had somehow forged higher before falling to their deaths.

Two days later, Frank Smythe made his own attempt along the same perilous traverse—solo, after his partner had to turn back in the grips of altitude sickness. Just as Harris and Wager had discovered, the going got scarier with each successive advance. At almost the same point his teammates had turned around, so did Smythe. He later wrote,

> I was a prisoner, struggling vainly to escape from a vast hollow enclosed by dungeon-like walls. Wherever I looked hostile rocks frowned down upon my impotent strugglings, and the wall above seemed almost to overhang me with its dark strata set one upon the other, an embodiment of static, but pitiless, force.

Smythe barely made it down the mountain alive, suffering not only from exhaustion but from hallucinations ranging from the delusion that he had a partner walking just behind him to seeing objects floating in the sky. (UFOs, fourteen years before Roswell?)

The team retreated to base camp just as the monsoon started to arrive, discouraged and worn out, but proud of their thrust toward the summit, and of the fact that no member of the expedition had lost his life.

• • •

During those expeditions in the 1930s, four preeminent British mountaineers came into their prime, and they brought with them a whole new style of alpinism in the great ranges. Had one of those attempts on Everest succeeded, it would have changed the course of mountaineering for good. The four men were Noel Odell, the last person to see Mallory and Irvine alive in 1924; Frank Smythe; Eric Shipton; and H. W. "Bill" Tilman.

Odell was a member of only the last of the four 1930s teams, but his bravura performance in 1924 gave him an authority on Everest matched by no other veteran. Tilman participated in two of the trips, leading the 1938 expedition. Though never the official leader, Smythe was one of the strongest climbers on three of the four ventures. But Shipton, who led the 1935 attempt, was the only man to take part in all four expeditions. If ever a mountain came to "belong" to a single individual, it was Everest and Eric Shipton in the 1930s.

The revolutionary new style that these men brought to the Himalaya would come to be known by the pithy epithet "fast and light." Since early in the twentieth century, when the first attempts on 8,000-meter peaks were launched, most of the efforts were organized along massive, quasi-military lines. The Italian expedition to K2 in 1909, for instance, led by Luigi Amedeo, duke of the Abruzzi, fielded twelve Italian principals, including four professional guides from the Val d'Aosta, a topographer, a doctor, the renowned photographer Vittorio Sella, and Sella's assistant. In the lowlands, the team hired no fewer than 260 porters to haul the team's tons of gear up the Baltoro Glacier to its base camp near Concordia.

It was Tilman and Shipton, above all, who pioneered the fast-

and-light alternative. As they perfected their style on small exploratory expeditions all over the Himalaya, in the process forging one of the storied partnerships in climbing history, those two men made a stirring case for an approach to tackling the biggest and highest mountains in the world that, ultimately, would not come into vogue for another forty years.

The early chapters of Tilman's official 1938 Everest account comprise a diatribe against the traditional slow-and-heavy style of Himalayan expeditioneering. The gathering tension between Great Britain and Germany, which would erupt in World War II within the coming year, and which had already rent a schism in the climbing world, compelled Tilman to train his guns on the ponderous German expeditions to Nanga Parbat and Kangchenjunga that were also taking place during the 1930s. And Tilman keenly realized that the slow-and-heavy military style brought with it all the ugly trappings of nationalism. "I think it is true," he wrote, "that the big German expeditions received financial as well as moral backing from their governments and certainly the Tibetans themselves are convinced that we are sent to climb Everest at the bidding of our Government to enhance national prestige. One result of this is that mountains tend to become national preserves."

How prescient these words are! Alas, from 1950 through 1964, when all fourteen 8,000ers received their first ascents, all but one of those campaigns was conceived in terms of massive buildups of supplies and camps, employing hundreds of porters and Sherpas, organized with military rigor, and tacitly aimed at proclaiming national glory. It was the Austrians and Germans against the French, the Brits against the Swiss, the Italians against the Americans, and the Chinese (who bagged Shishapangma, the last of the fourteen to fall) against the world. The sole exception to the slow-and-heavy style was the first ascent of Broad Peak, the twelfth-highest in the world, by four Austrians in 1957, including the legendary Hermann Buhl and Kurt Diemberger.

Tilman, however, was not comfortable in the role of polemicist. In his seven mountaineering chronicles, and later, in his equally blithe accounts of exploratory sailing in the polar regions, he perfected an understated, laconically humorous style that makes every page a delight to read. Simply put, Tilman is one of the finest mountain writers ever—and Shipton is not far behind. Thus Tilman mocks the traditional Himalayan style not only for its inherent nationalism, but for its inefficiency: "Indeed, there is more to be feared from underwork than from overwork on these expeditions. Far too many off-days are forced upon a party and much time is spent lying about in sleeping-bags. Mr Shipton, who has taken part in two of the large expeditions, has remarked that there is sometimes a grave risk of contracting bed sores."

Chronicles from the first ascents of 8,000ers in the 1950s, such as Ardito Desio's *Ascent of K2*, often read like grim nationalistic manifestos, full of the metaphors of war. Tilman's humor, in contrast, portrays the 1938 Everest expedition as a happy outing shared by friends, full of the joking camaraderie of a vacation lark. One example:

> *Over the first few days of any march [to base camp] it is wise to draw a veil. The things that have been forgotten are gradually remembered, and the whole organization creaks and groans like your own joints. You wonder if man was really intended to walk, whether motoring after all is not his natural mode of progression, and whether the call of the open road is as insistent as you yourself thought or as the poets of that school sing. Nothing much happened. It rained.*

About their fast-and-light modus operandi, however, both Shipton and Tilman were dead serious. Somewhere Shipton laid down the dictum that if an expedition could not be planned on the back of an envelope in a few hours in a pub, it wasn't worth going on. And there's a great anecdote from one of Tilman's lectures, this time to an audience of army cadets. After the recital, a young soldier rushed up to the podium and earnestly asked, "But sir, how does one get to join an expedition such as yours?" "Put on your boots and go!" Tilman roared.

The 1933 expedition had gotten three men to 28,200 feet without bottled oxygen. Hopes were high in Britain that the next attempt on Everest would succeed in claiming the summit. It was curious, then, that the 1935 attempt, led by Shipton, was organized as a "reconnaissance," charged, like the very first attempt in 1921, with surveying and mapping the surrounding valleys and peaks as much as attempting Everest itself. Curious, too, that despite the hard-won wisdom about the vicissitudes of the monsoon gleaned by the 1922 and 1924 teams, the 1935 expedition chose to explore in June and July. Not surprisingly, the team got no higher than the North Col at 23,000 feet.

From the 1935 expedition an unexpected harbinger of Everest's future arrived, cloaked in virtual anonymity. In Darjeeling, at the outset of the journey, Shipton chose fifteen Sherpas out of a pool of a hundred eager applicants. One of the last to be selected was a lad only nineteen years old, whom Shipton chose, he later wrote, "largely because of his attractive grin." His name was Tenzing Norgay. The 1935 venture was the first of seven expeditions to Everest on which Tenzing would serve.

In 1936, a strong team including Smythe and Shipton set out with the unalloyed ambition to reach the summit. But this time weather did the party in. The conditions were abominable, with deep, soft layers of new snow threatening major avalanches even well below the North Col. The monsoon arrived on May 25, earlier than any party in the Himalaya had ever experienced. Despite narrowing their margin of safety to the thinnest possible edge, the party got no higher than the North Col. The members returned to England seething with frustration.

George Finch, still smarting from the class-based prejudices that had almost excluded him from the 1922 expedition, scolded his peers. "We ought not to treat the climbing of Mount Everest as a domestic issue," he wrote in a newspaper article. "It is an issue of National and Imperial importance. The present position is that we are beginning to make ourselves look very ridiculous." Finch went on to warn that if British climbers kept making such a botch of Everest, perhaps the mountain should be turned over to Germans and Americans. (Climbers from both countries had expressed the desire to have a go at Everest.)

Noel Odell and Bill Tilman had been invited on the 1936 expedition, but they chose another goal instead. With two compatriots, they joined four Americans to attempt Nanda Devi, a beautiful mountain in northern India. Their expedition was the antithesis of the sort of military campaign urged by Finch, so casual and collegial that the men did not elect a team leader until late in the trip. And it was fast-and-light in spades. On August 29, 1936, Tilman and Odell stood on the 25,643-foot summit. Nanda Devi was the highest mountain climbed anywhere in the world, and would remain so for the next fourteen years. In the expedition book, Tilman recorded the pair's joy on the summit in one of the most memorably understated lines in mountaineering literature: "I believe we so far forgot ourselves as to shake hands on it."

In 1938, the fourth British Everest expedition of the decade unfolded. Under Tilman's leadership, the fast-and-light credo was applied to every facet of the team's logistics. Tilman later bragged that the expedition cost only one-fifth as much as the preceding efforts, with one-fifth as much baggage. Nonetheless, the team was the strongest yet thrown at Everest, with all four stalwarts—Odell, Smythe, Shipton, and Tilman—aboard. They reached base camp on the Rongbuk on April 6, ten days earlier than any previous expedition, and started up the well-worn route to the North Col full of optimism. Against the better judgment of the purist Tilman, the team carried bottled oxygen, which they would use higher on the climb.

By now, three men—and maybe five, depending on Mallory and Irvine's high point—had climbed to within 800 feet of the summit. If ever a team seemed destined to succeed on Everest, it was the 1938 expedition. But the mountain would have the last say.

Through the rest of April, temperatures stayed frightfully cold, colder than any previous party had undergone. It took a desperate effort simply to establish Camp IV on the North Col, an achievement forged only weeks later, after the temperatures had moderated. But on May 5, it started snowing . . . and didn't stop. It is hard to judge from the hindsight of seventy-five years, but either the monsoon, which two years earlier had arrived on May 25, engulfed the mountain in 1938 three weeks before that unfathomably early date, or the party had the worst possible luck with snowstorms in May, normally a relatively calm and clear month on Everest.

After several retreats to base camp to recuperate, the men made a final effort to get above the North Col. In extraordinarily bad conditions, Smythe, Shipton, and several Sherpas, the strongest of whom was Tenzing Norgay, reached 27,200 feet, where they pitched a shaky Camp VI. The Sherpas descended while the two Englishmen spent the night in their tent, hoping for a last chance to go to the top in the morning. It was June 8, and the smothering monsoon was now unmistakably here.

In the morning, setting off before dawn, Smythe and Shipton found the cold so intense they were sure they would suffer serious frostbite if they continued. They retreated to the tent, then made a second start at sunrise. Sinking to their hips in soft powder snow, the men took a full hour to gain a mere 120 feet. Above that floundering crawl, they found themselves on steeper, downsloping slabs of rock, covered with snow that seemed poised to avalanche at any moment. "Convinced of the hopelessness of the task," as Shipton put it, he and Smythe turned around. "It was bitterly disappointing, as we were both far fitter at these altitudes than we had been in 1933, and the glittering summit looked tauntingly near."

So ended the seventh British attempt on Everest. "It is difficult to give the layman," Shipton later wrote, "much idea of the actual physical difficulties of the last 2,000 feet of Everest. . . . [A] climber on the upper part of Everest is like a sick man climbing in a dream."

With the onset of World War II in September 1939, mountaineering worldwide was pretty much shut down. And it would take several years after V-E and V-J days in 1945 before climbers returned in force to the Himalaya. It is possible that the assaults on 8,000-meter peaks between 1950 and 1964 would have been organized along nationalistic and military lines even if Tilman's fast-and-light ethos had won Everest in 1938. After all, the war had pitted nations bitterly against one another. The French success on Annapurna in 1950—the first 8,000er to be climbed—took on the aura of a huge patriotic victory for a country that had been humbled and shamed by the German occupation. Likewise the Italian triumph on K2 in 1954, for a nation on the losing side of World War II.

But I'd like to think that if Tilman's team had pulled off the first ascent of Everest, big-range mountaineering would have pursued an entirely different course during the following decades. By the mid-1950s, Tilman and Shipton and their fast-and-light doctrine had slipped into the shadows. It is only in the last several decades that those two men and the way they approached the biggest and hardest mountains have taken on the prophetic aura they deserve. Nearly all climbers today look back on them as heroes and visionaries, way ahead of their time.

Among all my expeditions to 8,000-meter peaks, only Jim Whittaker's International Peace Climb took on the trappings of nationalism. Jim's intention, of course, was to promote internationalism, not nationalism, but, as I made clear in chapter three, it didn't quite work out that way, with the Soviets banding together in a clique frequently at odds with us Americans. For myself, making a political statement on that expedition—even as a plea for harmony among former Cold War enemies—was pretty low on my agenda. I didn't climb Everest in 1990 as an American, but simply as a mountaineer.

I did, however, carry an American flag to the summit, simply because the other teams took their flags to the summit as well, and I felt that it was the right thing to do. (Years later, when I appeared on *The Colbert Report*, Stephen Colbert asked me if I took the American flag with me to the summits of other 8,000-meter peaks. I said no. He asked, "Why not?" I answered, "Because America didn't support or sponsor my climbs." True to his onscreen persona as the über-capitalist, he was delighted with my reply.)

Nowadays, there's precious little nationalism involved in mountaineering. Yes, certain individuals will still tout themselves as, say, the first Malaysian to climb K2 or the first South African woman to get up Everest. But thank God I never had to sign a pledge of unwavering allegiance to a leader, as the French did to Maurice Herzog in 1950, or follow commands typed up at base camp by a lead-from-the-rear dictator like Ardito Desio on K2 in 1954. Instead, I've relished the chance to climb with brilliant mountaineers from other countries, even when the linguistic difficulties reduced our communication to sign language and rudimentary English. One of the best and most congenial expeditions I ever went on was on the east ridge of Annapurna in 2002, where our four principals were a Frenchman (Jean-Christophe Lafaille), a Basque (Alberto Iñurrategi), a Finn (Veikka Gustafsson), and an American (me).

Like most climbers my age or younger, I believe that nationalism should have nothing to do with mountaineering. Had I been climbing in the 1950s and '60s, I might have had a different attitude, although I think most of the mountaineers of that generation simply went along with the nationalism imposed on them by the clubs and committees that organized their expeditions. For the likes of Hermann Buhl or Edmund Hillary, the climbing itself was the important thing.

The whole question runs deeper than personal predilections. Throughout history, exploration has been wedded to national ambition. In conquering Mexico and Peru, the conquistadors Hernán Cortés and Francisco Pizarro boldly claimed ownership for Spain of the Aztec and Inca empires they had subjugated. That trend persisted into the twentieth century. We tend to look on such great Antarctic explorers as Robert Falcon Scott, Ernest Shackleton, Roald Amundsen, and Douglas Mawson as purists interested only in adventure and discovery, but they were very much caught up in the game of claiming new land for the countries they came from. The names they left attached to vast stretches of barren polar plateau bespeak their nationalism: King George V Land, Princess Elizabeth Land, Queen Maud Land, and the like. Before the International Geophysical Year of 1957–58 declared that the southern continent would belong to no country and would be preserved for science, British, Norwegian, French, German, Russian, American, Australian, and Japanese governments seriously intended to mine Antarctica for minerals, oil, whales, and seals.

Every mountaineer has to ask him- or herself what the ultimate motivation for risking one's life again and again might be. Until about forty years ago, it was common for climbers to talk about "conquering the mountain." That kind of military metaphor is, fortunately, completely out of vogue today. Yet there's no getting around the idea that fame is an intoxicating spur in the mountaineering game. Even in recent years, such bold alpinists as Tomaž Humar, Catherine Destivelle, and Oh Eun-Sun returned from triumphs in the Himalaya to cheering crowds in Slovenia, France, and South Korea, respectively, and it was clear that they basked in that acclaim.

Reporters always ask us climbers why we climb. It's a reasonable question, one we find it strangely hard to answer. I've pondered my own motivations as deeply as I know how, and what I've come up with is that it's vital to my whole makeup to pose tough challenges to myself and not to quit until I've solved them. Skeptics have tried to get me to admit that the modest fame I've earned, as the first and still the only American to reach the summit of all fourteen 8,000ers, must have been the carrot that lured me along on my race against my own limitations. But I have to disagree. I became the sixth person worldwide to climb all the 8,000ers without supplemental oxygen. But in the eyes of the media and the general public, only the guy who was first—Reinhold Messner—really registers. Coming in second, as Buzz Aldrin and Robert Falcon Scott recognized, let alone sixth, hardly matters.

What fame I do have, I did not seek out. It was generated instead by the media and by the marketing departments of my sponsors. I welcome it only insofar as it enables me to go on further adventures, to make a living, or to inspire others to overcome the challenges in their own lives. I never raced anyone else to be "first" in anything. (Well, except for swim meets in high school!) I became the first American to climb the 8,000ers virtually by default: no one else was actively pursuing this goal at the time. Although some people still question my true motivation, I insist that I did all my mountaineering simply to test myself against my heroes and my own ideals.

So it's the Tilmans and Shiptons, disdaining their own fame and disavowing nationalistic goals, not the George Finches, whom I admire and have strived to emulate. Mallory, in his characteristically aphoristic way, said it best: "Have we vanquished an enemy? None but ourselves."

The aftermath of the war changed the Himalayan game in a profound way. According to the historian Walt Unsworth, the Dalai Lama had his horoscope cast in 1947, and the result was the gloomy prediction that Tibet would soon be threatened by foreigners, so he decreed a ban on all non-native travelers in Tibet, to last at least until 1950. In that year, the Chinese invaded the ancient autonomous homeland, fulfilling the prophecy. The Dalai Lama would flee to India in 1959, but with the Chinese takeover, foreigners were all the more strenuously banned from Tibet. The north side of Everest, by which seven British expeditions had sought to find a way to the summit, was off-limits indefinitely.

Yet at the same time, insular Nepal began to open up, in part because the rulers, fearing a Chinese takeover, sought allies in the West. Gradually, the possibility of approaching the world's highest mountain from the south dawned in the minds of Everest's most ardent suitors—not the least of them being Tilman and Shipton.

Only a handful of Westerners had ever seen those southern approaches. In 1921, Mallory had crested the Lho La on the border of Tibet and Nepal, from which perch he had stared down at the Khumbu Icefall and named the Western Cwm, the U-shaped basin above the icefall. But he deemed the cliff leading from the pass down to the Khumbu a "hopeless precipice."

In 1935, Shipton and Dan Bryant had made the first ascent of Lingtren, the 21,730-foot summit just west of the Lo Lha. From the top, Shipton got an even better look than Mallory's, as he saw the whole of the Khumbu unfold before him, all the way to the South Col linking Everest and Lhotse. His estimation of the southern approach was more optimistic than Mallory's. "As far as we could see," he wrote, "the route up it did not look impossible, and I should very much like to have the opportunity of one day exploring it."

It took the American expedition leader Charlie Houston to organize the first reconnaissance of Everest from the south. Actually, it was Charlie's father, Oscar Houston, who pulled the mysterious strings that opened the doors of permission to Kathmandu and beyond. One of the finest American mountaineers of his day, Charlie had led the 1938 K2 expedition, which reached the remarkable altitude of 26,000 feet on a peak much harder to climb than Everest.

And he had been one of the strongest climbers on Nanda Devi two years before. He had in fact been pegged to go to the summit with Noel Odell on August 29, but on the eve of the summit dash, he got food poisoning from a tainted can of bully beef. Tilman took his place in the summit pair.

By 1950, Oscar Houston was sixty-seven years old. He had never been a climber of the caliber of his son, but he had a zest for exploration and adventure, and had co-organized with Charlie the first ascent of Mount Foraker, the second-highest peak in the Alaska Range, in 1934. And Oscar had the kinds of connections in high places that made all the difference.

The 1950 reconnaissance unfolded as something of a lark. The Houstons invited several friends who were only casual mountaineers, but when Charlie accidentally bumped into Bill Tilman in Kathmandu, he spontaneously invited his former teammate to come along. Straight off a grueling reconnaissance of his own in the Annapurna region, Tilman accepted without hesitation.

The team set out so late in the autumn season that they knew they would have no chance of penetrating even Everest's lower defenses. Simply finding their way *to* the mountain posed a major challenge. The villages up the Dudh Khosi and Khumbu valleys, so thronged with trekkers today—Lukla, Namche Bazaar, Thyangboche, Dingboche, Pheriche, and the like—were so unknown to the outside world in 1950 that few of their inhabitants had ever seen Westerners before.

On November 18, Tilman, Charlie Houston, and a single Sherpa pushed on through the upper Khumbu valley to the foot of the great icefall. They were stunned by the magnificence of their surroundings, but, perhaps surprisingly, took a dim view of the southern approach. Tilman declared the icefall "impracticable," and Houston guessed (without gaining a clear view of the obstacles) that the slopes leading up from the Western Cwm to the South Col would be steeper and more difficult than the northeast ridge approach first reconnoitered in 1921.

The major contribution of this first stab at Everest from the south was sorting out the approach march. That Tilman and Houston's assessment of the Khumbu route ultimately proved to be unduly pessimistic in no way diminished the joy of the voyage. For the rest of his days—he died in 2009, at the age of ninety-six—Houston swore that the Everest reconnaissance was one of the best trips of his life.

The 1950 thrust inevitably led to a more thorough reconnaissance, led by Eric Shipton. Although most of the team was British, Shipton extended an invitation to two New Zealanders—one of them a tall, fit beekeeper named Edmund Hillary. The 1951 team took a month to hike from the lowlands to Namche Bazaar, a trek made miserable by spanning the sodden weeks of August, with the monsoon still in force. But that decision meant the climbers would reach the foot of the Khumbu Glacier in early September, at the relatively mild onset of the autumn season in the Himalaya.

Several members of the team scouted a devious and dangerous route through the icefall, while Shipton climbed partway up the satellite peak of Pumori to get a good view of the whole route on Everest from the south. Unlike Tilman and Houston, he was encouraged by what he saw. But he did not like the icefall at all. Though willing to run its gauntlet of crevasses and teetering seracs himself, he declared that it would be unethical to subject Sherpas to the dangers of that passage. Hillary disagreed. "In my heart," he later wrote, "I knew the only way to attempt this mountain was to modify the old standards of safety and justifiable risk and to meet the dangers as they came; to drive through regardless."

How different the history of Everest would be if Shipton's ethical qualms had won the day! Nowadays, every spring and fall, Sherpas make scores of load carries through the Khumbu Icefall. A small contingent of them, nicknamed the "Icefall Doctors," are jointly hired by all the expeditions on the mountain to scout and secure with fixed ropes and ladders a new route each year through the labyrinth of ice. It's the most dangerous job on the mountain, but the Sherpas who sign up for the task go about it with the confidence of seasoned veterans. They're not oblivious to the hazards, just more comfortable in that environment, thanks to years of experience in that gauntlet of crevasses and seracs. Indeed, the icefall has proven over the last sixty years to be every bit as dangerous as Shipton feared. Starting with Jake Breitenbach on the 1963 American expedition, an inordinate number of climbers have fallen to their deaths in crevasses or been crushed by collapsing ice towers or avalanches in the Khumbu Icefall. And an inordinate proportion of those deaths have befallen Sherpas, simply because more of them make more trips through the icefall than do most of their Western employers.

In 1951, it was not until October 28 that the whole team, aided by three experienced Sherpas, forced a route completely through the icefall. They emerged from the maze to stand on the brink of the Western Cwm. As Unsworth writes, "They had turned the key that unlocked the door to Everest." But faced with two enormous crevasses that blocked their path, Shipton ordered a retreat—a decision that did not sit well with some of his teammates, particularly Hillary.

His whole life, Shipton was more interested in exploring unknown terrain than in making first ascents. On this, his fifth Everest expedition, he had performed one of his finest reconnaissances, proving that the southern approach to the world's highest mountain was feasible. But Everest was under his skin, and he longed keenly to lead the team that would ultimately claim its summit.

Mountaineers of my own generation often feel that we were born too late. On all my expeditions around the world—not only on 8,000ers, but in Alaska, the Andes, the Arctic, and Antarctica—I've never had the chance to discover unknown land. There are today, alas, no more blanks on the map. To be sure, there are still lots of unclimbed peaks around the world, but I was always drawn to the fourteen highest. Thus I envy the pioneers who first explored the 8,000ers. The joy of discovery that so motivated Shipton and Tilman is a reward that I, and nearly all my contemporaries, will never know. To critics who say, "Hey, Ed, you've never even made a first ascent," I answer, "Every ascent I make is a first for me." But there's no getting around the truth that explorers such as Shipton and Tilman were able go where few or no humans had ever been— a fantasy that I nursed as a kid, when I first heard the siren call of adventure. (Shipton even titled one of his books, about a 1937 reconnaissance north and west of K2, *Blank on the Map*.)

Back in Britain, public interest in Everest was at a fever pitch. The Himalayan Committee of the Alpine Club and the Royal Geographical Society appointed Shipton to lead a 1952 expedition that, nearly everyone assumed, would finally reach the highest point on earth.

There was only one problem. The Swiss would beat the British to the mountain.

• • •

Just as Great Britain once boasted that the sun never set on its empire, so British mountaineers blithely assumed by 1952 that Mount Everest "belonged" to them. But the Swiss had been trying to get permission to go to Everest since 1926, and the Nepalese government finally heeded the pleas of the Swiss Foundation for Alpine Research. For a while, the Brits lobbied for a joint British-Swiss assault, with Shipton himself as their trump card. But in the end, it would be an all-Swiss team that made the first serious attempt from the south—not once, but twice, on expeditions in both the premonsoon spring season and the postmonsoon autumn.

Like the British expeditions of the 1920s, the Swiss parties were led by men whose talents lay more in the realm of organization than technical climbing. But both teams included a pair of superstars. One was the brilliant alpinist Raymond Lambert, thirty-seven years old when the team left Kathmandu in late March 1952. Lambert had under his belt a number of exceptional ascents in the Alps, but his tour de force was a survival feat, when with two companions he was trapped in a storm on the first winter ascent of the Aiguilles du Diable in the Mont Blanc massif in 1938. The trio took refuge in a crevasse at more than 13,000 feet, where they languished for five days. In the end, Lambert made a desperate foray out into the storm to locate rescuers, thereby saving the lives of all three men. But he paid a dire price, as all his frostbitten toes were later amputated. Despite this severe handicap, he continued to climb, and on Everest he was the driving force.

The other superstar was Tenzing Norgay, thirty-eight years old that spring, participating in his fifth Everest expedition. Recognizing his abilities, the Swiss appointed Tenzing sirdar on both the 1952 attempts.

On April 26, the team attacked the icefall. In a scheme that seems almost suicidal today, they established their Camp I in the middle of that seething, groaning chaos of crevasses and seracs. I can't imagine trying to sleep in such a place—on every trip I've made through the Khumbu Icefall, I've moved as fast as was possible without being reckless. Each year, there are a few places within the icefall that look large and flat enough to accommodate a camp without the threat of serac fall from above. But often I've climbed past these seemingly benign places one day, only to find the entire area to be a shattered chaos of debris the next.

In 1952, somehow the Swiss got away with their risky gamble. During subsequent weeks, they laboriously built a string of camps across the Western Cwm and up the Lhotse Face, crossing the Yellow Band and climbing a buttress they named the Geneva Spur, which took them to the South Col at 26,000 feet. It's commonly forgotten today that it was the Swiss, not the British, who pioneered the route by which Everest would finally be ascended.

Nowadays, Camp IV is normally pitched on the South Col, but for the Swiss, doggedly ferrying supplies, it would take five intermediate camps, some pitched in precarious places, before they established Camp VI on the col. And they planned yet another camp, at around 27,500 feet, before going for the summit. Nowadays, with the development of lightweight equipment, warmer boots and clothing, and headlamps, we can tackle Everest with just four camps above base camp, instead of the original seven or more. Lighter gear allows us to climb faster and farther each day, so we can place camps farther apart. Warmer clothing and headlamps allow us to make predawn starts, rather than having to wait for the morning sun for warmth and light.

It was May 26 when the Swiss team finally gained the South Col, which they accomplished only after enduring a sleepless bivouac high on the Geneva Spur. All the climbers were aware that the days were numbered before the monsoon might arrive, shutting down their campaign. By this time, Tenzing and Lambert had forged a tight bond, despite sharing only a few words of English (French being Lambert's native tongue). On May 28, four men set out for the top, carrying only a single two-man tent and one day's food. Lambert and Tenzing took the lead, while two Swiss teammates followed close behnd.

At 27,500 feet, they stopped to pitch the tent. The two teammates volunteered to return to the South Col to wait in support of the summit duo. Of that night's vigil, Unsworth writes: "Lambert and Tenzing spent a miserable night in the little tent. They had no sleeping bags, no Primus stove, very little food. By using a candle flame they managed to melt a little ice in an empty tin to help relieve their raging thirst. Of sleep there was no question."

At 27,500 feet on the southeast ridge, there aren't many places to pitch a tent. I can only imagine how cold and uncomfortable that camp must have been, especially without sleeping bags or a stove. The most logical place for their tent would have been on a shelf now called the Balcony, where the top of a rocky triangular face meets the base of the southeast ridge. With some work, a small platform could be hacked out of the snow. Shivering with cold through a sleepless night is hardly a good recipe to prepare you for one of the most grueling physical efforts of your life. And I can only imagine the guts and fortitude it took for a man who had lost all his toes to frostbite to endure such cold again in pursuit of the summit of the world.

Full of hopes depite the grim night, Tenzing and Lambert set out at dawn on May 28. But the weather began to deteriorate. Even with bottled oxygen, the men moved at a snail's pace, sometimes literally crawling on all fours. In early afternoon, the clouds dispersed, and they caught a glimpse of the South Summit, still 650 vertical feet above them. Since it had taken them five hours to climb the 650 feet from Camp VII, Lambert and Tenzing knew they had no chance of reaching the top. They wisely turned around.

The two men had reached an altitude of 28,210 feet. Depending on Mallory and Irvine's high point, it seems likely that no one had ever climbed higher on earth. Yet as they moved carefully down the ridge, Lambert and Tenzing tasted only disappointment.

History is fickle. Mention the name Raymond Lambert to the average British or American climber today, and you will likely draw a blank. But had those two men reached the top of Everest on May 28, 1952, Lambert, not Sir Edmund Hillary, would reign today as the most famous mountaineer of all time.

Still, the Swiss had every expectation, now that they had pioneered the southern route to within 800 feet of the summit, of finishing the job on their postmonsoon expedition.

Fickle fate again intervened. The fall 1952 effort was jinxed from the start. The leader fell ill early on and had trouble recovering. Just below the Geneva Spur, Mingma Dorje, one of the strongest of the Sherpas, was struck and killed by falling ice. It was not until November 19 that Lambert, Tenzing, one Swiss teammate, and seven Sherpas reached the South Col—far too late. The weather, which had stayed ferocious throughout the autumn, never relented. During the single night the men spent at the South Col, the temperature fell to minus 30 Fahrenheit, with winds of sixty miles an hour. The next day, it took the men an hour just to cross the flat shelf of the col itself. Lambert threw in the towel.

In the *Himalayan Journal*, Edmund Hillary later confessed that he had fervently hoped the Swiss would fail, despite the age-old sporting convention of wishing one's mountaineering rivals suc-cess. "Let them get very high—" Hillary wrote, "good luck to them in that but not to the summit!"

It seemed that Everest belonged to the British after all.

While the Swiss had attempted Everest in the spring of 1952, Eric Shipton had led a British team to Cho Oyu, at 26,906 feet the sixth-highest mountain in the world. Lying just inside the border of newly annexed Tibet, Cho Oyu had never been attempted. The British team, which included Edmund Hillary, was thwarted not so much by the difficulty of the mountain as by the uncertain politics of intruding upon Chinese Communist territory. (Cho Oyu, I've concluded, is actually the easiest of the 8,000ers to climb. Its first ascent would be achieved in 1954 by an Austrian party led by Her-bert Tichy.)

In any event, the Cho Oyu venture had served as a useful shake-down for the 1953 British campaign against Everest. It would be Shipton's sixth expedition to the mountain that he knew better than anyone else in the world—better even than Tenzing Norgay, who would be the sirdar on his own seventh Everest expedition. Given how close the Swiss had come to reaching the top in 1952, the whole of the British mountaineering world was confident of suc-cess in 1953.

Shipton viewed the upcoming campaign as the pinnacle of his career. Although he was forty-five years old, he was as fit as any of the candidates for inclusion in the all-star British team. But then strange things began to happen.

Behind the closed doors of the Himalayan Committee, the grand pooh-bahs started questioning Shipton's fast-and-light style of mountaineering. Was he too casual in his preparations, too laissez-faire with his teammates on the mountain? Some of the committee's pundits began to argue for a larger, more regimented, military-style expedition. Everest could not be conquered, they implied, by notes jotted on the back of an envelope in a pub.

The scuttlebutt ever since 1953 has swirled around another possible reason for choosing a leader other than Shipton. An immensely charming and handsome man, Shipton had a bit of a reputation as a womanizer. There were no particularly scurrilous rumors imputing clandestine affairs—it was simply that Shipton's bohemian lifestyle stuck in the craw of certain strait-laced committee members. Shipton's very charm was viewed almost as a failure of character. The committee began to consider other candidates, among whom the most promising was Colonel John Hunt. Only three years younger than Shipton, Hunt had a modest alpine record and had participated in five expeditions to lower peaks in the Himalaya. But he was a graduate of Sandhurst and had served with distinction in the British Army in India and in World War II on the Italian front. An expedition led by an officer such as Hunt would be the antithesis in style from one led by Shipton.

The hard news came in September 1952, when the Himalayan Committee asked Shipton to co-lead the 1953 expedition with Hunt. Cut to the quick, Shipton refused, and then declined to go along as a mere member of the party. It was the most painful setback of the man's whole life. Many of Britain's foremost climbers, as well as Hillary, voiced their outrage, but the committee had made up its bureaucratic mind.

In Shipton's 1969 autobiography, *That Untravelled World*, he handles the mess with his characteristic dignity and pride, but the pain of rejection leaks from his sentences: "The chagrin I felt at my sudden dismissal was a cathartic experience which did nothing to increase my self-esteem. I had often deplored the exaggerated publicity accorded to Everest expeditions and the consequent distortion of values. Yet, when it came to the point, I was far from pleased to withdraw from this despised limelight; nor could I fool myself that it was the manner of my rejection that I minded."

The choice of Hunt over Shipton had far greater consequences than hurting the feelings of one of the twentieth century's finest explorer-mountaineers. The ultimate success of Hunt's massive, regimented assault on Everest fixed the pattern of big-range mountaineering for the next three decades. Fast-and-light as an approach to the world's highest mountains slipped into a limbo from which Shipton (and Tilman) would not live long enough to see it reemerge.

So the 1953 expedition left Kathmandu in early March with 14 principal climbers, including Tenzing; 19 crack high-altitude Sherpas; 362 porters; and 7.5 tons of gear and food.

The story of the first ascent of Everest has been told and retold so many times, there is little point in rehashing it here. As a commander, Hunt indeed proved himself to be a master of logistics. With no major mishaps and no acrimonious fallings-out among the teammates, the small army of climbers built its pyramid of supplies through the Khumbu Icefall, across the Western Cwm, up the Lhotse Face and the Geneva Spur to the South Col. Outdoing even the Swiss in the tight spacing of camps, the British established their Camp VIII on the South Col, and managed to erect a Camp IX at 27,900 feet on the southeast ridge—400 feet higher than the sketchy tent platform from which Lambert and Tenzing had set out the year before.

On May 26, Charles Evans and Tom Bourdillon launched the

first summit attempt from the South Col. With a gutsy effort, they reached the South Summit at 28,700 feet, setting a new record for the highest humans on earth, before having to turn back. Three days later, taking advantage of the high Camp IX, Hillary and Tenzing crested the South Summit, traversed the final ridge, solved the tricky obstacle that ever since has been called the Hillary Step, and stood on the summit at 11:30 a.m.

At base camp, James Morris, working for the London *Times*, used runners and coded messages to get word of the triumph back to Britain at the very moment that Queen Elizabeth II was being crowned. An already giddy crowd went wild at the news. Some wit later called that event "the last great day in the British Empire."

The expedition was carried out so efficiently that it seemed to proceed like clockwork. Hunt's straightforward account of the climb, *The Ascent of Everest*, with its zest for logistical detail, reads at times as a methodical narrative of inevitable success. If there was high drama within the party, most of it escapes the book.

The most piquant details from the expedition were left out of Hunt's book, to emerge later only in rumor or in the retrospective musings of the climbers. As he descended from the summit, Hillary's blunt yet immortal first words to his teammate and fellow Kiwi George Lowe were "Well, George, we knocked the bastard off!" For several years, journalists frenziedly sought to learn which one of the conquerors was the first to set foot on top. Climbers know that that precedence was irrelevant, but Hillary and Tenzing had pledged each other to secrecy on the matter. It was actually Tenzing, in *Tiger of the Snows*, the biography written by James Ramsey Ullman, who first revealed that Hillary had been first on the rope and had stood on top moments before Tenzing had.

Hillary's first act on reaching the summit was not to cheer with joy or embrace his partner, but to peer down the northeast ridge, hoping not to find any sign that Mallory and Irvine might have gotten there twenty-nine years earlier.

One of the few hints of discord came from Tom Bourdillon, the strongest technical climber on the team. He told his best friend on the expedition, Michael Westmacott, that he was sure he could have made the summit, had Charles Evans not run out of energy on the South Summit. Turning around, Westmacott recalled fifty years later, "was a decision Tom always regretted." Others in the team, however, were convinced that both men would have perished had they pushed beyond the South Summit.

Bourdillon was killed in a fall in the Swiss Alps in 1956. Outside the world of Himalayan connoisseurs, he remains a forgotten figure today.

For the rest of his life, Tenzing resented the fact that the ascent of Everest had made Hillary the most famous climber in history, while he, as a Sherpa, became not even a close second. Recognizing that injustice, the expedition leader Russell Brice (himself a New Zealander), who has often been criticized for taking large sums of money to guide relatively inexperienced climbers up Everest, recently quipped, "You know who the first guided client on Everest was? Ed Hillary." (Tenzing, after all, had climbed all but the last 800 feet of the route the year before.)

Perhaps the most beguiling anecdote from the expedition emerged in the words of Hillary himself. To my co-author, David Roberts, Hillary remarked in 2002, "Both Tenzing and I thought that once we'd climbed the mountain, it was unlikely anyone would ever make another attempt. We couldn't have been more wrong."

5

▲ ▲ ▲

Something About That Mountain

After finally getting to the summit of Everest in 1990 on my third try, the last thing I had in mind was going back to the mountain anytime soon . . . if ever. There were so many other peaks I wanted to climb, and among them all, K2 loomed as the next challenge.

But at the same time, I needed to make a living. I'd pretty much given up any hope of crafting a career as a veterinarian, and guiding Mount Rainier in the summer, though it was still fun and kept me in good shape, couldn't pay my bills for a whole year, no matter how frugally I lived. In the fall of 1990, I took a construction job that paid twenty bucks an hour, offered to me by a friend who was starting his own building business. Though I was no master carpenter, I learned by doing, just as I had with mountaineering.

Lots of climbers end up pounding nails to make ends meet. It's the ideal job in a way, because you can usually take off on a moment's notice for the next expedition. But building houses can be brutal work, as it often was during the freezing rain that's so common in a Seattle winter. I'd also moved into a real dump of a basement apartment, just because the friend who had rented out the rest of the house offered it to me for fifty dollars a month.

Phil Ershler, who was three years older than me, was a veteran RMI guide whom I looked up to as a mentor. He'd actually started guiding on Rainier way back in 1971, when he was only fifteen—eleven years before I started. By no means an imposing-looking guy, Phil had a calm, calculated demeanor that made him a safe and successful climber.

For the spring of 1991, Phil had organized a guided expedition to Everest with only two clients. They were Hall Wendel, the CEO of the Polaris snowmobile company, in his late forties, and his twenty-five-year-old daughter, Amy, an aspiring RMI guide. Hall had become a private client of Phil's, and they had climbed together around the world. At some point that winter, Phil invited Robert Link and me to sign on as his assistant guides.

Given my financial situation, it was the proverbial offer I couldn't refuse. On top of a free trip to the Himalaya, I'd earn a small salary. And there was a certain appeal to the project, since Phil was heading for the standard route on the south side of Everest—the side I'd never been on. A whole different approach, via the Khumbu valley in Nepal, which everybody who'd hiked it said was far more interesting and pleasant than the jarring truck ride to the desolate Tibetan plateau north of Everest. And a whole different route, through the Khumbu Icefall, across the Western Cwm, up the Lhotse Face, and from the South Col to the summit, if we could make it. I'd never even seen the south side of Everest, except in a glimpse from the summit in 1990, but I felt as though I knew the route step-by-step, ever since I'd read Sir John Hunt's *The Ascent of Everest* as a teenager. For me, the chance to retrace what was probably the most famous route on any mountain on Earth had a powerful allure.

Phil had introduced me to Hall Wendel in the parking lot up at the Paradise trailhead on Mount Rainier during the summer of 1990. I'd sized Hall up as an affable, very fit, successful business-man who had recently gotten the climbing bug in a big way. He had a wry sense of humor, and I liked him immediately. I already knew Amy through RMI. At the time there were very few women guides on Rainier, but she held her own amid that fraternity of tough mountain men.

Sometime during the winter, however, Hall and Phil had a seri-ous falling out. I never did learn the reasons for it. What it meant, though, was that the expedition was off—unless Robert Link and I were willing to lead it by ourselves.

Guiding on Everest, of course, was a far more serious business than guiding on Rainier. The first guided client to get to the sum-mit was the millionaire Dick Bass in 1985, when David Breashears shepherded him to the top. Six years later, guiding on the highest mountain in the world was still a relatively rare exploit. It would take another five years to produce the phenomenon of whole teams full of clients vying for places in the traffic jam on the standard Everest routes, as chronicled in Jon Krakauer's *Into Thin Air*.

Since Hall and Amy were still keen to climb Everest, Robert and I took charge of the logistics. During the winter of 1990–91, I rented a small warehouse in Seattle and ordered all the food and supplies we would need for our expedition. Robert came up to Se-attle from his home near Rainier to help out whenever he could, but I took on the brunt of the planning. Packing everything into heavy-duty waxed fish boxes took an inordinate amount of time and energy. Each loaded box had to weigh very close to 65 pounds, a standard porter load. I bought the fish boxes cheap, but they came as flat sheets, so I had to fold them into shape and then staple the ends with a big foot-operated stapler. I spent many a weary night alone in the warehouse with the radio blasting away as the stapler went *ka-thunk, ka-thunk, ka-thunk.*

For safety and strength in numbers, we hired two more RMI guides, Darrin Goff and Dave Carter, to join the team. And two of the guys who'd been with me on the Peace Climb the year before also came on board. Steve Gall, who would also serve as a guide, was a strong climber from Aspen who'd gotten to the top with Robert in the first American team on May 7, the day before I did. Although he didn't summit in 1990, Kurt Papenfus was a doctor. Having him along to take care of our medical needs gave me considerable peace of mind.

We got an early start, leaving Kathmandu on March 10. By the twentieth, we'd set up our base camp just below the snout of the Khumbu Icefall. It was a smooth-enough beginning to an expedition, but on rereading my diary, I find that I was constantly disappointed by my teammates' occasional lack of energy or drive. On the very first page, like an epigraph to the whole diary, appears my exhortation:

I. STRENGTH
II. PERSISTENCE
III. DETERMINATION

WHEN THE GOING GETS TOUGH, THE WEAK MAKE <u>EXCUSES</u>!!

And some of my diary entries are pretty sarcastic. On April 4, when we were supposed to make a carry through the icefall, three members of our party (as I wrote) "didn't 'feel well' so they didn't go. When do they realize the vacation is over and they have to earn their way to the top?" Ten days later, when most of us dropped down from Camp II to Camp I to pick up loads despite strong winds, one member never budged from the tent. "So much for the big talk [before the expedition]," I wrote witheringly in my diary. These less than stellar efforts simply reinforced the maxim I'd learned on my very first Himalayan expedition in 1987: Everest requires a level of effort that some climbers simply can't deal with their first time "on the hill."

The truth is, though, that the wind that spring was some of the nastiest and most relentless I'd yet experienced in the Himalaya. On April 19, I wrote, "Fuckin' Nukin'!!! This wind is really slamming us! I'm the only one that made it to Camp III today. Took me 4:15 [four and a quarter hours], carried 15 propane cartridges. Wind blasted all day, but I was too stubborn to turn. Robo [Robert Link] was sick so he stayed at Camp II. Steve turned with Chuldum & Tamding [two of our Sherpas] at the base of the bulge. Darrin & Dave got about ¾ of the way and then dumped [their loads]."

Neither Robo (as we all called him) nor I expected Hall and Amy to be as strong as us guides. It was our job to find the route, fix ropes, and establish camps. But we did hope that our clients could help carry some of the gear and food from one camp to the next. I didn't want to overwork anyone, but a minimal show of strength and tenacity on Hall and Amy's part would be critical to our success and safety. Everything gets much harder as you move up the mountain, and if you can't perform on the lower slopes, there's no way you'll do well up high.

Thus it was disturbing when our clients gave up short of the day's goal several times, even with empty packs. My diary entry sounds peeved, but it was more a feeling of alarm, as I wrote about Hall on April 19, "If he can't get to Camp III the show is <u>over</u>!"

Hall had plenty of determination and ambition, and as he doggedly plugged along, he kept up a positive attitude. It was his hope, in fact, to complete the Seven Summits by reaching the highest point on every continent. But I began to worry that he was underestimating the mountain while he overestimated his own capabilities. As early as April 28, before he'd even reached Camp IV on the South Col, Hall was talking about putting in a Camp V between the col and the summit. I suppose he thought the higher camp would give him a better chance of summitting. The Swiss in 1952 and the British the next year had placed a camp between the South Col and the summit, but after 1960, nearly every party on the south side of Everest had decided that an intermediate camp would create more hassles than it solved.

Indeed, Hall's plan struck me as a logistical nightmare. Just getting Camp IV established on the South Col was already taking a tremendous effort. Planning a Camp V 1,200 feet higher seemed utterly premature. I was beginning to feel that guiding on Everest was a no-win proposition. I wrote in my diary, "If we don't put in a C-V and Hall fails, he'll blame it on not having a C-V. . . . Gotta talk to Robo about [this]."

Yet by the next day, I'd agreed to put in a Camp V at around 27,200 feet. My diary recorded our rationale: "If Hall is so-so getting into C-IV, they [he and a guide or two] can use C-V. If he's doing OK, they won't use C-V. I say 'they' cause I <u>won't</u> be on the first summit team. I'm in charge of putting in C-V with 2 Sherpa."

As it turned out, we didn't make our first carry to the South Col until May 1, when I alone got a load up to the site where we hoped to pitch Camp IV. After that, we all retreated to base camp for three and a half days of rest and recuperation. Camp IV didn't get occupied until May 14. Meanwhile, the wind continued its fierce attack on the mountain. On the South Col on May 4, an Australian team and an American party led by the New Hampshire guide Rick Wilcox really got hammered. They retreated, the Aussies all suffering from frostbite. "They're lucky to be alive!," I wrote. "Nobody waits for the mountain to let 'em climb. They just blast up and try to fight it."

Besides ourselves, there were four other teams that spring trying the South Col route. Compared with the mobs that descend on the route today, the sparse concentration of climbers in 1991 seems almost antiquated. One of the teams on the mountain that really impressed me was an all-Sherpa expedition—one of the first of its kind ever to try Everest. On May 8, three members—Ang Temba II, Sonam Dendu, and Apa Sherpa—reached the top without incident. None of the rest of us were even in position to make an attempt by that date.

Apa Sherpa was twenty-nine years old that spring, when he first reached the highest point on Earth. He would go on to become an Everest legend. In 2011, he reached the summit for his twenty-first time.

The strain of guiding in such an uncertain season was getting to me. On May 9, Robo and I, along with Hall and Amy, spent the night at Camp III at 24,500 feet on the Lhotse Face. Once again, our clients had been unable to carry any loads themselves. I recorded the tension in my diary:

> Got into a shouting match with Hall. Now he wants Tamding [a Sherpa] to come up tomorrow to carry Amy's gear to the col. I lit

into him about him & Amy not proving that they're strong enough to climb this thing and that Robo & I will draw the line anywhere above here if we think it's too dangerous. Hall barked something about paying $200,000 to get up this thing and then we all started yelling.

By the next day, Amy had developed the telltale symptoms of acute mountain sickness. Both "Doc" Papenfus and I tried to convince her she had to descend immediately and that she should not attempt to go high again, but for two days she adamantly insisted that she could give it another try. I hated being stuck in this bind. Hall was paying the bills for the whole expedition, but Amy's stubbornness could endanger the lives of all of us.

Battered by the wind, we decided to go down one more time. On May 11, we left Camp III, as some of us descended all the way to base camp, while others, including me, went just to Camp II. If only the weather would cooperate, and we could recover our health and energy, we could set out on the thirteenth on what we now knew would be our sole chance to go for the summit.

It wasn't only Hall and Amy who were suffering. Steve Gall and Robert Link, who'd been so strong the year before, were, as I put it, "ill and mentally fried." Only Darrin Goff and I, among the guides, were in anything like reasonable condition. But on May 13, we climbed back to Camp III. Hall and Amy once again dragged way behind, carrying no loads of their own. But the wind had died somewhat, which gave us hope. The plan was to reach the South Col and establish Camp IV the next day, then get up early on the fifteenth and go for the summit.

That evening in Camp III, however, Dave Carter started feeling weak, dizzy, and "out of it," with a pulse of 120 beats per minute. We gave him bottled oxygen to breathe and diamox and dexamethasone to swallow, but he decided to go down the next morning. Then Amy came over to my tent. Sticking her head inside the door, she confessed that she'd changed her mind. She no longer had any motivation to go on, she said, so she'd descend with Dave in the morning. I tried not to show how relieved I felt.

On the fourteenth, I reached the South Col first, at noon, and set up a tent. Darrin got there an hour later and pitched a second shelter. Pury, one of our Sherpas, was the next to arrive, carrying Hall's personal gear. To my alarm, Pury said that even though Hall was climbing without any load and with bottled oxygen, tended by another Sherpa, Wong Chu, he was still three hours away and running out of O's. Despite feeling worn out by what I called in my diary an "ass-buster day," I promptly grabbed a bottle of oxygen and started back down the Lhotse Face.

At the bottom of the Geneva Spur, I met Hall and Wong Chu. Hall was moving slowly and looked spent. He admitted that the climb had taken everything out of him—all he wanted now was to get to the South Col. And I told him in no uncertain terms that I wouldn't let him go any higher than that. We finally reached Camp IV at 6:30 p.m. I was wasted from an eleven-hour non-stop day.

It seemed that all the spirit had drained out of our expedition. Robo was still at base camp, and over the radio he sounded listless. "He just wants to pack up and get out of here," I wrote in my diary. Steve Gall was also at base camp and seemed unmotivated to go higher. Amy and Dave Carter were out of the running. Doc Papenfus was content to go no higher than the Western Cwm.

Once he arrived at the South Col, however, Hall had yet another change of heart. He'd invested so much money and ambition in trying to climb Everest that he asked for one more chance. I told him that based on his performance the day before, as well as the days before that, I simply couldn't risk taking him higher. I based my decision on his safety, not on his huge investment of time and money. I knew that I wasn't the first guide to find himself in such an awkward position, nor would I be the last. Still, the whole situation really stressed me out. My heart wanted to take him higher, but my instincts told me to stop him there and then. To his credit, though he begrudged my ultimatum, Hall accepted it.

It was all too clear what a huge disappointment it was to Hall not to get up Everest. But it would not be the end of his quest.

So only Darrin and I were left to try for the summit on May 15. I could hardly believe that no one else in our team wanted to go for the top. After all our efforts over more than two months, I felt we owed it to ourselves to try for some sort of success, even if only one or two of us could get to the summit. Fortunately, the wind had at last dropped to zero. I decided to sleep breathing bottled oxygen to maximize my recovery for the morning, and to use it on my summit attempt. I had always felt that I would never use supplemental oxygen when I was climbing for myself. But if I was guiding, then it was not only permissible but responsible to use it. That way I'd be in better shape to go to the aid of a teammate or client in trouble. With bottled O's, I could rest in place for as long as an hour at a time without getting too cold. (This whole question of whether or not to guide with supplemental oxygen would be thrust to the fore during the disaster of 1996.)

Darrin and I got going at 1:00 a.m. Four members of the Wilcox party had set out an hour and a half before us. The weather was perfect, and I had high expectations, but when I felt the weight of eighteen pounds of oxygen apparatus on my back, I was hit with a new wave of discouragement. Only ten minutes into the climb, gasping for breath, I discovered that my regulator was broken. In disgust, I returned to camp and got another one. Then, still early in the morning, the flow of oxygen abruptly stopped. The gas, I found out, had been leaking out of a faulty hose. I was only too glad to chuck the whole apparatus and go on without artificial aids.

From the start, Darrin had complained of really cold feet. After I passed him, he faded into the distance behind me. During the previous night he had voiced trepidation about the summit day, and perhaps those doubts took some of the wind out of his sails. After only an hour or so, I saw him turn back and descend to camp. It was a wise decision—discretion the better part of valor. No mountain is worth losing your toes for.

The weather was indeed perfect, but the snow conditions were terrible—"dry, unconsolidated shit," I called it in my diary. "Wouldn't even hold a step." Fortunately, I had the Wilcox party's broken trail to follow.

Climbing with bottled oxygen, Mark Richey, Yves La Forest, Rick Wilcox, and Barry Rugo got to the top between 8:30 and 9:45 a.m. They passed me on their way down, each giving me hearty encouragement. Now I was truly alone on the upper part of the mountain. I struggled on. The psychological strain of the last two months of guiding on a team that was starting to come apart at the seams was now taking its toll. I was physically and mentally fried. I'd already lost close to twenty pounds. Only my congenital stubbornness kept me going.

The last stretch from the South Summit to the top almost turned me back, as blowing snow decreased the visibility. "The ridge seemed never-ending," I later wrote in my diary. "But I was too close to quit even 100 yards short. I wouldn't have been able to live with myself." At around 1:00 p.m., I was clumping, exhausted, up the last few steps. "Hardest day of my life!" I would pronounce it in my diary, and twenty-two years later, I can look back and agree: that summit push at the age of thirty-one was indeed the most difficult and strenuous effort of my career to that point.

All day, I'd assumed I'd have the summit to myself, even if only for half an hour, as I had the year before. But to my annoyance, as the top grew near, I saw a guy standing there. He must have come up from the opposite side, via the northeast ridge. To my further annoyance, he was photographing my every move.

The down suits Robo had ordered for us were supposed to be "magenta" in color, but the real thing was closer to a garish pink. I later learned that the guy on the summit sized me up and thought, *Hmm, climber without bottled oxygen, solo, pink suit—must be French.*

On top, I awkwardly shook hands with the stranger. A balaclava covered his face, all except for the mouth. But there was something awfully familiar about that mouth, that smile. Suddenly it hit me.

"Andy?!"

"Ed?!"

By the most improbable of coincidences, it was Andy Politz, my partner from the Kangshung Face, my RMI buddy from our semi-legendary "load wars" on Rainier. He'd gotten to the top about an hour before, as part of an expedition led by Eric Simonson on the northeast ridge. We hugged and whooped with laughter.

Andy would have stayed there and chatted for hours, but I was obsessed with the need to head back down and help our crippled expedition get safely off the mountain. And the weather was deteriorating by the minute. "I'll give you a call when I get home," I yelled back as I started down. But only moments later, I thought, *Hey, was that a perfect ending to two months on Everest, or what?*

From the moment I'd first stood on top of Everest in 1990, my main ambition had been focused on K2. I'd climbed Kangchenjunga in 1989. If I could get up K2, I'd become the first American to reach the summits of the world's three highest mountains. But that sort of "record" wasn't really important to me (unless it could help me attract sponsors). Ever since I'd read Charlie Houston and Bob Bates's classic *K2: The Savage Mountain* as a teenager, I'd dreamed of tackling that beautiful and forbidding pyramid in the heart of the Karakoram. I had come to think of K2 as the Holy Grail of mountaineering. For me, the peak loomed as an ultimate test of skill and nerve, but at last I felt ready to make the attempt.

At the end of a psychologically grueling three-month expedition in the summer of 1992, I accomplished my goal by reaching the summit of K2. That expedition was the most dramatic in my life to that date, and it formed a crucial turning point in my career. The trip turned into a genuine epic. On K2, I came closer to dying than I ever had in the mountains, and in pushing on with Charley Mace and Scott Fischer to the top in a gathering storm with hideous snow conditions, I committed what I still regard as the greatest mistake of my climbing life. Surviving the frightening descent from K2 will never cancel out my conviction that going to the top on August 16 was indeed a bad mistake. That's one area—judgment in the mountains—in which I know better than to cut myself undeserved slack.

I wrote about the K2 expedition at length in both *No Shortcuts to the Top* and *K2: Life and Death on the World's Most Dangerous Moun-*

tain, so I won't repeat the story here. What happened that summer, however, had a profound effect on the campaign I planned for 1993. In a nutshell, on K2 I had expended so much effort helping others get up the mountain, and in three cases, helping save their lives, that I nearly lost any chance of making my own push toward the top from Camp IV on the Shoulder at 26,000 feet. In addition, having had to buy a place on an expedition run by a Russian team, whose leader proved to be probably the most selfish jerk I've ever had to team up with, I came home from Pakistan that summer disillusioned with big expeditions composed of climbers who were strangers to one another before they gathered at base camp.

The answer that sprouted in my brain through the fall and winter of 1992–93 was to try to climb an 8,000er solo. As long as I was willing to spend as much energy on a mountain as I had on K2, I thought, why not expend it all on myself, instead of in the service of others—some of whom seemed only minimally grateful? My inspiration was Reinhold Messner's dazzling feat in 1980, when he soloed the Great Couloir on Everest during the monsoon season without supplemental oxygen—a deed regarded by many as the boldest in the history of mountaineering.

My plan was to go back to the north side of Everest in 1993 and attack the Japanese Couloir, a snow-and-ice gully that was one of the most direct routes on the north face. On a solo attempt on this route in 1987, Roger Marshall had died while I was on the adjoining Great Couloir, on my first attempt on Everest. The year before, two stellar Swiss climbers, Erhard Loretan and Jean Troillet, had dazzled the mountaineering world by dashing up the Japanese Couloir alpine-style in only forty-three hours.

My scheme for 1993 was to acclimatize on Everest by making

training jaunts up and down the lower part of the face, then to go fast and light alpine-style to the top and back in three days. At the same time, I recognized how scary a proposition any solo attempt on an 8,000er would inevitably be. Without a partner to rope up with, I knew every crevasse posed a potential death trap. And the psychological trial would be extreme. Still, I was psyched to try it. As I wrote in my diary early during the trip, while I was still in Kathmandu, "Tomorrow begins the biggest, most challenging adventure of my life."

Knowing that good snow cover on my route would make climbing faster and less technical, I decided to go to Everest in the autumnal postmonsoon season. (All through the summer, the monsoon smothers the high Himalaya in new snow.) The biggest challenge of mounting a solo expedition was paying for it. I made a rough calculation of the cost for everything from the Chinese permit to airfare to hiring porters and yak drivers, and came up with the ungodly total of $45,000. This, on top of still being in debt from my K2 expedition. The prospect of raising cash to repay my K2 debts as well as fund an Everest expedition overwhelmed me. Although I had now climbed the three highest peaks in the world, that feat had scarcely increased my fame. When *Outside* ran a short profile about me, the magazine titled the piece "Ed Who?"

The only answer was to spend the winter trying to get companies to sponsor me. Back then, I was a complete naif about how to do so. In a time before the Internet, the only tools at my disposal were the telephone and the post office. I wrote dozens of letters to companies without getting a single response. Or I'd cold-call a firm such as Coca-Cola, only to get some very junior staffer on the phone. In a breathless rush, I'd tell her what I would offer the company in exchange for their dollars. She would inevitably say, "I'll give this info to our head of marketing, and he'll call you back." And of course, nobody ever called back.

My whole fund-raising effort would have been a bust but for the timely intervention of two friends with great connections, Gil Friesen and Jodie Eastman. Thanks to them, I ended up with sponsorship deals with MTV and Polo Ralph Lauren. I also had a small stipend from a sleeping bag manufacturer called MZH. In the end, through various deals and promises, to my considerable surprise, I raised enough money to pay for the Everest expedition and settle some of the leftover bills from K2.

For my team on the mountain, I would have only two partners: Carolyn Gunn, a veterinarian friend from my days guiding on Rainier, who would serve as base camp cook and as doctor, and Tamding, one of the Sherpas from our '91 expedition. Since he was fluent in Tibetan, Tamding would prove very helpful in dealing with the Chinese bureaucracy and in communicating with our yak drivers.

The usual hassles—securing a permit, retrieving lost baggage, and hiking for days along roads washed out by monsoon downpours on the approach—threatened to derail my trip, but by August 24, we'd arrived at base camp at 17,000 feet well below the snout of the Rongbuk Glacier. Five days later, we headed up the valley to establish an advance base camp. I had hired only two yak drivers with six yaks, yet even so small an entourage succumbed to its own inertia. On the twenty-ninth, half in amusement, half in exasperation, I recorded in my diary:

Tons of fartin' around on the part of yakkers. They are in no hurry to go. Get up, scoot around, sit down, have tea, collect the yaks, smoke

In 1922, George Leigh Mallory (left), Teddy Norton, and Howard Somervell (who took the photo) reached 27,000 feet on Everest's northeast ridge.

1

The 1924 expedition group photo. Mallory is standing second from left, his boot on a teammate's shoulder. Sandy Irvine is standing first left.

2

The last photo ever taken of Mallory (left) and Irvine, as they set off from the North Col on June 6, 1924.

3

Eric Shipton gazes at the summit pyramid of Everest on the 1935 expedition.

5

Edmund Hillary (left) and Tenzing Norgay high on the South Col route in 1953.

Tenzing on the summit on the first ascent of Everest, May 29, 1953.

6

Two climbers dwarfed by the mountain as they approach the West Ridge in 1963. (© Barry Bishop, courtesy of National Geographic Society)

7

Tom Hornbein climbing high on the West Ridge, May 22, 1963. (Photo by Willi Unsoeld and used by permission of Jolene Unsoeld)

8

Dougal Haston climbs the Hillary Step very late on September 24, 1975, as he and Doug Scott complete the first ascent of the Southwest Face. Hours later, the two men would survive the highest bivouac ever attempted to that date. (© Doug Scott)

Krzysztof Wielicki, one of the two Poles who made the first winter ascent of Everest in 1980. (© Bogdan Jankowski)

10

Leszek Cichy, Wielicki's summit partner in the winter ascent. (© Bogdan Jankowski)

11

George Lowe leading the crux pitch on the Kangshung Face in 1981. (© Sue Giller)

12

A climber jumars the headwall on the Kangshung Face. Climbing of such a high technical standard had never before been accomplished on Everest. (1981 American Kangshung Expedition)

13

Erhard Loretan on the summit of Everest after he and Jean Troillet completed their astounding 1986 alpine-style ascent of the Japanese and Hornbein Couloirs in only 43 hours round-trip. (© Jean Troillet.)

14

The southeast ridge from the South Col, now the standard route on Everest. The British Southwest Face expedition ascended the couloirs and rock bands on the left. (© Ed Viesturs)

15

The Kangshung or east face of Everest. The American team in 1983 ascended the central buttress. (© Ed Viesturs)

16

a butt, argue & talk, scoot around, weigh the loads, sort the loads, smoke a butt, re-weigh the loads, recollect the yaks, on & on & on. Finally got loaded & moving @ 9:30. . . . The yakkers kept wanting to stop & camp but I pushed 'em on to this site @ 18,290 feet.

That month my former partners from Kangchenjunga, Jim Wickwire and John Roskelley, were making a two-man attempt on the traditional route via the North Col and northeast ridge. I spent some time chewing the fat with my old pals in their base camp. In the end, however, they got no higher than the North Col. Disgusted by the incessant snowstorms, they threw in the towel in early September. Wickwire later wrote in the *American Alpine Journal*, "The monsoon arrived late [in 1993] and was said to have been the worst in 40 years."

Indeed, the snow that fall seemed incessant. My diary records day after day of griping about the weather. On September 8, for instance, I wrote, "Snow, snow, snow! When will it stop?" With the slopes above me loaded with new snow, I watched as one avalanche after another shot down the Japanese Couloir. Because it was such a direct line, the couloir made a perfect funnel for snowslides. So I decided to abandon the route and focus instead on the neighboring Great Couloir, the route we had attempted in 1987. Although less direct, the Great Couloir promised to be a lot safer. If I could get up it, it would still constitute a solo ascent of the north face.

During the first week in September, the three of us managed to establish a second camp (we called it Corner Camp) at 19,000 feet, reached by a straightforward hike up the moraine on the main branch of the Rongbuk Glacier. We were still a full thousand vertical feet below the base of the true north face, and a discouraging 10,000 feet below the distant summit of Everest. Huddled inside our tent in Corner Camp on the evening of September 3, Carolyn and I had a close call of the sort I had never experienced before in the mountains. My diary:

Snowed like a mother most of the night. . . . I was heating water in my bivi tent & Carolyn came over. It was snowing so we had the mosquito netting up to keep the snow out. After a while we both got very dizzy and bolted for the door. Carolyn nearly passed out—her eyes rolled back into her sockets. I held her and kept telling her to breathe, breathe while I tried to regain my consciousness. Whew. We finally both came around again.

Through the fog of my dizziness, I had dimly realized what was happening: carbon monoxide from the stove, trapped inside the tent by the snow and two layers of roofing cloth, was poisoning us. I had read about other climbers and explorers dying from the very same insidious peril. Because carbon monoxide is odorless, you don't detect it. The feeling is very much as if you're simply falling asleep. And if you do give in to sleepiness, a simple mistake becames a fatal one.

By September 12, I had a real plan of action. I would climb with Tamding to a Camp II at 21,400 feet, finally coming to grips with the north face itself. This part of the route was dangerously crevassed, so by roping up with Tamding on my first probe, I could safely scout and mark the most hazardous places. Then Tamding would descend to base camp. The next day, I'd try to push all the way up to 25,000 feet by myself and, with luck, establish a Camp III there. Then come all the way back down to ABC to rest up for my summit push.

The first part of the plan went according to Hoyle, although

I wrote on the morning of September 13, "Didn't sleep great last night—too much goin' thru my head." Finally the weather had turned, with a clear, sunny morning. The great irony of the high Himalaya is that on such a day, you can actually be too hot! All day on the thirteenth, I sweltered under the blazing sun. The next day, I reached 23,500 feet before retreating to Camp II. And then it started snowing again. Even in my relatively secure perch low on the face, I worried about avalanches. I had carefully placed my camp in the middle of a field of huge crevasses, which I hoped would swallow any avalanches hurtling down the Great Couloir.

Nonetheless, all afternoon and through the night, I heard those avalanches crashing down from far above me. I got almost no sleep. In the dark, my imagination ran wild as I began to question the safety of my tent site. At times, the only way I could ease the anxiety was to put in my earphones and turn up the volume on my Walkman. The next morning, I was only too glad to bolt from Camp II back down to the safety and comfort of ABC.

It was, I had to admit, a discouraging start. As I would later learn, almost no one was having success on the north side of Everest that year, thanks to the snowfall. But I gave myself a pep talk in my diary on the fifteenth: "Now it's my turn! I feel ready mentally—just need a break in the weather so the snow can settle & I can go for it. . . . The familiarity of the Great Couloir [from my 1987 attempt] makes it a bit more comforting."

Well, it was not meant to be. During the next three weeks I made six separate attempts on the Great Couloir. On every thrust, I was defeated by the snow conditions above my high camp, so I'd retreat to base camp. The fickle weather only added to my doubts. Those three weeks were an ordeal by uncertainty, with fear the steady undercurrent. I vented my exasperation in diary entries.

Sept. 19
Snowing again! What's the deal? . . . This snowing shit is pissing me off big time. I come up, flail, get hammered by snow & bail on back to ABC.

Sept. 23
Same shit—different day! Ugh! Bored, irritated, frustrated, peeved, etc, etc. Can only read so much & listen to music for so long.

Sept. 24
This seems like a surrealistic dream—each day is the same, blending into the next, no difference. Days go by & nothing happens. Someone/ something is trying my patience.

Sept. 27
My mood cycles from very depressed to optimistic (on sunny days). Just hangin' around every day is killing me—what a waste of time!

I was playing a chess game with the weather. At base camp, I felt safe, with plenty of supplies to wait out the storms. But I'd begin to wonder whether it was clear and sunny at my highest camp, and the temptation was to head up and see. At Camp II I had only a minimal supply of food and fuel, so each trip up I had to carry more. I knew that even after a storm had passed, I needed to wait at least twenty-four hours for the fresh snow to consolidate. Then I'd race back up to Camp II.

In my little tent among the crevasses, I'd fall asleep full of hope and anticipation. Usually my alarm would wake me up around 1:00 a.m. Outside, everything was completely silent. *It's not snowing!* I'd think, only to zip open the tent door to see yet another dump of snow. The new snow that had settled on my tent walls had muffled the sound of the fresh storm. I'd sit it out for another day or two, then in frustration race back down to base camp.

On September 29, when I climbed back up to Camp II, I found the tent completely buried in new snow, with only the tip of the roof peeking out of the drift. It seemed like a warning sign, but I was still determined to go to 25,000 feet the next day. Now anxiety supplanted boredom. "A big mystery right now," I wrote about the route ahead. "I'm excited, scared, worried, apprehensive. . . . Anxious about the snow—it could be great or it could be hell."

"Hell" was the right guess. Despite leaving Camp II at 2:00 a.m. in hopes of better conditions, I found myself punching knee-deep through a crusty surface into unconsolidated powder beneath. It took only forty-five minutes of slogging for me to acknowledge another defeat, because the risk of triggering an avalanche was too great. I turned back at only 22,800 feet.

On October 9, I set out on my last attempt, still hoping to reach the summit in a three-day alpine-style push. By now, however, the strain of weeks of danger and solitude had gotten to me. As I wrote in my diary, "If anything [the snow conditions] have gotten worse. Agh! What to do? Rule #1—Don't get killed!"

With a 40-pound load on my back, I was off by 1:00 a.m. The sky was clear and the wind was down, but the snow underfoot was as unstable as ever. Angling up a steep diagonal slope, I took a few gingerly steps. All of a sudden the whole slope settled beneath me with a loud *whompf!* In that moment, I felt sheer terror. I knew that that kind of settling was the likely precursor to a massive avalanche. The whole couloir, it seemed, was ready to cut loose.

At least the mountain had forced me to make the decision I'd dreaded for the last month. I headed down, holding my breath with each footstep. I was finished with the north face. In six attempts, I'd gotten no higher than 23,500 feet—a colossal 5,500 vertical feet short of the summit. What was most frustrating was the knowledge that it wasn't my lack of technical ability or courage that had thwarted my attempt, but just lousy weather and insanely dangerous snow conditions.

I still wasn't willing to give up entirely. If I could switch my objective to the traditional route, head up the East Rongbuk Glacier to the North Col, and then climb along the northeast ridge to the summit, I'd feel that my campaign was a success. So, on October 10 and 11, Tamding and I blitzed our way up to the basin just below the North Col. On the twelfth, I climbed to the col and pitched my tent there. By now, however, the constant snowstorms had given way to fierce winds. On the thirteenth, I got to 25,600 feet on the face above the col, but had to turn back. I waited for the winds to die down through the night of the fourteenth, but it just wasn't in the cards. On the fifteenth, I made another try, but couldn't even match my high point of two days before. The wind was not only bitterly cold—it made simply moving upward scary and dangerous.

That evening I wrote in my diary, "The game is over. Everest wins/Ed loses."

On October 18, the trucks arrived at base camp to pick us up. Of all the parties on the north side of Everest that autumn, we were the last to leave.

I felt a deep disappointment, but I knew I'd given it my best shot. Unlike my try at the Kangshung Face in 1988, it wasn't objective danger or difficulty that turned me back in 1993. It was the ceaseless snowstorms that piled drifts into hair-trigger avalanche slopes throughout September, then wind too strong and cold to survive in mid-October. Later I would take some solace in the knowledge that of all the parties on the north side of Everest that autumn, including such world-class mountaineers as Jim Wickwire and John Roskelley, only two teams put any climbers on top. A total of six men reached the summit that season from the north, and none of them topped out after October 10.

Himalayan climbing is always a crap shoot. That autumn, the monsoon simply refused to loosen its grip on Everest. It would be presumptuous to claim that, given better weather, I would have succeeded—but at least I would have had a fighting chance. No matter how well you prepare, no matter what shape you're in, no matter how determined you are to succeed, an 8,000-meter peak can smack you flat. At least that autumn I'd obeyed my Rule #1: "Don't get killed."

My solo attempt on the Great Couloir represented my eighth attempt on an 8,000er. (In the spring of 1993, I'd tried Shishapangma, getting to the central summit, but balking at the horrendously corniced knife-edged ridge leading a mere hundred yards to the true summit.) I think it surprised even me that among those eight expeditions, five had been to Everest. I've never thought of Everest as the most interesting or challenging of the fourteen 8,000ers—those honors would fall to K2 and Annapurna. So why did I keep coming back to the world's highest peak? There were pragmatic reasons—a chance to guide in 1991, a place on a team organized by Jim Whittaker in 1990. But Everest had somehow gotten under my skin. There's something about that mountain that lured me back again and again . . . as it has lured other climbers, starting with Mallory.

By the end of 1993, I was still struggling to scrape together a living as a full-time climber. I actually considered resuming a career as a veterinarian. In low moments, I wondered whether I'd squandered an advanced education only to become a part-time carpenter supporting a climbing addiction. Thirty-four years old, I was still living in a basement apartment, although I'd upgraded my windowless cell to a place that had big windows opening on a lawn with a matchless view of Puget Sound. I'd recently ended a serious relationship, because my girlfriend couldn't suppress her animosity about my being away so often on long trips. The atmosphere between us had grown so tense that even talking about climbing or going to parties with other climbers got on her nerves.

Then, out of the blue, sometime that autumn, John Cumming, an RMI guide friend of mine, called me up and offered to cast me as the leading sponsored climber for a new outdoor gear company that his father was financing, to be called Mountain Hardwear. It was a kind of "Hallelujah" moment, and I accepted without a second's hesitation. I'll never forget that phone call, which, along with Gil Friesen's intervention the year before, which had won me MTV sponsorship, marked one of the true turning points of my career. Mountain Hardwear would continue to sponsor me through the completion of my Endeavor 8000 in 2005, and though I no longer represent the company, I'm lastingly grateful for the huge boost in my career those folks provided.

Soon after the call from John Cumming, Rob Hall invited me to guide clients on Everest in the coming spring. I'd met Rob on K2 in 1992, where he was climbing with his inseparable partner Gary Ball. Hall and Ball, as we called them, were arguably the leading team running guided trips on 8,000-meter peaks, having founded a firm called Adventure Consultants. I was in awe of this pair of famous Kiwi climbers when I met them at base camp, but we got along well on K2, and I played an instrumental role in getting Ball down the mountain alive after he was stricken with pulmonary edema in our highest camp, at 26,000 feet.

Sadly, the very next year Gary died on Dhaulagiri, when he again was felled by pulmonary edema. Unwilling to abandon Adventure Consultants, Rob invited me to help guide his clients in '94.

Everest for the sixth time, when I still had my sights set on other 8,000ers? Nonetheless, I didn't hesitate to accept Rob's offer. Guiding on Everest for a small salary sure beat slapping together houses in Seattle in midwinter sleet as a way to make ends meet. And as I contemplated the upcoming expedition, I came up with an idea that Rob quickly agreed to. If we got up Everest reasonably early in the season, and if we could buy places on someone else's permit, Rob and I could give Lhotse, Everest's neighbor and the fourth-highest mountain in the world, a shot. Acclimatized on Everest, we might be able to dash up Lhotse in alpine style in only a few days.

I got to base camp below the Khumbu Icefall by late March, well in advance of Rob and the clients. With our six Sherpas, I puttered around, making our base camp habitable, building benches and tables out of rocks, and even carrying loads through the icefall, along the route that another team of Sherpas had trailblazed with ladders and fixed ropes.

Our six clients were an intriguingly mixed bunch. There were two Americans, Dave Keaton and Dave Taylor, and two Germans, Ekke Gundelach and Helmut Seitzl. Back for a second go at Everest was my friend Hall Wendel, whom I'd turned back at the South Col in 1991. Since that expedition, we'd become great pals. After Everest, Hall had hired me to guide him on peaks in Mexico, Ecuador, and New Zealand, as well as on an attempt on 23,494-foot-high Pumori near Everest. He also invited me on several sailing trips in the Caribbean aboard his beautiful yacht, during which we spent many raucous days and nights island hopping and scuba diving. We became such good friends that eventually I quit charging him for my time as a guide and just had him cover expenses. This year, on Hall's return to Everest, I would be his staunchest supporter as he strived to attain the goal that he admitted was paramount in his dreams.

The sleeper in our bunch was a Norwegian, Erling Kagge. At age thirty-one, he was already renowned in his native country for his polar exploits. In 1990, with Børge Ousland, he had completed the first unsupported journey to the North Pole. Then in 1992–93, he made the first solo unsupported trek to the South Pole, covering 814 miles in fifty-two days. He'd brought his book about this feat, *Alone to the South Pole*, along on the expedition, and, as a longtime devotee of polar literature, I devoured it in what little spare time I had on the trip.

Yet Erling had never climbed a real mountain of any kind before. To make Everest the goal of your first mountaineering venture was pretty bold. But if he succeeded (with our help), he'd be the first person to claim the "three poles"—90 degrees south and north and the highest point on earth.

During those preliminary days, as I put it in my diary, I was "the only white boy on the hill." I amused myself by observing the Sherpas' antics as they carried loads through the icefall. "It's funny to see some of the Sherpas trying to look very fashionable and a bit glitzy . . ." I wrote of their dress and demeanor. "Too bad there aren't any women up there to impress! Then there's the old guard—climbing in tattered sweaters, old wool hats, & jeans." There was also a not-so-subtle rivalry to prove who was fittest and could move fastest. "Nima, Norbu & Ang Dawa are always battling for the lead.

Tashi & I are just behind them & then Chombi & Tenzing follow behind us. . . . It seems there is a bit of competition going on between the Sherps & also to show off for the white boy. I just hang with 'em to show that I'm not a pushover."

On April 6, Rob arrived with his wife, Jan Arnold, who would serve as our base camp manager, and the six clients. Hall and I reconnected immediately, although his hyperness got on my nerves a bit. As I wrote,

Hall always wants to play cards [at base camp]—I'm not always into it. I want some solitude, think time & relaxation. . . . Hall gets bored quickly, but he doesn't want to work or haul loads. So he gets antsy. He doesn't realize the amount of work that goes on while he's twiddling his thumbs. . . . Great guy, though—hopefully many more adventures together.

As I had first discovered in 1991, being a paying client can lend itself to a certain complacency; it's as if the money a guy forks out makes him think he's bought the privilege of being waited on. There were times in the first weeks on Everest in 1994 when this penchant drove me a little crazy. On April 24, I complained in my diary,

At lunch we discussed what [the clients] should carry to Camp III tomorrow to sleep. Food, tent, [sleeping] pads, bags—it's all up there. All they need to carry is clothes, headlamp, cup & spoon. Some balked because they had to carry their own fucking plastic cup! Come on!

Still, all six of our clients were good people, and they were performing well as we moved steadily through the icefall and across the Western Cwm. That spring we were blessed with some of the best weather I'd ever experienced on Everest, and Rob and I began to believe that we could make our summit attempt early enough to give the two of us ample "leftover" time for our crack at Lhotse.

After making a single push to Camp III at 23,500 feet to acclimatize, the clients and Rob headed all the way down to the hill town of Dingboche. It was Rob's idea that relatively thick air, good food and drink, and three days of rest would rejuvenate the whole team. In the meantime, the Sherpas and I kept hauling loads all the way up to the South Col at 26,000 feet. In the end, that splitting of forces maybe wasn't the best idea. At base camp, the Sherpas and I had control of our food preparation and kitchen hygiene, and we were relatively isolated from members of other teams who might be suffering from various illnesses. But at Dingboche, eating food prepared by locals, some of our clients came down with unpleasant gastrointestinal problems. "Most of the clients," I wrote on May 3, "didn't feel that the trip down valley was really worth it. It's humid, lots of yak shit, some got the shits, etc. They're all back [at base camp] and happy to be here."

Amazingly, the weather stayed almost perfect, day after day of clear skies with relatively light winds. Our plan was to leave base camp on May 5 to start our summit push, aiming for May 9 as the day to go to the top. Among the other teams on the south side that year was a party guided by Todd Burleson, as well as an Everest clean-up expedition that included my partner from K2, Scott Fischer. Despite the considerable experience of those climbers, they seemed to wait for Rob to give the signal when it was time to head up the hill.

This wasn't the first, nor would it be the last time that I bore witness to what I called "summit fever." As I wrote in my diary on May 4, "Tomorrow <u>we</u> go—the Swedes go; Scott's team goes! The lemming effect!! No one wants to be out front, alone. If I was alone I'd be up & gone Johnson—get away from the crowds. ('Herd' is more like it!)"

On May 5 our whole team climbed to Camp II at 21,000 feet in the Western Cwm. We rested there for a day, then moved up to Camp III on the Lhotse Face on the seventh. On the eighth, we climbed to the South Col. I'd decided to use bottled oxygen on this ascent, because as a guide, I thought it more responsible to use that aid in case any of the clients got into trouble. I first turned on my set as we moved through the Geneva Spur just below the South Col. The weather was still holding.

That night I tried to sleep with supplemental oxygen, but gave up—the apparatus has never felt comfortable to me. To Rob's and my delight, the clients were all faring well. Hall Wendel had learned from 1991. This year he was in far better shape and better prepared mentally. As we'd climbed through the Geneva Spur, he stayed right on my tail.

We awoke at 11:00 p.m., as the Sherpas served us tea. Rob always had two extra Sherpas at high camp whose chief role was to melt ice for water and keep everyone hydrated and fed. They would also act as back-up support in case we needed more manpower on the climb above the South Col. That night it was clear and starry, with virtually no wind. I couldn't quite believe our good fortune. Each client carried two bottles of oxygen, which at a rate of two liters per minute should last him through the whole twelve-hour trip to the summit. The Sherpas carried a third bottle for each client to be used on the descent. I carried three bottles myself, as did Rob.

Everything went as planned. Just behind Ang Dorje, our Sherpa who took the lead, Hall Wendel moved confidently upward. He seemed unstoppable, and I was quite impressed with his performance. Hall reached the summit at the early hour of 10:15 a.m. In the middle of the pack, I topped out at 10:30. I stayed there an hour with Rob, as one by one, all six of our clients reached the summit. Three of our Sherpas—Ang Dorje, Nima Norbu, and Norbu—also got to the top.

On the way down, Hall ran out of gas, but he was still able to move, albeit slowly, under his own power. I ran sweep for our team, arriving with Hall back at the South Col at 6:00 p.m.

The same day that we climbed to the top, Scott Fischer made his first ascent of Everest, doing so without bottled oxygen. I was really proud of my old buddy's achievement, and let him know. Four days later, Burleson's entire team summitted. All in all that spring, a total of thirty-seven men (no women) reached the top via the South Col route.

Everest is never easy, but that was by far the smoothest ascent of any 8,000er I'd had in the eight years since I'd started climbing in the Himalaya. It was very gratifying when Hall later told me, "Ed, you were right to turn me around in ninety-one. We did it right this time. I can't believe how great it feels!" The trickle of doubt I'd harbored since then now evaporated. Instead, my conviction that I should always listen to my instincts and never let myself be swayed by clients' or teammates' desires was reinforced.

As for Erling Kagge, he impressed all of us. He easily picked up the basic climbing skills, and he was so strong and so comfortable with Everest's "arctic" conditions that he fit in like a seasoned mountaineer. Upon returning to Norway, he would write a book about his triple triumph, called *Pole to Pole & Beyond*.

By May 11, all of us had arrived back at base camp, and the next day, the clients started the hike out, guided by the Sherpas and Jan Arnold. Rob and I still had as much as three weeks before the monsoon would hit. We rested for a day, then headed back up the route we knew so well.

In a mere four days from base camp to the top and back, we climbed Lhotse alpine-style, stopping to camp only twice along the way. We carried one small tent and a single sleeping bag that we zipped open and shared like a blanket. Rob used bottled oxygen; I didn't. We stood on the summit on May 16, just seven days after reaching the summit of Everest. By that date, the "herd" that had thronged the south side of Everest had vanished, everyone having headed down the Khumbu valley to civilization. Descending from Lhotse, Rob and I had the whole Western Cwm and the Khumbu Icefall to ourselves. It was a magical experience.

We nicknamed our feat a "twofer," as in "two for the price of one." I would go on to apply that tactic on a number of subsequent seasons in the Himalaya and the Karakoram. With Lhotse, I'd now topped out on four of the fourteen 8,000ers, and come within a hundred yards of the top of a fifth, Shishapangma. Even as I headed home from Everest, I was planning a trip to Cho Oyu with Rob for the fall of 1994. And for the first time, I really began to ponder the possibility of climbing all fourteen. With the four highest 8,000ers under my belt, and the security blanket of Mountain Hardwear sponsorship, I felt that this was a tangible goal. I didn't care so much about becoming the first American to climb all fourteen. What motivated me was the conviction that trying to reach the summit of all the 8,000ers was the kind of lifetime challenge I had always sought.

• • •

Things went so well in 1994 that Rob invited me to come back the next year and guide for Adventure Consultants again. It wasn't my ambition in life to become an Everest guide, running trips for clients year after year on the South Col or northeast ridge routes, as climbers such as Russell Brice and Eric Simonson had done, and as Rob and Scott Fischer were starting to do in earnest. But once more, I concocted a twofer. After Everest, if we had time, Rob and I would hike out to Lukla, where we'd board a prearranged helicopter to fly us to the base of Makalu, the world's fifth-highest peak. If our acclimatization held up in 1995 as it had in '94, we might be able to dash up Makalu alpine-style, just as we had Lhotse.

In fact, I had a hugely ambitious program for 1995, for after flying home from Nepal and recuperating for two weeks, I would meet Rob again in Pakistan, where we'd try to get up Gasherbrum I and Gasherbrum II. Two twofers, back to back. A "fourfer"?

In the summer of 1994, at a barbecue in Seattle, I'd met Paula Barton, with whom I fell in love almost at once. It didn't take long to realize that Paula was *the* woman for me, the one I could spend the rest of my life with. Assuming, of course, that I was lucky enough to have her reciprocate my feelings.

In *No Shortcuts to the Top*, I wrote at length about my courtship of Paula, our marriage, and the years thereafter during which, despite her fears for my safety, she was my number one cheerleader as I pursued Endeavor 8000. I won't repeat the story here, but it gives me immense pride to say that, nineteen years later, we're still in love with each other as we manage a family of four great kids. Whether or not our children ever become climbers, Paula and I will support them in the goals in life they choose. I have no investment in their following in my footsteps. Let them discover their own passions, just as I did.

Paula had little grasp of mountaineering before she met me, but she gamely climbed to the top of Rainier with me that summer. It was a grim outing, cold and windy, and on the summit, with her eyelashes covered in rime ice, she chewed on a frozen bagel without complaining. On this ascent and on a few other climbs in the Cascades, Paula gained a small understanding of what it was that I did in the mountains.

That autumn on Cho Oyu, I brought up with Rob the idea of Paula coming along to Everest base camp next spring to act as assistant manager. Even though Rob had yet to meet Paula, he agreed at once and offered to pay her expenses—this despite the fact that he already had a highly competent base camp manager in his friend Helen Wilton.

Paula had never traveled anywhere in the world as remote as Nepal. In March 1995, when we arrived in Kathmandu, I explained that if the food wasn't boiled, baked, or peeled, it was probably best not to eat it. One evening, against my advice, she had a chocolate sundae with whipped cream and a maraschino cherry on top. To me the dessert looked like a gastrointestinal time bomb, and I cringed with every bite she took. Sure enough, Paula was sick as a dog and stayed in bed for the next day or two. On the hike in to Everest, we ate in all the lodges. At Gorak Shep, only a day's march short of base camp, Paula was eating a bowl of rice for dinner when she found a huge dried spider in it. She plucked it out, tossed it aside, said "Yuck!" and just kept eating. I knew then that she was my kind of partner!

As I had the year before, Paula and I got to base camp below the Khumbu Icefall before Rob and the clients had arrived. Hiking in with us was Guy Cotter, a Kiwi friend of Rob's, who was along this year as a second assistant guide. I liked Guy immediately, and welcomed the added strength he'd give our party. He was an extremely competent and experienced climber, with a dry wit and little patience for whining and incompetent clients.

As I'd learned in 1994, Adventure Consultants was famous for its elaborate base camp dining quarters. The tent was a large, rectangular, heavy canvas contraption with vertical side walls. Whoever got to base camp first—in this case, the Sherpas, Guy, and me—was in charge of the monumental job of leveling a spacious platform for the dining tent, erecting and anchoring it against possible hurricane-force winds, and building solid stone benches with backs along three inside walls that surrounded a big central table also made of stone. We would shovel gravel in to fill the gaps between the rocks. Getting everything relatively flat took a ton of work. We covered the table with a large tarp and a plastic table cloth, and cushioned the benches with thick foam pads. We also set up a stereo system with speakers hanging from the ceiling, and electric lightbulbs run on batteries charged by solar panels.

We also erected a big kitchen tent with rock walls for our Sherpa staff, and made level platforms and set up tents for each of our clients. When they finally arrived at base camp, they simply "moved in." All that prep work was backbreaking labor at 18,000 feet, but I loved it, feeling that it would only make me stronger and help me acclimatize faster. And as with a construction job, at the end of the day you get a visual reward for your day's toil.

The prime reason for all this luxury was to make the clients as comfortable as possible during their down time and recovery at base camp. It served also to help them get fit and eager to be on the verge of coming to grips with Everest. But Rob also liked to throw a big party midway through the expedition so that everyone could let off steam. He'd invite climbers from other teams to come over and party with us. Many beers would be consumed and guys and gals would dance on the table well into the night.

Rob had begun to believe that, given enough time, careful management of logistics, and patience with even the slowest of clients, he could get almost anyone up Everest. In one sense, I admired that quality in Rob. He seemed to have a deep empathy for his clients, as he did everything he could to help them fulfill their mountaineering quests. On the other hand, I was more pragmatic about guiding, or perhaps I simply had less tolerance and patience than Rob did. No matter how much I liked my clients personally, I needed them to show me that they had the toughness and grit to earn a summit. My approach, I believed, gave the mountains their due respect, and was safer as well. But there's really no right or wrong in this matter. When I worked with Rob, I deferred to his style.

By 1995, after all, Adventure Consultants had become a hugely successful company, with many loyal clients who stuck with Rob for one adventure after another. Buoyed by our Everest triumph in 1994, Rob had actually started claiming a "100% success rate" in the advertising for his guided expeditions. I later thought that a certain overconfidence in this respect contributed to the tragedy of 1996.

In any event, the weather and snow conditions turned out to be far worse in 1995 than the year before. And the clientele ... well, what you might call a "colorful character" in normal life can become a real tribulation on Everest. One of our 1995 clients, in particular, proved to be a handful. She was a Polish woman whom I'll call Karina.

Karina actually had an impressive climbing résumé, but she was a huge pain in the ass. She climbed so slowly that Guy Cotter lost all his patience with her. On trips through the Khumbu Icefall, with

Guy escorting her, she would balk at a crevasse that was so narrow, all it took was a simple step or a short jump to cross. In addition, she was clipped into a fixed rope for backup. But Karina would wail, "I cannot do this. I cannot cross. You must help me. You are my guide and that is your job." Fed up, Guy would answer, "Okay, don't cross the crevasse. Go back down." Then he would keep walking up the hill. Sure enough, with no other options, Karina would step across the crevasse and follow. But she was excruciatingly slow. Guy would climb ahead for half an hour or so, stop, make himself comfortable, and read a book until Karina arrived. As she approached, he'd pack up, then continue for another half hour and repeat the process.

Two of our other clients were Doug Hansen and Chantal Mauduit. Doug was a postal worker from Washington State who was so keen about Everest that he'd taken the night shift at his post office while he worked construction in the daytime, just to save enough money to buy a place on the Adventure Consultants team. A single parent, Doug took great pains during the expedition to stay in touch with his daughter back in Seattle. He was an extremely nice guy, and we were all pulling for him to succeed, but Everest would reduce him to his last resources. Rob, I think, got so emotionally invested in Doug's eventual success that it played a fateful role in the 1996 disaster.

Chantal was one of the top women big-range mountaineers in Europe, and she signed on with us as a client only to minimize the permit fee. She announced that she would perform the climb on her own, independent of us guides, and she had an intense ambition to become the first woman to climb Everest without bottled oxygen. She would take advantage of Rob's logistics, sleeping in our camps and using the supplies we carried up the mountain. On summit day, she would climb with us, accompanied by two Sherpas, but eschewing the aid of us guides.

Or so she intended. Three years earlier, on K2, Scott Fischer and I had had to give up our first summit bid to help rescue Chantal after she had collapsed on her way down from the summit. An eerily similar scenario would play out in 1995.

It was great having Paula along at base camp. But the trip was frustrating for her. She knew she didn't have the experience to go up through the icefall, but there was too little to do down below while the rest of us were shepherding loads and clients slowly up the mountain. To stay busy she reorganized the food supplies and took day hikes down to the lower villages. She even organized aerobic classes for anyone stuck at base camp while we were "up on the hill"! Throughout the trip, Paula worried about my safety, but in radio chats from higher camps, I'm sure I minimized for her the inevitable dangers of climbing Everest.

Despite the shortcomings of Karina, our climb through the Khumbu Icefall, across the Western Cwm, and up the Lhotse Face to the South Col went reasonably well. By early May, we had five clients installed at 26,000 feet in Camp IV on the South Col. One of the spunkier clients was an orthopedic surgeon from Tucson named Abelardo. He and I were already friends, since I'd guided him on the Mexican volcanoes. One night, when I gave a talk in Tucson, I had stayed at Abelardo's house. When we went to bed, he said we'd meet in the kitchen for coffee and breakfast at 9:00 a.m. I thought, *Wow, that's a nice leisurely start to the day*. At 9:00 the next morning, as I showed up in the kitchen, Abelardo entered the house by the front door. I asked where he'd been. He said he'd already performed two hip-replacement surgeries that morning!

At the South Col, our team was strong in manpower, with all three of us guides and seven competent Sherpas ready to go, two of them assigned to accompany Chantal. Rob had targeted May 7 for our summit push. Still, the weather was iffy, and the snow conditions above the South Col were not nearly as advantageous as the year before.

On May 7, we got our usual early start in the middle of the night, but the day was cold and windy. Chantal and her Sherpas left camp before us, since she knew it would take her longer to reach the top climbing without bottled oxygen. I had misgivings about the conditions early on, but I felt that we might as well plug along, for often the winds die with the rising sun. We could still turn around if the weather got worse. In general, though, it seemed that our clients were slower and weaker than those on our team the previous year. Doug Hansen, in particular, was really hurting and moving slowly.

We got to the South Summit at 28,700 feet by 9:00 a.m. From there on, the snow conditions along the ridge leading to the true summit looked treacherous, and the wind was whipping in fierce gusts. Guy and our most talented Sherpa, Lobsang Jangbu, made a tentative scout of the ridge, but quickly decided it would be too risky for the clients. Getting everyone to the top and back safely would be a real stretch. The decision to turn around seemed obvious. I looked at Rob and pointed thumbs down. He nodded in agreement. Even so, it was tantalizing to get within 300 vertical feet of the top and have to give up, but it was the right decision. We started down with the clients.

Doug Hansen was in the worst shape, so I went ahead with him, tending him step-by-step. Rob, Guy, and several Sherpas were supervising the other clients. Doug was so wasted, he'd simply sit down in the snow. I had to yell at him to keep him moving, but by then, I'd lost my voice from breathing the dry, cold air. I put my face only inches away from Doug's and hectored him in a laryngitic rasp, "C'mon, man, you gotta keep going!"

In the midst of this grim retreat, Lobsang, who had ambitions of his own, decided to go for the top solo, rather than take care of the clients. He made the summit and caught up with us on the way down, but Rob was really pissed at him. It was for that reason that Rob didn't hire Lobsang in 1996. Instead, Scott Fischer did—and during the disastrous events that unfolded that May, Lobsang would play a pivotal but controversial role.

On my way down with Doug, I passed Chantal and her Sherpas, still moving upward. She was climbing very slowly and her lips were blue from hypoxia. We exchanged a few words, as I reminded her to make sure that she had enough energy in reserve to get down. It was the same advice I'd given her before her attempt, when she'd taken me aside and asked, "Ed, how do I do this? What are your tactics for getting up Everest without oxygen?"

Somewhat later, when Doug and I were well below the South Summit, I suddenly got a call over the radio from Rob, still at 28,700 feet. "It's Chantal," he said. "She's collapsed. We're going to have to get her down."

It was a replay of 1992 on K2. Once again, Chantal had used up every ounce of energy getting to the South Summit. And when she collapsed, she fell apart completely. She couldn't even walk, so Guy, Rob, and two Sherpas literally dragged and carried her down, as Guy later put it in disgust, "like a sack of spuds."

For all her vaunted independence as she planned to climb without our help and to make the first oxygenless female ascent of Everest, now Chantal said to Rob, "I signed up for your trip. You're responsible for me. You have to get me down."

Hearing the news over the radio, I decided to wait with Doug, even though he badly needed to get back to camp himself. When Chantal arrived, pulled and lowered down the slope by the Sherpas and Guy and Rob, I pitched in and helped drag her to the South Col. Through the night, Guy administered to her every minute, and at times he thought she was going to die. But by morning, she had recovered. She headed down from Camp IV under her own steam.

Chantal Mauduit was a very strong mountaineer, a beautiful woman, and a superstar in France. Those of us who knew her well, as I did, loved her dearly. But she had a vexing unwillingness to admit that other climbers more than once saved her life, or even to thank them for their crucial help.

Sadly, Chantal would die in her tent at 21,500 feet on Dhaulagiri in 1998, in circumstances that remain mysterious fifteen years later.

Doug Hansen made it through the night at the South Col, too. On May 8, exhausted by the dicey rescue, we all started down the mountain.

The year before, thirty-seven men and women had reached the top by the South Col route. In 1995, only six did so. Besides Lobsang, five members of another team topped out on May 15. By waiting eight days after our own attempt, they benefited from better snow conditions and weather up high. Once Rob had committed to May 7, there was no way we could take a second shot.

I'm often asked why, after investing so much time, energy, and money in an expedition such as ours, we couldn't make that second attempt. The answer is that it takes so much manpower just to get sufficient supplies and oxygen bottles to our highest camp for one summit attempt, that the prospect of resupplying that camp days or even weeks later is overwhelming. Having reached 28,700 feet on a first attempt, even the world's strongest climbers would be hard pressed to recharge for a second bid. With clients who barely got to the South Summit the first time, the task is unthinkable.

When you pick a summit date, as Rob did with May 7, you have to make an educated guess. Experience and a good weather forecast contribute to that choice, but so does luck. In the high mountains, it comes down to hit or miss. For that very reason, getting to the top of any 8,000er is such a rewarding event.

Still, it was maddening to have missed out on Everest by such a small margin. But on Makalu, Rob and I, climbing together with Veikka Gustafsson (the first of my thirteen expeditions with Veikka), got to the summit on May 18. The Everest acclimatization had paid off in spades, as we blitzed Makalu alpine-style in just four days.

Less than two months later, I got to the top of Gasherbrum II alone, as Rob, not feeling well, turned back at 23,900 feet. And only eleven days later, I topped out on Gasherbrum I with three new companions I'd met in the Baltoro, including two men who would soon achieve their own lifetime accomplishments by bagging all fourteen 8,000ers. They were the Pole Krzysztof Wielicki and the Mexican Carlos Carsolio, both incredibly strong and yet genial mountaineers.

Despite the near-miss on Everest, 1995 was my best year yet in the Himalaya and the Karakoram. I had now gotten to the summit of eight of the fourteen highest mountains in the world. I was well-launched on the path of Endeavor 8000.

As gratifying as that achievement was, I was equally proud of having performed as a caring, responsible guide on Everest. Getting both Doug Hansen and Chantal Mauduit down alive was as challenging a deed as climbing Makalu or the Gasherbrums. I'd still never lost a partner on any climb, and I'd like to think that wasn't just luck—that it sprang from a sense of duty to others, especially when they got into trouble, and from my steadily growing confidence that I needed to listen to my own instincts to tell me when to go on and when to turn back.

In mountaineering, I believe, that's a quality that's even more valuable than skill or nerve.

6

▲ ▲ ▲

The West Ridge

It took only three years to disprove Sir Edmund Hillary's prognostication that after the first ascent, no one would ever bother to climb Everest again. In 1956, a strong Swiss team put four climbers on the summit, and two other members made the first ascent of Lhotse, at 27,940 feet the fourth-highest peak in the world. That expedition approached the mountain as the British had in 1953, retracing their route through the Khumbu Icefall up to the South Col and on to the top of Everest. High on the Lhotse Face, part of the team diverged from that route to bag their secondary goal—or perhaps their primary, since the Swiss got to the top of Lhotse five days before they summitted on Everest.

After the Chinese invasion of Tibet in 1950, all approaches from the north were off-limits to Western climbers. So the north side, on which the seven British attempts in the 1920s and '30s had been prosecuted, would remain closed for another thirty years. Closed, that is, to all but the Chinese themselves—and to their on-again off-again allies, the Soviets.

Herein lies perhaps the strangest of all Everest mysteries. Persistent rumors over the decades have surfaced to the effect that a Soviet team composed of thirty-five climbers and five scientists attacked Everest from the north in 1952—the year before Hillary and Tenzing made the mountain's first ascent. Those rumors, which were substantive enough to appear in the pages of the London *Times*, had the team leaving Moscow on October 16, which seems absurdly late in the autumn. (If you're going to make a postmonsoon attempt on Everest, you need to start the hike in in August, as we did in 1988, in hopes of getting high on the peak by late September or early October.)

According to the reports, six climbers established a high camp at 26,800 feet on the northeast ridge. Then disaster struck. None of the six was ever seen again, despite exhaustive searches by their teammates. The whole party supposedly regained base camp on December 27, with winter in full force.

What makes this fugitive expedition all the more suspect is that later Soviet authorities denied that it had ever taken place. Of course, the eternally secretive Soviet Union might have covered up what could only be regarded by mountaineers the world over as a fiasco of the highest magnitude. Yet from those rumors leaked to Western newspapers and magazines, even the names of some of the lost climbers emerged—Datschnolian (the leader), Lanitsov, Alexandrovich, and Kazhinsky.

I don't know what to think about the whole business, and I've never felt any compulsion to look into it deeply. For that matter, I can't imagine how one would research such an event or nonevent, since Soviet sources from the early 1950s are not exactly open books even today. In his definitive history of Everest, Walt Unsworth grants the fugitive expedition a kind of plausibility:

The motive was certainly strong enough: had the Soviets been successful in snatching Everest it would have been an outstanding propaganda coup, comparable with Sputnik I. The political will to attempt the coup was not lacking either, particularly as this was during the Stalinist era and at the height of the cold war.

My own instinct is to regard that 1952 expedition as either a hoax or an elaborate rumor founded on misinformation. Although Russians had climbed a lot in the Pamirs and Caucasus, by 1952 the country had never launched an expedition to any of the major Himalayan peaks. And you'd think that a forty-man expedition would leave plenty of identifying trash behind, but as far as I know, no subsequent parties on the north side have found a single "artifact" that could be clearly linked to a 1952 Soviet team. It's possible that six climbers falling to their deaths from a high camp would never be found—there are quite a few Everest victims whose bodies have never been discovered. But the American 1999 expedition, on which Conrad Anker discovered Mallory's body, also found an oxygen bottle high on the northeast ridge that they proved had been left by a Chinese expedition in 1975. There's junk all over Everest, and you'd think that some of the trash that a big Soviet team might have discarded in 1952 would have Cyrillic writing on it!

The whole affair remains murky and bizarre. If no such Soviet expedition was ever launched, what was the source (or sources) of the rumors and reports, which go into such specific details as the date of leaving Moscow and the names of four of the dead climbers? An exploration hoax is usually the work of a single individual, whether delusional or simply dishonest, such as Dr. Frederick A. Cook with his bogus 1906 claim of the first ascent of Mount

McKinley. If the 1952 expedition was a hoax, it must have had multiple perpetrators.

I guess we'll never know.

We *do* know that a massive Chinese expedition attacked Everest from the north in 1960. But the fundamental truth as to what it accomplished remains, more than fifty years later, as uncertain and controversial as the shadowy Soviet venture. The expedition account was published in a Chinese propaganda journal called *China Reconstructs*, and a translation of the leader's report appeared in the British *Alpine Journal*.

According to these accounts, the astounding total of 214 expedition members traveled to the Rongbuk Glacier in March 1960. One-third of the delegation, which included both men and women, was made up of Tibetans. In the spirit of true Communist egalitarianism, acccording to *China Reconstructs*, the team included "workers, peasants, P.L.A. [People's Liberation Army] men, serfs who had just been freed from serfdom in Tibet, teachers, students, scientific researchers, medical workers and government functionaries from various parts of the country. In the expedition, there were seventeen Masters of Sports, eighteen First Grade Sportsmen and a greater number of Second Grade Sportsmen. The whole group averaged 24 years of age." The leader of the team was one Shih Chan-chun.

Over the course of the next two months, this veritable army established a series of seven camps up the East Rongbuk to the North Col, then up the north face and northeast ridge. Progress was painfully slow. Simply getting to the North Col nearly defeated the team. The advance guard of three, all Masters of Sports, took three days to climb 1,800 feet, and still gave up 160 feet short of the col. As Unsworth writes, "From the Chinese accounts, which always lack essential details, it is not possible to determine whether the reconnaissance party were ultra-cautious or merely inept."

Bouts of activity on the mountain were interrupted by lulls during which all 214 members retreated to base camp. Somehow, though, on May 3, three climbers pitched tents at a Camp VII at 27,900 feet, just below the daunting Second Step. There is no reason to doubt the truth of this claim, but that camp remains today one of the highest ever established on Everest (as opposed to open bivouacs by climbers caught by storm or darkness).

That same day, May 3, the leader Shih Chan-chun and a climber named Wang Feng-tung tried to climb the Second Step. The account of this assault is cloaked in propagandistic vagueness: "We pressed on with great determination and care," wrote Shih, "boldly using the necessary mountaineering techniques." By 9:00 p.m., the duo had allegedly climbed all of the Second Step but for a final ten-foot-high vertical cliff of rock. Again according to Shih, the two men dug a hole in the ice in which they bivouacked, taking turns sitting in each other's lap. They decided not to use supplemental oxygen, despite temperatures of minus 40 Celsius (equal to minus 40 Fahrenheit). In the morning, "Our physical condition . . . was perfectly all right except for sheer exhaustion."

Once again, however, the entire team headed down to base camp. It was not until ten days later that the principal climbers headed back up the mountain, restocking camps as they went.

By the night of May 23, four climbers had reoccupied Camp VII. The next day, they tackled the Second Step. This time, all four were breathing supplemental oxygen. They got to the final ten-foot wall.

One climber, Liu Lien-man, fell four times as he tried to scale the blank cliff. After the fourth try, he was too exhausted to make another attempt.

It's at this point (if not sooner) that the Chinese account begins to strain credibility to the breaking point. Another Chinese, Chu Yin-hua, now tried to lead the ten-foot cliff. To do so, he supposedly took off his boots and socks and attacked the wall barefoot! Even this desperate tactic failed to solve the crux.

Finally, the four men resorted to a climbing technique that dates back to the nineteenth century: the shoulder stand. The exhausted Liu crouched against the cliff as Chu (with his boots back on) clambered up his legs and stepped onto his shoulders.

He trembled all over, short of breath, but clenched his teeth and steadily stood up, with much heroic effort. Liu helped Chu Yin-hua to the top of the slab. Finally with the help of a rope paid out by Chu from above, the three others climbed the cliff one after another. Only when they had reached the top of the Second Step did they find that it had taken them three hours to climb this three-metre slab.

Liu was too exhausted to go on. The three Chinese—Liu, Chu, and Wang Fu-chu—and a Tibetan whose name is alternately given as Gonpa or Konbu, now held what they called "an open Communist Party meeting." They decided that Liu would stay where he was, at the top of the Second Step, while the other three went for the summit. "After the three others left, Liu Lien-man, at the risk of his life, switched off his oxygen in a heroic, self-sacrificing spirit to save the last few dozen litres of oxygen for his comrades assaulting the summit."

For some reason, the men had no flashlights. Yet they managed to navigate "with the help of the twinkling stars and the reflection of the snow." Reduced at times to crawling on all fours, they ran out of bottled oxygen at 28,950 feet. The following exchange took place:

> It was Wang Fu-chou who spoke first: "We are shouldering the glorious task of storming the summit. Can we turn back?"
> "Press ahead!" was the determined answer from Chu-hua and Konbu.

The Tibetan took the lead. At 4:20 a.m., he stood on the summit of Everest. His partners joined him.

In the darkness, it was impossible to take photos that might have proved the truth of the Chinese ascent. The three men spent fifteen minutes on top, planting a Chinese flag and burying a bust of Mao Tse-tung in the snow. (Neither object has since been found, but that does not in itself disprove the claim, as the snows and winds of summer and winter can drift over or tear loose anything left on top of a Himalayan peak.) As they descended, the three summiteers found Liu still alive. All four men got back to Camp VII, then, despite their exhaustion and frostbite that would later cost them amputated toes, immediately headed down the mountain.

Thus the Chinese claimed to have made the third ascent of Everest, and the first from the north. At once, Western experts cast doubt on the ascent. As Ad Carter wrote in the *American Alpine Journal*, "The details are such that mountaineers in nearly all parts of the climbing world have received the news with considerable skepticism."

Photos from Camp VII published in various journals were intensely scrutinized and compared with photos taken in the 1930s. The gist of the analysis was that the Chinese indeed had reached an altitude of 27,900 feet, where they said they had pitched their highest camp. But the tale of conquering the Second Step seemed far-fetched. Surviving an open bivouac without bottled oxygen at 28,200 feet? Climbing *barefoot* at that altitude? Crawling to the summit in the dark without flashlights?

As mentioned in chapter two, in 1975 another Chinese expedition bolted a ladder to the crux cliff at the top of the Second Step. Not only those summiteers but every subsequent climber who got to the top via the northeast ridge scaled the ladder rather than the cliff itself. Until 2007, that is, when Conrad Anker got permission temporarily to remove the ladder and free-climbed the Second Step, rating it 5.10.

In 1960, 5.10 was at the upper limit of the best rock climbers near sea level on cliffs such as Yosemite and the Shawangunks. Neither the Tibetans nor the Chinese were known for their rock climbing skills, and it seems doubtful that they could have surmounted a 5.10 pitch (even with a shoulder stand) at 28,200 feet in subzero cold. What's more, the objection Anker raised to the notion of Mallory climbing the Step in 1924 applies to the Chinese effort in 1960 as well. Even if they managed to get up the cliff, how did they get back down it? The Chinese report is silent on this subject. As Anker pointed out, there are no places just above the Second Step where a decent rappel anchor could be placed. And you don't down-climb a shoulder stand!

There's yet another reason to doubt the Chinese claim. On the opposite side of Everest at the same time, an Indian team was trying and failing to reach the summit. They reported that on May 25, the weather was bad, and that on the twenty-sixth the monsoon broke in earnest. This is in flat contradiction to the "twinkling stars" that supposedly lit the Chinese crawl through the night of May 25–26 to the top of Everest.

Given all these reasons to question the Chinese claim, it puzzles me that Unsworth, who raises many objections, still concludes, "There seems little doubt now that the Chinese did climb Everest in 1960."

On this matter, my co-author, David Roberts, and I tend to part ways. David has always had a nose for the fraudulent and years ago wrote a book called *Great Exploration Hoaxes*. He's told me that he doesn't believe there's a chance in hell the Chinese accomplished what they claimed in 1960. In contrast, I tend to give climbers the benefit of the doubt. There's a long tradition in both mountaineering and exploration of taking climbers and voyagers at their word— unless, as in the case of Frederick Cook and Mount McKinley, the evidence of fraud is simply overwhelming. I'm not willing to go on record as calling those Chinese propagandists liars. It's within the realm of the conceivable, as Unsworth states, that they did indeed make the first ascent of Everest from the north in 1960. Exactly how they did so would be interesting to learn—I sort of wish I could have been there to see how they might have done it.

When I climbed the Chinese ladder in 1990, I had a good look at the Second Step. It was clear to me that it would be very difficult at best to climb this cliff at sea level with proper rock shoes and warm weather, let alone at 28,240 feet in temperatures below zero, wearing bulky high-altitude gear. Even with the ladder, it was quite a struggle for me without supplemental oxygen. The ladder is more or less vertical, not leaning into the wall at an angle, which makes climbing it strenuous and awkward.

As with the Russians in 1952, I guess we'll never know the

truth—unless somebody digs the bust of Mao Tse-tung out of the summit snows.

It may seem curious that Americans showed so little interest in Mount Everest before the 1960s. Over the decades, leading American mountaineers had made important contributions to climbing in the great ranges. The first ascent of Minya Konka in western China, a remote mountain once rumored to be higher than Everest, was pulled off in a brilliant tour de force by a four-man American team in 1932, with Terris Moore and Richard Burdsall reaching the summit. (Minya Konka was one of the few great mountains in the world climbed on the first attempt, and Chinese authorities later tried to discredit the well-documented American triumph.)

The first ascent of Nanda Devi in 1936, which for fourteen years would remain the highest summit yet reached, was organized by four young Americans who invited four more senior Englishmen along on the expedition. It was the two Brits, Bill Tilman and Noel Odell, who reached the top, but the Americans, particularly Charlie Houston and Ad Carter, played crucial roles in this smoothly orchestrated ascent.

The three American attempts on K2, in 1938, 1939, and 1953, paved the way for the Italian first ascent in 1954. In the 1950s, another pair of American expeditions made breakthroughs in the Karakoram. The 1958 expedition to Gasherbrum I, led by Nick Clinch, succeeded in placing Pete Schoening and Andy Kauffman on the summit. That was the only one of the fourteen 8,000-meter peaks whose first ascent was achieved by Americans. Two years later, another American team made the first ascent of Masherbrum. Though slightly lower than 8,000 meters, at 25,660 feet, Masherbrum was a formidable and dangerous challenge that had previously turned back such world-class mountaineers as Don Whillans. On July 6, Willi Unsoeld and George Bell reached the summit, followed the next day by Nick Clinch (once again the expedition leader) and the Pakistani Jawed Akhter.

Two attempts on 8,000ers in the 1950s that included Americans have faded into the limbo of almost-forgotten exploits. The first attempt ever made on Makalu, the world's fifth-highest mountain, was undertaken by an American team led by Will Siri in 1954. The climbers reached a shelf at 23,300 feet before being turned back by storms. Makalu's first ascent would come the next year at the hands of a crack French team led by the Annapurna veterans Lionel Terray and Jean Couzy.

And in the autumn of 1955, an international team led by the German-born American Norman Dyhrenfurth attempted Lhotse. Among their members were three Americans: Fred Beckey, George Bell, and Dick McGowan. The team made an admirable effort, reaching 26,600 feet—only 1,300 feet short of the summit—before being defeated by cold and high winds. The intended summit push would have been made by Beckey and the Swiss climber Bruno Spirig. It was a Swiss team the next spring that made Lhotse's first ascent.

By 1960, Dyhrenfurth, who would become a kind of professional leader of large-scale Himalayan expeditions, had his eye on Everest. It would take him and others two and a half years to organize what became the American Mount Everest Expedition (AMEE). And when it finally came together, it would amount to the most complex and expensive American climbing expedition ever launched anywhere, before or since. (Most expensive, if you adjust 1963 dollars to reflect later inflation.) In the 1960s, nationalistic efforts to climb the highest peaks were the norm, and high costs were taken for granted in other countries as well as America. Think how much money the United States spent on its Apollo program, just to get the first men on the moon!

Dyhrenfurth's rationale was that only big expeditions had a good chance of succeeding on 8,000-meter peaks. According to James Ramsey Ullman, the AMEE's official historian, during the planning stages Dyhrenfurth and Charlie Houston had a lively debate about big-versus-small. To Houston, a huge crowd on Everest would violate what he called "the true mountaineering spirit." Ullman later explained Dyhrenfurth's thinking:

Norman, for his part, begged to differ. Though yielding precedence to no one in the "purity" of his mountaineering spirit, he believed that a major objective called for a major campaign. True, he conceded, there had been some notable climbs by small expeditions, among them Houston and Bates's own forays on K2. But the fact remained that they had not reached K2's summit. It was a large Italian party that finally did it. And on Everest itself, the British, after their many gallant but unsuccessful tries by comparatively small teams, had at last triumphed only when they put a powerful task force in the field.

Dyhrenfurth's argument could have been contested. His own excellent 1955 attempt on Lhotse had been with a team of only eight climbers. Masherbrum had been climbed in 1960 by a team of ten, three of whom were Pakistanis (among whom only Jawed Akhter was expected to go high). As for K2, in all likelihood the 1953 team would have made its first ascent had Art Gilkey's thrombophlebitis not turned the expedition into a desperate fight for survival. For that matter, Dyhrenfurth had before him the shining example of the Austrian first ascent of Broad Peak, pulled off in 1957 by Hermann Buhl, Kurt Diemberger, Fritz Wintersteller, and Marcus Schmuck, using neither bottled oxygen nor high-altitude porters.

Dyhrenfurth evidently felt so much pressure to succeed that he decided to stick to the conventional norm of a large team with massive logistics. Given the thinking of the day, that's a rational decision. If the AMEE launched a small, compact expedition and failed, he'd catch the brunt of the blame. Others might say, "The Americans just aren't up to the challenge of Everest. Leave it to us Europeans."

Big Himalayan expeditions persisted well after 1963, but by now, massive logistical assaults have fallen out of favor. My only experience with the mob approach came on Jim Whittaker's Peace Climb in 1990, and as I said in chapter three, I never really felt much of the spirit of international brotherhood that was Jim's goal for the expedition, and I would far rather have gotten up Everest for the first time as part of a small group of friends who'd climbed together before the expedition.

Once the machinery of AMEE massiveness started cranking, however, there was no stopping it. In the end, Dhyrenfurth and his deputy leader, Will Siri, chose a team of twenty Americans. On the hike in, the expedition's gear, weighing a total of 29 tons, was subdivided into no fewer than 909 porter loads. The total cost of the expedition rounded out at $430,000 dollars—the equivalent today of $3,233,000!

Not surprisingly, fund-raising for such an extravagant venture soon proved to be the chief hurdle. The AMEE received critical help in the form of a hefty contribution of $114,719 from the National Geographic Society, provided its own staff photographer, the first-rate climber Barry Bishop, go along as the official cameraman on the expedition. Other major supporting institutions included NASA, the National Science Foundation, and the U.S. State Department's Bureau of Educational and Cultural Affairs. In the appendix of Ullman's *Americans on Everest*, no fewer than 185 donors of gear and food are thanked. They range from the momentous (Eddie Bauer sleeping bags for the whole team) to the humble (mashed potatoes from Carnation).

Man, if I thought stuffing individual man-day food packs in that Seattle warehouse before the Peace Climb was drudgery, I'm sure glad I didn't have to run the gauntlet of two and a half years of getting the AMEE's logistics in order!

It was characteristic of the grandiose scale of the AMEE that the team hired James Ramsey Ullman to write the expedition book. Ullman had been a climber of very modest accomplishments, but he had become the most famous mountain writer of his day, after his 1945 novel, *The White Tower*, hit the bestseller list. (In 1950, it was made into a movie, starring Glenn Ford, Claude Rains, and Lloyd Bridges, among others.) By 1963, Ullman was fifty-five years old and not in good health. He hobbled along for a single day of the hike in from Kathmandu, before the team doctors declared that poor blood circulation in his right leg might pose a risk to his life. He ended up writing *Americans on Everest* from his armchair (as it were), poring over the diaries and reports of the team members. It's a tribute to Ullman's storytelling skill that the account feels as you-are-there real as it does.

The AMEE climbers varied widely in technical skill and mountain experience. Several had done little more before Everest than guide Mount Rainier or hike up Colorado's highest peaks. At the other end of the spectrum were driving, talented climbers such as

Willi Unsoeld and Tom Hornbein. And as the AMEE progressed in the field, it began to split along the lines of that dichotomy. The majority of the team wanted only to get up Everest by the South Col route. The minority, made up of the most ambitious and the technically boldest, hungered for a loftier goal. They wanted to pull off a climb the likes of which had never been accomplished in the Himalaya.

Curiously, Dyhrenfurth himself initially suggested a more ambitious goal for the AMEE than simply making the third ascent of Everest (or the fourth, if the 1960 Chinese ascent was genuine). He proposed a triple assault on Everest, Lhotse, and Nuptse. Had the team succeeded in that campaign, it would indeed have been a major accomplishment. But few of the members showed much enthusiasm for Dyhrenfurth's trifecta. Lhotse, of course, had been climbed by the Swiss in 1956, and the first ascent of Nuptse had come in 1961, when two members of a British expedition—the Englishman Dennis Davis and the Sherpa Tashi—had reached the summit.

The bold new idea that did catch hold with the team was also partly Dyhrenfurth's inspiration. As Tom Hornbein recalled its gestation in *Everest: The West Ridge*, on a visit to San Diego, Dyhrenfurth laid out maps and photos of the mountain, then queried Hornbein: "What do you think of trying the West Ridge?" At first Hornbein thought the idea *too* daring. "Wasn't it enough," he remembered thinking, "to climb by the regular way?"

Yet "Norm had planted the idea and a boyhood dream was alive again: Everest, and by a new route." For weeks, Hornbein kept an Indian Air Force photo of Everest from the west on his desk, as he brooded over the possibility, until he knew that the West Ridge was a challenge he was born to pursue.

Ullman's *Americans on Everest* is the official expedition account. But Hornbein's *Everest: The West Ridge*, not published until 1965, when Sierra Club Books brought it out, is a priceless complement to Ullman. Just last spring, Hornbein's memoir was republished by Mountaineers Books in a splendid new edition to mark the fiftieth anniversary of the AMEE. In my opinion, *The West Ridge* may be the best book ever written about Everest, though many would put Jon Krakauer's *Into Thin Air* in first place.

Ullman quotes Dyhrenfurth from a taped discussion of expedition planning, voicing his perspective on the West Ridge: "If we can pull it off it would be the biggest possible thing still to be accomplished in Himalayan mountaineering." But the caveat that follows prefigured the division that would split the team into two camps. In response to Hornbein's suggestion that the AMEE throw all its resources into the West Ridge attempt, Dyhrenfurth rejoined, "This we cannot do. I'm all for making a serious stab at the West Ridge—a thorough reconnaissance to see if it's feasible. . . . [But] we have—almost *have*—to have a success. If later on we say, 'We tried the more difficult route of the West Ridge and bogged down,' that will be a very lame excuse for all the people who backed us."

In other words, the South Col route came first. The West Ridge attempt could take place simultaneously, but it would get distinctly second billing, in terms not only of food and gear but of Sherpa support.

Those would become fighting words to Hornbein, and to the contingent of other members who became his West Ridge allies.

From the start, Dick Emerson, Willi Unsoeld, and Hornbein declared themselves West Ridgers. All three had been teammates on the Masherbrum expedition, where they became the closest of friends. A sociologist from Cincinnati, Emerson had spent summers in the Tetons as a climbing ranger and was regarded as perhaps the most talented rock climber there at the time. On Masherbrum, Hornbein had sacrificed his own chances for the summit after he stopped a teammate's long fall with an anchorless belay, then escorted the injured man down the mountain.

Two young Dartmouth graduates and friends since adolescence, Barry Corbet and Jake Breitenbach, signed on to the West Ridge effort as well. In 1959, at ages twenty-two and twenty-three, respectively, Corbet and Breitenbach had formed half of a tight-knit four-man team that made the first ascent of the West Rib of the south face of Mount McKinley, the hardest route done to that date on North America's highest mountain.

Barry Bishop was on board, too—at least at first. In 1951, at the tender age of nineteen, he had joined Brad Washburn's party making the first ascent of the West Buttress on McKinley—the standard route on Denali today. Ten years later, he had made the first ascent of the striking Ama Dablam near Everest, perhaps the hardest Himalayan peak climbed by 1961. Bishop turned his efforts to the South Col route only when it began to seem doubtful that a West Ridge climb might succeed. As the team's official photographer and representative of the National Geographic Society, which had kicked so much money into the expedition, Bishop knew he had to be in place when any summit attempt got launched.

The division between West Ridgers and South Colers (as they called themselves) never amounted to a true schism. It was a united party of twenty under Dyhrenfurth's competent leadership that established base camp below the Khumbu Icefall on March 21. The next day, several members reconnoitered a route through the icefall. And the day after that, disaster struck.

On March 23, three members and two Sherpas set off up the route pioneered on the twenty-second to a gear dump in the icefall, hoping to improve the wanding and securing of fixed ropes along the way. The lead rope of three was composed of Dick Pownall, Jake Breitenbach, and Ang Pema. At about 2:00 p.m., belayed by the Sherpa, Pownall started to climb a 30-foot-high ice cliff. Suddenly the men heard a noise that one of them later described as "a deep ominous rumbling, then a shattering roar." From out of sight above the cliff, a gigantic serac—"about the size of two railroad cars one on top of the other"—spilled over the rim.

The second rope of Gil Roberts and Sherpa Ila Tsering was knocked off its feet by the tumbling ice debris. They slid 40 feet, but emerged uninjured. When they scrambled back up to look for their teammates, they found Pownall buried up to his chest in ice, but no sign of Ang Pema or Breitenbach. It took ten minutes to dig Pownall out of his near-tomb. Then the men heard a groaning sound, and located Ang Pema buried facedown under nearby rubble. They dug him out in another fifteen minutes. Miraculously, Pownall had not been seriously hurt, though Ang Pema had a dislocated shoulder and blood streaming from his head.

But the only sign of Breitenbach was the rope linking him to Pema, which disappeared under what evidently was tons of ice blocks. The men shouted, pulled on the rope, and dug frantically with their axes, to no avail. At last, Gil Roberts cut the rope that had linked Pema to Breitenbach—a deed that would haunt him for the rest of his life.

Back at base camp, as the news spread, the whole team received the secondary shock. Worst afflicted was Corbet, Breitenbach's best friend in the world, who collapsed in weeping and screaming out loud to no one in particular: "Stupid goddamned gentleman's sport that kills people in their prime and happiness."

One of the worst decisions expedition members ever have to face is what to do after a teammate dies on the trip. I'm eternally thankful that I've never lost a partner on any climb.

There have been expeditions that have shut up shop and gone home after such a death. Chris Bonington's team on K2 in 1978 did just that after Nick Estcourt was killed in an avalanche, though not before taking a vote on the question that found the members evenly divided as to whether to continue or go home. It may be cynical, but the outcome seems directly propotional to the size of the expedition. The larger the team (and the more money invested in the project), the more likely the expedition will still pursue its goal. In 1963, with Breitenbach killed on only the second day of climbing, there seems to have been no suggestion made by any member (not even Corbet) of calling off the show. I suspect that had I been on the 1963 expedition, I would have decided to stay on as well.

Jake Breitenbach was the first climber ever killed in the Khumbu Icefall. There have been many deaths in that chaotic labyrinth of ice since 1963, and it's now recognized as perhaps the most dangerous place on Everest—at least on the two "standard" routes. His teammates judged that Breitenbach's body was buried under so much debris that it would never be found, but the constant movement of the icefall disgorged it only six years later, when a Japanese party discovered the corpse.

During the month of April, the team slowly built its pyramid of supplies and camps through the icefall, across the Western Cwm, and up the Lhotse Face. Midway across the cwm, the West Ridgers took a hard left and started climbing slopes that had never before been trodden, as they worked out a line up 2,400 feet of steep snow and ice to a shoulder on the west side of Everest. Their numbers, however, were badly depleted. Not only had Breitenbach, one of the most enthusiastic West Ridgers, been killed, but Dick Emerson was having a very hard time acclimatizing. Barry Corbet had his troubles, too: acclimatization difficulties of his own, on top of the shattering psychic blow of losing his best friend. It was now that Hornbein and Unsoeld surged to the forefront of the effort.

But it was also now that Dyhrenfurth decreed that the vast majority of manpower and supplies be devoted to the climb by the original South Col route. In *Americans on Everest*, Ullman soft-pedals the conflict this decision spurred, making it sound like a polite debate between Hornbein and Unsoeld on the one hand and Dyhrenfurth and the deputy leader, Will Siri, on the other. Hornbein was convinced that both routes could be pushed at the same time, but Dyhrenfurth disagreed. Invoking the "backers" of the expedition again—all the societies and companies that had donated food and gear and money to the AMEE—he emphasized the catastrophe that would ensue should nobody on either prong of the assault reach the summit. The West Ridge, he agreed, was "a great challenge, a great adventure." But he was going to pour the team's resources into getting at least two men to the summit via the South Col route. The West Ridge was a secondary priority.

In *Everest: The West Ridge*, Hornbein is more candid about this rift. On April 3, Hornbein observed, "This was the first sign of a conflict that was inevitable between the two routes. From now on we would be competing for manpower and equipment to accomplish our separate goals." Over the radio, voices grew strident, as "each team found the other increasingly more vigorous and dogmatic in its own defense. The thing that saved it was that usually we were aware we overstated our cases." Privately, even Hornbein and Unsoeld had grave doubts as to whether the West Ridge would go.

It was not surprising, then, that through April the procession up toward the South Col proceeded with military efficiency, while the West Ridge assault suffered one setback after another. On April 16, Barry Bishop and Lute Jerstad, accompanied by the Sherpas Nima Tenzing and Chotari, reached the South Col, where they left a small depot of supplies. It was earlier than any of the five previous expeditions to assault Everest from the south in the spring season (two Swiss, one British, two Indian) had gotten to that crucial staging point. But then bad weather intervened, as progress ground almost to a halt. It would not be until April 27 that the team's Camp V would be established on the col.

Like the British in 1953, and the Swiss the year before them, the AMEE planned another camp between the South Col and the summit. That was finally accomplished on April 30, though it took ten men two hours to carve a suitable tent platform out of a steep snow slope at 27,450 feet, where they erected Camp VI.

Dyhrenfurth had already chosen the duo to make the first attempt. They were Jim Whittaker and the Sherpa Nawang Gombu. Big Jim, as everybody called him because of his six-foot-five stature, had proved a workhorse on the mountain and seemed unstoppable. In the spirit of the 1953 first ascent, which had paired Hillary with Tenzing, the AMEE wanted to have a Sherpa collaborate with an American to reach the summit first. But Gombu deserved the place on his own climbing merits. On the 1960 Indian expedition, with two Indian military officers, Gombu had reached an altitude of 28,300 feet on the southeast ridge before the trio was forced back. It was no coincidence that Gombu was Tenzing Norgay's nephew.

I was only three years old when the AMEE took place, but I later got to know Big Jim very well, through our Mount Rainier and Seattle connections. Jim's twin brother, Lou, ran RMI, the outfit that first hired me as a guide in 1982. And in the 1960s, Jim became the CEO of Recreational Equipment, Inc. (REI), at the time the leading outdoor equipment firm in the country. Jim and I have always gotten along well, and he was completely supportive of my first efforts in the Himalaya. And, of course, in 1990 he invited me along on the Peace Climb. By then he was sixty-one years old, but he still managed to reach an altitude of 23,000 feet on the north side of Everest, carrying a load to our camp IV at the North Col in support of us summiteers. Big Jim was in fact legendary for his stamina and drive in the mountains. After Everest, he continued to grow REI even while he mingled with movie stars and politicians, but I was impressed by how comfortable he seemed in his own skin. Knowing what he himself had achieved in the mountains, he was unstintingly complimentary toward younger climbers as he encouraged them in their own goals.

The first attempt on the summit was originally supposed to include Barry Bishop and Sherpa Ang Dawa, but the team had decided that it would be vital to try to film the summit push. Dyhrenfurth himself was the only filmmaker on the expedition besides Dan Doody, and Doody was *hors de combat* after April 21, when he developed thrombophlebitis in one leg. His life was saved by anticoagulants administered by the expedition doctor, and by ten days "flat on his back." With no hard feelings, Bishop agreed to swap places with Dyhrenfurth in the first summit party.

In a bravura performance of his own, Dyhrenfurth made it to 27,450 feet, where he helped chop out the site for Camp VI, even though he was "utterly exhausted and barely able to crawl into our tent." As Dyhrenfurth later wrote, "I had no illusion about making the summit. My 45th birthday was only six days off." The next day, roped up with Ang Dawa, the leader of the AMEE reached 28,200 feet on the final ridge. The Sherpa wanted to go on, but Dyhrenfurth knew that at the pace they were climbing, both men would run out of supplemental oxygen, and the wind was blowing hard. Sadly, the semiwhiteout stirred up by the wind prevented any filming of their two teammates going for the summit.

Big Jim and Gombu had set off from Camp VI at 6:30 in the morning. That's relatively late by today's standards, but it was the norm until well after the 1960s, as climbers were convinced that the brutal cold and darkness of a predawn start would defeat their best efforts. Given that hour of departure, the placement of Camp VI relatively close to the summit made all the difference.

No one had ever set out for the top of Everest as early as May 1. Hillary and Tenzing had claimed the first ascent on May 29. The year before, Tenzing and Lambert had made their bid on May 27. The four Swiss who had reached the top in 1956 did so on May 23 and 24. Even the controversial Chinese assault in 1960 had climaxed with a putative summit push on May 24.

The day that Jim and Gombu set out for the summit was really marginal, with a fierce wind that never let up. A midday temperature of minus 20 Fahrenheit was recorded at the South Col, leading Whittaker to estimate the temperature near the summit at minus 30. Each man carried two bottles of oxygen, which they breathed at the relatively rich rate of three liters per minute. In his pack, besides the bottles, Jim carried rope, a little hardware, two water bottles, a camera, food, and extra clothing. The total weight was an ungodly 45 pounds. That's far more than summit climbers lug today, and far more than I've ever carried to the top of any 8,000er, let alone Everest. The consequence was that the men moved very slowly.

At least the snow was in good step-kicking shape. Jim and Gombu took turns breaking trail. As they climbed, the men searched for traces of the 1953 expedition's Camp IX, which had been pitched a full 450 feet higher than the AMEE's Camp VI, but found none. Apparently the tents and discarded gear had been blown off the mountain during the intervening decade. In mid-morning, to lighten their loads, the men cached one half-depleted oxygen bottle each, planning to pick it up and use it on the way down.

Jim and Gombu reached the South Summit at 11:30 a.m., later than they had hoped. The final ridge leading only 300 vertical feet to the top looked daunting. Now they roped up, with Jim in the lead, belaying each other on the more exposed passages. According to Ullman, back home in Seattle Big Jim had pledged to his family and friends that he would step on the summit of Everest, and Gombu had promised his uncle, "I will go where you have gone."

Mercifully, the Hillary Step was an easier climb in 1963 than it had been in 1953, thanks to a thick coating of snow. Jim surmounted it by kicking steps in the snow, then scrambling left onto a rock platform at the top of the Step. Gombu followed on belay. They trudged on, sure now that they would succeed. Jim stopped, brought Gombu up to him, and said, "You first." The Sherpa answered, "No, you." They walked the last few yards to the top side by side.

It was 1:00 p.m. Jim got an American flag out of his pack, attached it to a four-foot aluminum stake, planted it on top, and took a picture. There followed a panoply of flag photos—the ensigns of Nepal, India, the National Geographic Society, and the Himalayan Institute of Mountaineering. Many photos of each other, and of lower mountains stretching into the distance in all directions. Then the two men probed the snow with their axes, in an effort to excavate the bust of Mao Tse-tung that the Chinese claimed to have buried there three years earlier. They didn't find it.

It had been a smooth, if slow, climb to the summit, but the descent verged on desperate. Because the water in their bottles had frozen solid, neither man had drunk a sip all day. Jim has retold this story many times, but he still wonders why he put those bottles in an outside pack pocket, where he knew they would surely freeze. In fact, fairly soon after he and Gombu began their ascent, he knew the water had frozen solid, yet he still decided to carry the useless bottles all the way to the top and back!

Even after retrieving their half-empty oxygen bottles, the men soon ran out of gas. For hours, they stumbled downward, hypoxic and dehydrated. A chunk of cornice broke loose between them, from which they jumped away in terror. Then, at the worst possible moment, Jim had to heed what Ullman euphemistically called "undoubtedly the highest call of nature in mountaineering history." The hardest going of all came on the mere 30-foot rise back up to the South Summit. Both men were taking about twenty breaths per step.

I can sympathize with that minor ordeal. Coming down from the summit of Everest, it feels as though the climbing is over. Just when you think that you're completely done with having to go uphill, you're confronted with that climb up and over the South Summit. It's all you can do to grit your teeth, put your head down, and plod upward again. Once you pass the South Summit, it's downhill for

3,000 feet to the South Col. Many people assume that going down is easy. Yes, it's easier and faster than going up, but by this point of the climb you're often running on fumes. You've used nearly every ounce of energy just to get to the top, and it's all you can do to keep your balance and check your downhill speed as you stumble along. The tents below become your beacons of safety and rest.

It was not until 5:45 that Jim and Gombu regained Camp VI. They had been going steadily, except for their pause on the summit, for more than eleven hours. In the second tent, the men found Dyhrenfurth and Ang Dawa, already in their sleeping bags. "All I could do," Dyhrenfurth later reported, "was croak my congratulations."

So, by the early date of May 1, the AMEE had succeeded in its primary goal. The team had pledged to keep the names of the climbers who first reached the top a secret from the outside world. Even in intercamp radio calls, the members camouflaged the identity of the victors. Gil Roberts, at advance base camp, announced to the others scattered around the mountain, "The Big One and the Small One made the top!"

By May 9, however, porters had carried the news of the AMEE success out to Kathmandu. As Dyhrenfurth later wrote, "The pressure from the outside world to release the names of the first summit team became unbearable." That day he radioed the truth to the outside world.

The impact of the news on the American public was more powerful than anyone on the AMEE had foreseen. As a national triumph, the first American ascent of Everest ranked not far below putting the first men on the moon. And Big Jim Whittaker became

Neil Armstrong. For at least two decades after 1963, Jim remained not only America's most famous climber—he was for thousands of casual observers the only American climber they could name.

Throughout the April build-up on the South Col route, the West Ridgers were suffering one setback after another. The shortage of manpower had effectively stalled their progress. But on learning of Whittaker and Gombu's success, Hornbein and Unsoeld were overjoyed, assuming that now the combined efforts of the AMEE could be devoted to the West Ridge.

It would not quite turn out that way, however. A premonition of what was to come arrived on May 2. During a rest stay at base camp, Hornbein and Unsoeld overheard Maynard Miller talking to Will Siri in a tent fifty feet away. A competent climber when he was in his twenties, Miller, now forty-one, had turned all his attention to glaciology. He told Siri, "Now that the mountain is climbed we've got to put our major effort into research." Siri's answer was inaudible.

By mid-April, the West Ridgers had established a Camp 3W at 23,800 feet on the west shoulder, but all the serious difficulties lay ahead of them. Finally, however, Dyhrenfurth provided Sherpas to help push the West Ridge assault. With Hornbein and Unsoeld in the lead, the team got Camp 4W pitched at 25,100 feet, and they reconnoitered farther up a "Diagonal Ditch" to 26,200 feet, where they thought they might be able to place another camp. From that point, a couloir led straight upward toward the distant cliffs of the Yellow Band, a stratum of rock that girdles Everest on all sides. After 1963, that gully would forever be known as the Hornbein Couloir.

But in the middle of the night of May 16, a near-catastrophe took place. Huddled in their tents at 4W, eight men—four Americans and four Sherpas—listened as the wind rose to a thunderous roar. Suddenly two of the tents were ripped from their moorings. Inside them, the Sherpas and Barry Corbet and Al Auten tumbled helplessly down the slope. A void of 6,000 feet down to the Rongbuk Glacier lay beneath them, but a narrow shelf of snow stopped the slide a hundred yards below the camp. From the wreckage, only Auten was able to escape. He clumped up to the two-man tent containing Hornbein and Unsoeld, who put on clothes and boots and went out in the dark to rescue their teammates.

As Unsoeld later wryly reported, "Corbet and the Sherpas seemed comfortable enough, buried securely in the wreckage, and besides if we had dug them out, there would have been nowhere to put them. We therefore contented ourselves with lashing the flapping rags to axes with climbing ropes and telling the boys not to run off as we would be back in the morning."

Despite the jocular tone of that account, the tent disaster came close to ending the whole West Ridge venture. The next day all eight men limped down to Camp 3 W. The Sherpas, badly spooked, wanted nothing more to do with the assault, so continued down to Camp II in the Western Cwm. Those Sherpas had been the best available. "This left only a mixed handful of old-timers and raw beginners upon whom it was unwise to depend for the sustained effort called for by repeated carries," Unsoeld later wrote.

In *Everest: The West Ridge*, Hornbein revealed how low the men's morale plunged during that retreat: "We were finished, demolished, literally blasted off the mountain. We hadn't even sunk our teeth solidly into the climb."

Dyhrenfurth had scheduled a second team, composed of Lute Jerstad and Barry Bishop, to head up the South Col route, aiming for a summit date of May 18 or 19. The original plan, if the

West Ridgers could get up their new route, was to have them meet Bishop and Jerstad on the summit and descend the other side. But after the tent catastrophe at 4W, such a schedule was impossible.

The conflict between the members at base camp who wanted to wrap up the expedition and head home and the West Ridgers came to a head in a radio conversation between Barry Prather (speaking for Dyhrenfurth, whose voice was hoarse with laryngitis), and Hornbein:

> *Prather:* The porters are coming in on the twenty-first and we're leaving Base Camp on the 22nd. Over. . . .
> *Hornbein:* O.K., we realize time is running out but we envisioned that there were a few more days beyond the twentieth or twenty-first so far as summit attempts by our route are concerned. . . . How do you read that? Over.
> *Prather:* Only comment is, there are three hundred porters coming in here on the twenty-first. Over.
> *Hornbein:* Well, I guess we'll see you in Kathmandu then.

On the next day, Dyhrenfurth agreed to postpone the Jerstad-Bishop attempt to a summit date of May 22. This meant leaving advance base camp on the eighteenth. Hornbein and Unsoeld still doubted that they could pull their tattered contingent together in time to meet a May 22 summit deadline.

But now the whole West Ridge team—Hornbein, Unsoeld, Corbet, Auten, Emerson, and five game Sherpas—spurred themselves to extraordinary efforts. They had originally planned two more camps above 4W, but now Hornbein boldly proposed a single Camp 5W, to be pitched as high as possible, maybe even partway up the Hornbein Couloir. The Sherpas got caught up in the fervor of the campaign. One of them, Ila Tsering, jokingly told Unsoeld, "All good Sherpas down Base Camp. All bad Sherpas up here 4W."

On May 21, Corbet and Auten led up the Diagonal Ditch, followed by all five Sherpas roped together. Hornbein and Unsoeld came last. In a spirit of true brotherhood, the seven supporting teammates were carrying the gear and food to allow the two leaders to make their bid for the summit. By late afternoon, they had all reached 27,200 feet, where they pitched a single two-man tent on what Unsoeld called "the first possible campsite since entering the couloir." It was a ledge only eight feet long, narrowing from a width of twelve inches to only three. Unsoeld and Hornbein shook hands with their gutsy supporters, who headed down in the gathering dusk to Camp 4W.

After too short a night, the two men set off from Camp 5W at 6:50 in the morning of May 22. They had a discouraging start. Despite their breathing bottled oxygen, the terrain was so difficult that after four hours, they had gained only 400 feet. They still had 1,400 to go to reach the top.

Somewhat higher, they confronted the Yellow Band. The rock was so loose that it offered, as Hornbein put it, "an unlimited selection of handholds, mostly portable." Hornbein exhausted himself leading most of the crux pitch, then lowered off so Unsoeld could finish it. Once the Yellow Band was behind them, the men realized, they had passed a point of no return. There would be no hope of getting rappel anchors in the rotten rock, and it was too difficult to down-climb. The only option left was to get to the summit and head down the South Col route.

Slowly the tricky mixed ground gave way to easier snow slopes. Inexplicably, both men felt a burst of new energy as they got near the summit. "The going was a wonderful pleasure, almost like a day in the Rockies," Hornbein later recalled. They reached the summit at 6:15 p.m.

I've always deeply admired the West Ridge exploit. I never knew Willi Unsoeld, who was killed in an avalanche on Mount Rainier in 1979, but Tom Hornbein, who's still climbing well at age eighty-two, has become a good friend of mine. He's one of the most intelligent and thoughtful people I have ever met—not the sort of guy to make a rash decision. He and Willi must have very carefully calculated their odds of success and survival. Yet given my relatively conservative approach to climbing 8,000ers, I think I might have turned back on May 22, 1963, when I realized that if I got up the Yellow Band, I wouldn't be able to get back down it. That's exactly the decision Eric Simonson and I made even closer to the summit of Everest in 1987. And yet. . . . Perhaps my perspective would have been different in 1963, and I might have pushed on. That's something I'll never know.

It would never occur to me to second-guess Unsoeld and Hornbein. In climbing past a point of no return, and in reaching the summit as late as 6:15 p.m., they were really sticking their necks out. But they were superb mountaineers, and they knew what they were doing. I'll always believe that I can't prescribe safety limits for anyone else. That margin is a very personal thing, one that every climber has to figure out for himself. I truly believe that what Unsoeld and Hornbein did that day was beyond spectacular. They made a 100 percent commitment and climbed toward the heavens.

On top, Hornbein later wrote, "We hugged each other as tears welled up, ran down across our oxygen masks, and turned to ice." They spent twenty minutes on the summit, then, with the sun setting, started down the southeast ridge, a route they'd seen only from 8,000 feet below it in the Western Cwm.

On reaching the top, Unsoeld and Hornbein had found fresh footprints in the snow. They had to be those of Jerstad and Bishop, who had in fact reached the summit at 3:30 p.m. With only a single flashlight, whose batteries were fading, Hornbein and Unsoeld crept down the Hillary Step and the knife-edged ridge below it, peering into the gloom for footsteps and the scrape marks left by ice axes. And they kept yelling *"Hellooo!"*

At last they heard an answering cry. When they caught up to Jerstad and Bishop, who had no flashlight at all, they found that their friends were in worse shape than they were. All four staggered down another few hundred feet until, deciding it was too hard to find the route, they stopped to bivouac at 28,000 feet—higher than anyone had ever spent a night out and survived (unless the two Chinese in 1960 had really bivouacked just below the Second Step).

The four men had the great good fortune to have a clear and windless night. They laid their pack frames down in the snow, then half-sat, half-lay atop them. All four men had lost feeling in their feet. Unsoeld offered to warm Hornbein's feet on his stomach, which seemed to help, but, misreading the absence of pain in his own toes, declined the reciprocal favor.

They got through the night, then hobbled down toward camp VI on the South Col route, when they met Dave Dingman and Girmi Dorje coming up, looking for Bishop and Jerstad. Eager to get low and warm up, they kept going, making it all the way down to advance base on May 23. Both Bishop and Unsoeld would later have many toes amputated because of severe frostbite.

On the twenty-fifth, the whole AMEE team started the hike out. From Namche Bazaar, Unsoeld and Bishop were helicoptered to a hospital in Kathmandu.

In the eyes of the public, Hornbein and Unsoeld's feat never won them even a fraction of the fame that Whittaker earned for being the first American on top of Everest. But in the minds of climbers all over the world, the fast-and-light, do-or-die ascent of the West Ridge, in an era dominated by ponderously equipped, slow-moving expeditions, seemed truly revolutionary. As Doug Scott, himself a genius of Himalayan ascents, declares today about the West Ridge exploit, "In terms of sheer commitment, it's the finest climb ever done on Everest."

Many years later, Hornbein told my co-author, David Roberts, that he still felt guilty about Unsoeld losing his toes. "For a long time," he said, "I had a really potent feeling that I failed to recognize the condition of Willi's feet. I felt, if only I had done something differently."

Despite the competition that persisted throughout the AMEE, the former teammates stayed in touch with one another over the decades after 1963. In 1999 the surviving members held a reunion in a mountain hut near Vail. "For the first time," Hornbein told Roberts, "I walked away feeling I'd been part of one expedition, not two."

7

▲ ▲ ▲

Death and Survival

Is there anything new to say about the disaster on Mount Everest in the spring of 1996? I doubt it. Many years from now, armchair pundits will still be arguing about exactly what happened during the storm that struck late on May 10, and even for those of us who were there at the time, essential questions about the tragedy will remain unanswered.

That was the Everest season made famous, of course, by Jon Krakauer's number one bestseller, *Into Thin Air*. Seventeen years later, Amazon lists no fewer than eleven books still in print about that chaotic spring. Besides Jon's account, they include memoirs by the survivors Beck Weathers and Lene Gammelgaard, as well as Anatoli Boukreev's ghost-written *The Climb*, essentially a point-by-point rebuttal of Jon's critique of Anatoli as an irresponsible, glory-seeking guide. After Anatoli's death on Annapurna in 1997, *Above the Clouds*, a collection of his writings translated from the Russian, was published. That book casts further light on his role in the catastrophe and furnishes a more articulate rejoinder to Jon's charges than does *The Climb*.

Also still in print are memoirs by Göran Kropp, the guy who bicycled to Everest from his native Sweden and tried to climb Everest solo, without accepting so much as a candy bar from anyone else on the mountain; Matt Dickinson, who was on the north side of Everest that spring, where other deaths occurred; and Jamling Norgay, who reached the summit with our IMAX team. Not only these, but a pair of accounts from members of the South African team (which Jon also criticizes in *Into Thin Air*)—a bland, self-serving narrative by Ian Woodall, the team leader, and a tell-all exposé by Ken Vernon, the unfortunate journalist assigned to the expedition.

I confess I haven't read most of these books, even though I was on Everest myself that spring. (Maybe *because* I was there!) It's safe to say that no season in any year on any mountain in the world has ever generated so much written scrutiny. I suppose in that sense Everest '96 has a kind of mythic status. It's reminiscent, in a minor way, of all the ink that's been spilled trying to untangle the JFK assassination.

Everest '96 even has its conspiracy theorists! Just last year, a book appeared by yet another climber who was on the mountain at the time, who has apparently spent the last fifteen years trying to dig up proof that the leaders of the three main expeditions— Rob Hall, Scott Fischer, and David Breashears—knew beforehand that the storm of May 11 was coming and failed to warn anyone else, thereby plunging others into desperate struggles for survival. I won't dignify this preposterous book by mentioning its author or title here.

Even the first ascent of Everest in 1953—arguably the most celebrated event in mountaineering history—produced only four books by expedition members. And those books, rather than quarreling with one another, rounded out the full story handsomely. Sir John Hunt wrote the official narrative, *The Ascent of Everest*. Hillary told his own version in *High Adventure*. Wilfrid Noyce's *South Col*—a sadly neglected minor masterpiece—presents a deeply personal, philosophically reflective account of the climb by one of Britains's finest mountaineers. And James Morris's slender *Coronation Everest* details the brilliant logistical scheme by which he got word of the great success to the London *Times* at the very hour of the coronation of Queen Elizabeth II.

In *No Shortcuts to the Top*, I devoted a long chapter, called "Time to Say Good-bye," to my own role on Everest in 1996. I won't repeat that account here, and by 2013, there seems to be little hope of uncovering any crucial new details about all the turns of bad luck and the unfortunate decisions that cascaded into catastrophe that spring. Blaming others when people die on a mountain is not my cup of tea. (Even Jon Krakauer, who in a sense started the furor by writing such a compelling book, is fed up with the whole subject, and refuses to talk about Everest anymore in public.)

What lastingly disturbs me about the 1996 controversy is the smug accusation voiced so often by folks who barely understand mountaineering or Everest that the whole disaster was caused by incompetent clients paying big bucks to get dragged to the summit. When I'm giving a talk about the 8,000-meter peaks, someone in the audience invariably raises that canard. It's all I can do to grind my teeth, smile politely, then explain the actual reality of guiding on Everest.

I recently reread my 1996 diary, however, and it prompted me to a few new ruminations about that terrible season. Those, perhaps, are worth sharing. And no matter how much time passes, I'll never get the tragedy out of my head, for on Everest that year, in Rob Hall and Scott Fischer, I lost two of the climbing partners who were closest to me, with whom I'd performed some of my finest ascents.

After getting up three more 8,000ers in 1995—Makalu, Gasherbrum I, and Gasherbrum II—I was on a roll with my Endeavor 8000. Only six summits remained for me to round out the fourteen. They were Shishapangma, where I'd come within a hundred yards of the top in 1993, Manaslu, Broad Peak, Nanga Parbat, Dhaulagiri, and the one that would become my personal nemesis, Annapurna.

That successful 1995 campaign engendered my plan to go back to Everest for the eighth time, in the spring of 1996. Guiding with Rob Hall again, I'd use Everest as a springboard to get acclimatized for a try at Manaslu. Another twofer, with Rob and Veikka Gustafsson as my Manaslu teammates. Rob would pay my guiding salary and the cost of travel to Nepal. Scott Fischer had also asked me to guide for him on Everest in 1996, but it seemed logical to stick with Rob.

But there was another opportunity on the horizon. David Breashears, whom I'd first met on the north side of Everest in 1990, came to me with the kind of proposal that in the end I couldn't turn down. MacGillivray Freeman Films had asked him to make an IMAX film of climbing Everest, all the way to the top. At first the project seemed absurd and impossible, if for no other reason than the sheer weight of the camera gear. But the idea got under his skin, and David accepted the challenge. When he asked me to come along as the official climbing leader of the expedition, and to serve in effect as one of the film's on-camera "stars," I couldn't say no.

Eric Simonson in the Great Couloir at 27,500 feet, on my first attempt on Everest in 1987.

1

Success at last! My self-portrait on the summit of Everest in 1990, on my third try.

2

Wong Chu, our head Sherpa, carries a load across a crevasse in the Khumbu Icefall in 1991.

3

4

Top: Camp III at 24,000 feet in 1991, with new snow dusting our tents. A cloud bank creeps up the Western Cwm below us.

Right: In 1991, a line of climbers ascends the Lhotse Face near the Yellow Band. In 2012, that line would include more than 200 climbers!

5

An accumulation of discarded oxygen bottles at the South Col as seen in 1991. In recent years these bottles have all been cleaned up due to an incentive to pay Sherpas to bring them down.

6

Summit day, 1991, high on the southeast ridge. Makalu in the background, far-distant Kangchenjunga on the left.

7

On my solo attempt from the north in 1993, my lonely camp after a snow storm.

8

The final section of the summit ridge in 1994.

9

Rob Hall (right) and me on the summit, 1994.

10

I'm climbing the last few feet to the summit of Lhotse in 1994, with Everest in the background. (© Rob Hall)

11

Doug Hansen (front) in 1995, climbing at about 27,000 feet in 1995. Doug would die on Everest next year in the tragedy that also took the lives of Rob Hall and Scott Fischer.

12

In 1996, Paula Viesturs checks expedition food and gear lists in Kath-mandu.

13

Paula and myself at base camp in 1996.

14

Our team moves in front of Ama Dablam in 1996. (© Paula Viesturs)

15

David Breashears wielding
the IMAX camera at 25,000
feet.

16

Going for the top in 1996. The
rest of our IMAX team is visible
in the lower left.

17

Left to right: myself, Paula,
Araceli Segarra, and David
Breashears in Deboche, relieved to be heading home
after the tragedy of 1996.

18

19

Top: The shadow of
Everest from 27,500
feet, just after dawn on
May 23, 1997.

Right: The South
Summit at dawn in
1997.

20

Veikka Gustafsson and
myself on the summit
in 2005.

21

I'm approaching the South Col on my last attempt on Everest in 2009, just before my 50th birthday. (© Eddie Bauer First Ascent/Jake Norton)

22

On the summit in 2009, for the seventh time. (© Eddie Bauer First Ascent/Jake Norton)

23

A fond farewell—Everest from Kala Patar in 2009.

24

When I told Rob about this new project, he graciously stepped aside, hiring other guides to replace me on his Adventure Consultants team. The technological challenge that intrigued David hooked me as well. And being put in charge of nearly all the equipment and logistics for this gigantic undertaking seemed a logical next step in my expedition career.

Sweetening the deal was David's acceptance of Paula as our base camp manager. In 1995, Paula had only been Helen Wilton's assistant at base camp; this year, she'd run the show. In the midst of hectic preparations for the IMAX trip, Paula and I blocked off ten days in February to get married and spend our honeymoon in Mexico. (Scott Fischer, my partner from K2 in 1992, came along as our "official" wedding photographer.) Afterward, I joked that Everest would be our real, extended honeymoon, albeit a fairly rigorous one. I had no idea. . . .

At base camp that March, for the first time I really felt that there were too many climbers on the mountain, nearly all of them aiming at the standard South Col route. Rob Hall was there with his biggest Adventure Consultants entourage ever—twenty-six souls, including assistant guides, Sherpas, clients (among them Krakauer, on assignment for *Outside*), and base camp personnel. Scott Fischer, leading his own Mountain Madness team, had a contingent of twenty-three. The veterans Todd Burleson and Pete Athans were leading four clients. There was a South African team of twenty-one, a Taiwanese team of five, a loose assortment of other climbers, and our own IMAX team of ten. Base camp became an international village inhabited by a diverse and colorful cast of citizens.

It was inevitable that Rob and Scott would feel a keen rivalry to get the most clients up the mountain. Success one year was great for business the next. As for David Breashears, the mob posed a huge cinematic quandary. The IMAX film had to create the illusion that we were alone on the South Col route. The last thing we needed were "extras"—clients, Sherpas, guides from other teams— showing up in the corners of our film footage. Our job was to stay out of the way of all the other teams, or else time our shots when nobody else was in sight.

Very early on the expedition, I had a setback that shocked me. Planning to carry a load through the Khumbu Icefall on April 9, I came to a small depot where some of our team had cached our crampons at the foot of the icefall. But mine weren't there— somebody had stolen them! It turned out that David Breashears's crampons had been stolen too, as well as those of Robert Schauer, the very experienced Austrian climber who was part of our team. I registered my outrage in my diary: "Of all the places in the world, I would hope that my gear on Mt. Everest would be safe. Not anymore I guess. A very sad day in Everest's history."

Later we had a base camp meeting of the leaders and sirdars of the various expeditions to discuss the problem of thievery. We never did find out who stole our crampons, so our Sherpas insisted that we lock our tent zippers as we pitched camps higher on the mountain. It seemed a sorry solution to the problem of keeping our gear intact, and I opposed the proposal, because I had always believed that in an emergency, climbers in trouble should help themselves to whatever they need in other teams' tents. But the majority ruled, and we started to lock our tents. With that decision, we acknowledged that here and now on Everest, the age-old tradition of respect for one another among mountaineers, whether strangers or not, had been irredeemably violated.

Besides Robert and me, our IMAX team consisted of three other climbers: Araceli Segarra, a Spanish mountaineer and part-time model; Jamling Norgay, the son of Tenzing Norgay, who made the first ascent with Hillary in 1953; and a Japanese climber named Sumiyo Tsuzuki. The multiethnic makeup of our party was essential to David's conception of the film, and it wouldn't hurt to boost sales in the international market. Early on, I assessed the strengths of our six climbers. David, Robert, and I, I was pretty confident, would be able to get to the summit, weather and snow conditions permitting. Araceli also had a strong chance—"very motivated, great attitude & strength," I noted in my diary. About Jamling, I was less certain. "Nice guy," I wrote, while wondering just how motivated he really was. His role in the IMAX narrative was to follow quite literally in his father's footsteps. But I had no idea how well Jamling would perform up high, and in my diary I gave him only a fifty-fifty chance of getting to the top. Sumiyo was the weak link, as she'd already shown in the early stages of the expedition. "Not strong mentally or physically" was my blunt diary judgment.

During the rest of April, we progressed slowly but steadily up the mountain. Everything was far more complicated, however, than on my previous expeditions, because David was filming constantly. We had to figure out which angles and which places on the mountain would best carry the narrative, then stop for hours to get the footage. Shooting with an IMAX camera and huge film magazines was an extraordinarily difficult job that David carried out brilliantly. Some days, especially overcast ones with leaden skies, were simply worthless for filmmaking.

The added stress and toil of making the film, staying out of the other parties' way, and yet establishing camps as we would on a normal expedition left me little time to reflect. My 1996 diary, not surprisingly, is skimpier than any of the ones I'd kept on my previous expeditions to 8,000ers. Still, there are episodes I recorded there that I'd all but forgotten in the years since '96.

To make a coherent IMAX film, David had to decide which of us "talent" to focus the filming on. That meant calculating who had the best chances of summitting. Robert Schauer, as David's camera assistant, was never intended to be an on-screen personage, no matter how well he climbed. On April 22, I noted David's thoughts: "He's more concerned with [filming] Araceli & me and not really with Jamling and Sumiyo. He realizes their chances are slim, but Araceli & I have a greater chance at the top & that will make the movie."

My diary also reminds me of a macabre episode I never mentioned in *Shortcuts*. On April 23, somewhere above Camp II, "David told me of a body that we should deal with. I went over to it. It was ½ body—waist down. I grabbed its suspenders and dragged it for 10 min[utes] to a crevasse and dropped it in—rest in peace." We could not even guess at the identity of this Everest victim. The mountain is not, as the press sometimes puts it, littered with dead bodies, but the chances are that sooner or later you'll stumble upon one. Greg Child once took a photo of a corpse on Everest still attired in its down suit, from which a skeletal head stared at eternity. When *Life* published the photo full-page, both Greg and the magazine were pilloried. Yet all he was doing was recording the reality of Everest.

The overcrowding on the mountain produced unseemly conflicts beyond the dispute over our stolen crampons. On April 23, I climbed up toward Camp III on the Lhotse Face, trailing some Sherpas from another expedition. We'd already cached our tents and gear at III, claiming sites for our camp. The slope there is quite steep, and finding a good campsite is difficult. With all the teams vying for spots at Camp III, people were racing up the hill to claim their places. But, as I wrote that day, "I had a sneaky suspicion that [the other team's leader] had sent the Sherps to scam our tent spots. . . . I got to CIII at 9:30 and found the 2 Sherps trying a squeeze play—man did I give them an earful! . . . They didn't argue cause they knew I was right."

On April 29, I headed up from Camp III, hoping to reach the South Col. Various Sherpas had already prepared the route and fixed ropes up to what would serve as all the teams' Camp IV. But it was a cold and windy day, and, feeling my feet grow numb, I turned around at 25,000 feet, just above the Yellow Band. Even so, I felt great, acclimatizing without bottled oxygen as well as I ever had.

On April 30, our whole team returned to base camp to recuperate. The plan was to rest there for a few days, then make our push for the summit. We all felt optimistic, since despite the burden of filming, we were right on schedule. Paula exuded confidence in our success, as she recognized the strength and competence that David and Robert brought to our party.

Despite the occasional friction between teams, we'd worked out an amicable arrangement. Rob had a feeling that May 10 was his lucky Everest summit day—that date had worked for him in the past. Now he and Scott decided to join forces, with their teams going for the summit together. In theory, that may have sounded like strength in numbers and psychological support. But privately, I questioned the plan. With so many people clambering up the summit ridge on the same day, a bottleneck would become inevitable. Thus our IMAX team decided to head out before Rob's and Scott's, claiming the first shot at the summit, so that we could film in relative isolation. Our plan was to head back up the mountain on May 5, hoping to go to the summit on May 8.

None of us had any premonition of the disaster that was about to unfold.

Preoccupied with planning for the summit and filming the whole way up, I didn't make a single entry in my diary between April 30 and May 5. I was determined to try Everest again without supplemental oxygen. That, in fact, had been part of the IMAX plan, as David and the producers felt that such an effort would add color to our story. I was more than happy to climb once more without the burden of carrying oxygen bottles or the nuisance of wearing a claustrophobic mask.

On May 5, our IMAX team left base camp at 5:45 in the morning. I arrived at Camp II in the Western Cwm at 10:45. Taking only five hours to climb 3,700 feet, from 17,800 to 21,500, proved to me that I was in great shape. Robert, David, and Araceli got to camp an hour later. Sumiyo and Jamling didn't arrive for another several hours. David initially hinted at going on to Camp III on the Lhotse Face the next day, but changed his mind, declaring May 6 a rest day. "Okay," I wrote in my diary, "I don't care either way. Sum & Jam would be blown away if we went tomorrow. A day of hangin' is fine by me."

On May 7, we all reached Camp III, as the weather steadily improved. I was psyched for the summit push, but Sumiyo was hurting, getting to camp a full three hours after I arrived. "She'll probably have to go on O's to get to C[amp] IV," I observed in my diary.

During the night, however, the wind picked up. At 5:30 a.m. on May 8, as we roused ourselves to climb to the South Col, the wind was howling high on Everest, with a giant plume of snow streaming from the summit. David, Robert, and I held a council to decide what to do. Since we'd get only one shot at making a film, we thought the odds were too long to risk a summit attempt in high winds and cold. The weather felt unsettled, and we all knew that most years a calm period came sometime in May, so we decided to wait for better conditions. "Bummer to go down," I wrote, "but it was the only reasonable option." On May 8, we descended to Camp II. On the way, we passed all the other teams, including Rob's, Scott's, the Taiwanese, and the South Africans, heading up. It was frustrating to see them confidently climbing toward their own summit pushes, but we were pretty sure we'd made the right decision. There's always a temptation to follow the crowd, out of a nagging fear that they know something you don't, but in the end, one's instincts are the best guide. We'd rest a day at Camp II, then, if the weather held, go back up the mountain, hoping to push from the South Col to the top on May 12, two days *after* all the others had made their attempts.

Well, the rest is mythic history—or at least the next four days on Everest are. The whole world seems to know how the various parties set out from the South Col early on May 10. How twenty-three members of Rob's and Scott's teams (including Sherpas) reached the summit, as well as a single Taiwanese, "Makalu" Gao Ming-Ho. How others turned back, or were "parked," like Beck Weathers, partway up, ordered to wait for his team leader to escort him down the mountain. How the weather deteriorated in the afternoon as a sudden, violent storm swept in. How the descent turned into chaos. How "the Huddle," as David later called it, formed in the night only a few hundred yards from the South Col tents, as a group of clients and a single guide got lost in the whiteout, and how Anatoli Boukreev went out in the storm and brought all but two in to safety. How Beck Weathers, given up for dead, roused himself in a last-ditch effort and stumbled back to Camp IV. How Scott, who must have been suffering from some kind of edema, pushed himself to the summit, the last of his team to top out, but never made it back to the South Col. How Rob, who was too determined to get Doug Hansen to the top, waited too long and died near the South Summit, not before having his poignant good-bye conversation via patched-through radio to his pregnant wife, Jan Arnold, in New Zealand. How the rest of us rallied to save the lives of the most severely frostbitten, including Beck Weathers and Makalu Gao.

Through a telescope at Camp II, I watched the drama unfold. The slowness of so many of the climbers, all on the same route, created the "traffic jam" that had so much to do with the catastrophe. I had always set 2:00 p.m. as my own summit turnaround deadline on an 8,000-meter peak, which gave me enough time to get back to high camp before dark. But on May 10 at 2:00 p.m., there was a whole string of climbers still moving upward, many of them well below the South Summit. Actually, for them the turnaround deadline was perhaps irrelevant, since running out of bottled oxygen was their greatest threat, not returning after dark. By now that procession of climbers had been moving uphill for more than fourteen hours. They were simply too slow, and they were running out of energy as well as oxygen.

I couldn't help myself—as I looked through the telescope, I muttered out loud, "Guys—you left at midnight. It's two o'clock!" And, "Dudes, what are you doing? Wake up! Turn around, turn around!"

My diary entries at the time sound in retrospect like a telegraphic announcement of impending tragedy:

May 10 (Late):
Rob & Scott's team[s] caught out late in wind/whiteout. People tired/running out of O's, can't find camp/cold/tired, very windy. Big mistake today—climbed too late, bad weather/too long, [therefore] running out of oxygen.

May 11:
Up @ 6 AM. Veikka monitoring radio all night from Rob's tent. Rob called @ 5:30 AM from S. Summit. Doug died during the night. Rob in bad shape—HACE [high-altitude cerebral edema]/weak/ hypothermic/hypoxic/tired. We tried to get him to keep moving— after 3 hrs he still hasn't moved. I tried to kick his butt into gear over radio. Very emotional for me—& everyone. Jan called and we broke down. Very tough to hear. Tried to get 2 Sherps to Rob—high winds turned them back.

Not surprisingly, my diary ends with this entry. I simply didn't have the time, the energy, or the heart to record either what I was feeling or what we did after May 11. We had suddenly found ourselves in the vortex of a whirlwind of shock, sorrow, and desperate rescue efforts.

Of course the tragedy put our own IMAX ambitions in limbo. David at once donated the oxygen bottles we'd cached at the South Col to the effort to save the weakest survivors. Now the locks on our tent zippers, which I had thought ridiculous in the first place, proved only a minor hindrance, as we told Jon Krakauer to go ahead and slice through the tent walls with a knife to get the oxygen. We left the IMAX camera behind as we climbed up the Lhotse Face toward the South Col. At 25,000 feet, we took over the shepherding of Beck Weathers all the way down to Camp I, at the upper lip of the Khumbu Icefall, where a very gutsy Nepali pilot landed to pick him up and whisk him to a Kathmandu hospital. MacGillivray Freeman might well have welcomed David's filming the rescue, but they put no pressure on him to do so, and he decided it would be morally indefensible to capture such agony on film. Our focus now was not on filming, but on helping others. There was no way to do both.

At base camp, Paula had been following the disaster with mounting alarm and horror. For the first time, she truly recognized how dangerous Himalayan mountaineering was. In the unfolding drama, she played a key role, monitoring radio calls and keeping many of the teams up to date on what was happening on the mountain. But to Paula it was unimaginable that after the deaths of so many climbers, including our friends Rob and Scott, we might still think of trying to complete our IMAX project. Then she overheard David casually remark on the radio, "When this is all over, we'll regroup and go back up." Privately, I had made the same decision. I wanted to go back up and finish what we had started. Not in spite of what had happened, but to turn the disastrous season into something more positive. Had we gone home at that point, as most of the others on Everest had done, our only option would have been to come back the next year, with a smaller team, to finish our IMAX film. Why not finish it now?

Paula, however, simply lost it. David's fiat seemed premature to her, as she assumed that at least we'd have a team meeting to discuss what to do. But in the end, she realized that the decision was not one in which she even had a vote. She stayed at base camp for the memorial service, then hiked down to Dingboche with some of the surviving clients from Rob's team. The warmer, thicker air and the greenery of the forest helped to calm her nerves. After a few days in the lowlands, while she struggled with her feelings, she hiked back up to base camp. And from that moment on, she poured her heart into supporting my effort to make the IMAX film happen and to climb to the summit once more.

In *No Shortcuts to the Top*, I recounted our successful climb back up the mountain, more than a week after nearly everyone else had gone home. We got all our climbers to the South Col, but David "parked" Sumiyo there, knowing she'd never make it to the summit.

In the middle of the night of May 22–23, I left camp before anyone else, since climbing without bottled oxygen and breaking trail, I would, we all thought, be slow enough that David, Robert, Araceli, Jamling, and the Sherpas would catch up. Somehow, though, the camera crew never caught up to me. Despite all the emotional strain I'd gone through during the previous two weeks, I never climbed better at high altitude than I did that morning. I had the feeling that nothing could stop me, not even the knee-deep snow that I plowed through with a vengeance. Reaching the summit at 10:00 a.m., I radioed Paula, and she cheered my triumph wholeheartedly.

David caught up to me on the summit, where we congratulated each other with tears in our eyes. But it was too cold to wait for the others, so I started down. Ironically, this meant that none of the IMAX footage from the summit day had me on camera. That didn't matter to me. What did matter was that David, Robert, Araceli, and Jamling got to the top and back safely, and that David got the footage he needed. The film that resulted, called simply *Everest*, remains the highest-grossing IMAX movie yet made.

The hardest part of that otherwise glorious summit day—

indeed, one of the hardest experiences of my life—was passing the bodies of Rob Hall and Scott Fischer. On the way down, I stopped and sat beside each of them, as I struggled with my emotions. Sitting next to Scott's frozen body at 27,300 feet, I couldn't help speaking out loud to him. "Hey, Scott," I said, "how you doing?" Of course there was no answer but the wind.

"What happened, man?"

There was of course no time left in the spring of 1996 for Manaslu, and after Rob's death, Veikka and I would not have had the heart for another expedition even if there had been time. In terms of my Endeavor 8000, I was in a sense "stuck" on eight of the fourteen highest peaks, with six to go. But I was in no rush to finish my campaign: no matter how long it took, I relished the journey. Thus in the fall of 1996, rather than go after one of the six, I returned to Cho Oyu, which I'd already climbed in 1994. Doing so was in part to honor Rob, for we had agreed to co-lead an Adventure Consultants team to the seventh-highest peak in the world, and clients had already signed up for the expedition.

Rather than let the company founder, Guy Cotter took over the running of Adventure Consultants. The Cho Oyu trip went smoothly, and I was happy to reach the summit on September 29 with two of the clients.

Already in the works for the spring of 1997 was yet another film project on Everest. With the runaway success of the IMAX movie, David Breashears had come into his own as a filmmaker. *Nova*, the highly acclaimed PBS series out of Boston, approached David about making the first serious cinematic exploration of what happens to the human body and mind at the most extreme altitudes on earth. The project was the brainchild of Liesl Clark, a talented director who, though not a climber herself, had a passion for making documentaries about outdoor adventure.

Either just before or during the 1997 expedition, David and Liesl became a couple. Personal relationships can sabotage an expedition, but in this case, their pairing would only enhance the making of the film that was later titled *Everest: The Death Zone*. David would shoot with a video camera all the way up the mountain, while from base camp, Liesl and our doctor, Howard Donner, would direct the rigorous testing that revealed just what happened to our brains and bodies as we climbed above 26,000 feet.

I was David's first choice to be the guinea pig for the film. Although I might otherwise have been tempted to plan an expedition to Manaslu or Shishapangma for the spring, once more David's offer was too good to refuse. And once again, I would use Everest as a springboard in another twofer, with an attempt on Broad Peak in Pakistan scheduled for the summer.

The story line of the *Nova* film dictated the premise that David's crew had come along to study climbers making an otherwise routine attempt on Everest from the south. So Guy Cotter put together another Adventure Consultants team, with me as the assistant guide. Three clients signed up, one of whom was Dave Carter, my former RMI buddy who had helped me guide Hall Wendel in 1991. Dave hadn't reached the summit that year, so he was eager to give Everest another shot. And I was confident that he was strong enough to get to the top, unless really bad weather or snow conditions shut us down. Dave would stand in as our "client" for the film.

Liesl's presumption was that experienced high-altitude veterans such as David and myself ought to test better than someone like Dave Carter, no matter how fit he was. So David, even while making the film, would also have to submit to the sometimes maddening battery of tests Liesl and Howard inflicted on us at each camp.

Another "project" claimed my attention that spring, one that had little to do with mountaineering. In February, on the first anniversary of our wedding, Paula and I went to Mexico for a brief vacation. She had just turned thirty. I had known since the first days that we dated that having kids was a number one priority for her, and now she decided it was time to start. I wanted kids myself, but wasn't sure exactly when. But when Paula suggested that we start to build a family, I thought, *Why not?*

Paula got pregnant during the early part of 1997. I knew it would be really hard on both of us to be separated while the baby grew inside her, but a quite deliberate calculation went into our timing. It was utterly essential that I be there when Paula gave birth. If she got pregnant in February, the child would be born in late October or early November, months during which I had lined up no expeditions. (We would subsequently plan the births of all four of our children around just such a schedule.)

Rounding out our party was Veikka Gustafsson, who would be neither a guide nor a true client. Using our camps and supplies, Veikka hoped to get up Everest without supplemental oxygen. When he'd summitted as Rob's client in 1993, he'd breathed bottled gas, and though as the first Finn to climb Everest, he immediately became one of his country's top sports heroes, Veikka had the same kind of purist ideals that I'd always espoused. For him, the bottled oxygen was a nagging asterisk. Trying Everest without the stuff was a preliminary step in his own campaign to reach the summit of all fourteen 8,000ers, every one of them without supplemental oxygen—a goal he finally achieved in 2009.

On April 4, I reached base camp below the Khumbu Icefall, once more ahead of the rest of our team, who would arrive a few days earlier. This was my ninth expedition to Everest, my fifth on the South Col route. And it was my fourth straight spring season on the mountain. It all seemed so familiar, the routine of setting up a comfortable base camp, the sizing up of the other parties camped nearby. I might have felt that Everest was getting *too* routine—was I in danger of becoming one of those one-mountain specialists who keeps returning to guide clients up a route he believes he's got "wired"? I didn't think so, since each trip had a different objective, and I could never afford to become complacent on Everest. Paula frequently reminded me of this with an aphorism she had come up with: "Just when you think you have it all figured out, you don't."

A rigorous study of high-altitude physiology actually appealed to me immensely. After all, in vet grad school I'd studied a lot of physiology. And just the year before, two doctors from the University of Washington Medical Center—one of them being my hero Tom Hornbein—had put me through a grueling workout to gauge such measures of my physical capacity as VO_2 max, lung capacity, and anaerobic threshold. (It turned out that my very high scores were probably mostly due to the luck of my genes. Thanks, Mom and Dad!)

This year at base camp, however, there were haunting memories of the tragedy of 1996. The events of the previous year were still fresh in my mind, yet it was hard to believe that they had really happened. Not watching Rob putter around base camp or Scott saunter by with his "What, me worry?" grin on his face felt distinctly odd. And I knew that if I got to the summit again, I'd once more have to pass by the frozen bodies of my two former comrades.

That would be an emotional tribulation I'd have to prepare for days in advance. Since no one had been back up there since the previous spring, David Breashears and I hoped that if we found the bodies, we could investigate them more carefully than the year before, in hopes of gleaning new insights into what had gone wrong for Rob and Scott.

One reason I think I've avoided serious climbing accidents is that I never take mountains for granted. Each time I tried to climb Everest, it was as hard and as dangerous as the first time. No peak ever becomes a Yellow Brick Road, as Scott had half-jokingly called the South Col route. I knew that there was no way to reduce the risk on Everest to near zero, no matter how well prepared I was, and in my very first diary entry in 1997, I made a resolve about the Khumbu Icefall, the most dangerous part of the route. "Going up yesterday," I wrote, "I decided to minimize my times through the icefall. I'm here to guide & not schlep loads." On past expeditions I had always volunteered to carry many loads through the icefall, not only to do more than my fair share of the work, but to get as fit as possible. Now, on my fifth trip to the south side of Everest, the risk of traveling again and again through the perilous labyrinth of the icefall seemed hard to justify.

On April 8, David, Liesl, the rest of the film crew, the Sherpas, Veikka, Guy Cotter, and our clients arrived. It's really hard to judge the capabilities of clients you've never met before. You have to take them at their word on the résumés they submit. It turned out that the two clients besides Dave Carter who'd signed on with Adventure Consultants were relatively weak. One of them, named Peter, had trouble acclimatizing from the start. On April 20, less than two weeks into the expedition, he came down with pulmonary edema at base camp. Guy had to put him in a Gamow bag, a portable pressure chamber that artificially simulates a lower altitude with thicker air. That action probably saved his life. Only a couple of days later, Peter got heli-evacuated to Kathmandu.

The other client was a real piece of work. He was a Spaniard whom I'll call Jorge. Guy told me that, according to his résumé, Jorge had traveled to both the North and South poles, and that now he wanted to add the "third pole" to his credentials. I thought, *Wow, Jorge sounds like the second coming of Erling Kagge.* But we learned early on that the guy had been flown to the South Pole, and that his Arctic exploit consisted of being flown to within one degree of the North Pole and skiing the last sixty-nine miles (with guides)—a fairly popular tourist option.

When I met Jorge at base camp, I was surprised and disappointed to greet a sweaty, pudgy, obviously out-of-shape fellow. Sure enough, on the mountain he never got higher than Camp II. Guy, who doesn't suffer fools gladly, invented a string of nicknames for Jorge, which included "the Gimp," "Fatso," and "the Penguin."

Back home, Jorge had already made quite a fuss about his impending triumph on Everest. His wife was pregnant, and Jorge had actually planned with doctors, via sat phone calls from the expedition, to have them induce the birth to coincide to the minute with Jorge's final steps to the summit!

The guy had another habit that was peculiar at best. He was fixated on his bowel movements, and always told us when he was heading off to go, as well as how it went after he got back. Veikka and I turned Jorge's toilet routine into a private joke that we kept using on many later expeditions. Whenever one of us had to take a crap, we'd announce, "I'm going to have a meeting with Jorge."

On returning, the other guy would ask how it went. The answer involved reporting that the meeting with Jorge had required a lot of paperwork.

In *Into Thin Air*, Jon Krakauer created the indelible cartoon portrait of the client so helpless he can't even put on his own crampons, but whom leaders like Rob and Scott coddle up the mountain, and in some cases, into death traps. With Sandy Pittman, Jon perfected the vignette of the Manhattan socialite with her espresso coffee maker at base camp, who gets short-roped by a Sherpa to ensure her success on Everest. Actually, though, Sandy had climbed some creditable mountains before Everest, and while she may have been a bit full of herself and entitled, she wasn't a clueless novice who had no business on Everest.

As far as I know, no client has ever been pulled, carried, or dragged by a guide or a Sherpa to the top of Everest. Yet thanks to the cleverness of Jon's caricatures, and to a morbid armchair desire to see rich fat cats who plunk down sixty-five grand for a shot at Everest get their due by dying on the mountain, the nonclimbing public assumes that all Everest clients fit that stereotype. This really bugs me. It doesn't even begin to fit the mold of the folks I've guided on any of the 8,000ers. In 1997, in Peter and Jorge, we did indeed have clients who weren't equal to the challenge of Everest. But we never guaranteed them the summit, and we never encouraged them to try to exceed their limits. When it became clear that they couldn't go high, we sent them back to base camp—or, in Peter's case, to Kathmandu.

For me, guiding on Everest is a huge responsibility. I'm not in it just to make money—I feel a constant obligation to watch out for each client's safety, and if one of them succeeds in reaching the summit, I share fully in his or her joy. It's an ethic I first learned on

Mount Rainier, and it's an integral part of why I climb. Not just to notch summits for myself, but to enable others to achieve what for most of my clients turn out to be goals that are among the high points of their whole lives.

One of the side benefits of all the technical apparatus *Nova* brought to the expedition was the relative ease with which I could stay in touch with Paula back in Seattle. I missed her badly, and it was tough not to be with her as the baby gestated inside her. My diary entries recorded those bursts of happiness when we could talk by sat phone or trade e-mails.

April 8
I was glad to hear she & baby are fine & everything is OK. We talked for 18 minutes. . . . I love her [here I drew the sign for "infinity"]!!

April 14
Called Paula but we kept getting disconnected at the end because of a battery glitch. But she's fine & it was great to hear her laugh.

April 28
Called Paula—I love to hear her cheerful voice. Baby's got a heartbeat! We'll do an ultrasound June 12th. Got her Care package from NOVA—beautiful letter & great pics. . . . Can't wait to get back to Paula & home.

After the expedition, once Paula had her ultrasound, we knew that we were expecting a boy, and we started thinking about what to name him.

Except for Peter's edema and Jorge's limitations, our climb went smoothly through the first weeks. We got Camp III established on the Lhotse Face by the relatively early date of April 26. After a descent to base camp for R & R, we were ready to make our push. In my optimism, I anticipated a summit day on May 7, which might allow me to be home as early as May 18. On May 3, eagerly gearing up for the push, I wrote in my diary, "It's been a beehive of activity here this morning—packing, showering, shaving, getting ready to go. We're ready to get movin' so it worked out great. Let's hope that the weather stays with the forecast."

Well, Everest is fickle. Extremely high winds during the following days put an end to our plans for an early dash. My spirits drooped. "Way too many people at base camp!" I griped in my diary. And after making another trip up to Camp II, I wrote, "Icefall is getting very funky this time of year. Only wanna do one more round trip and then that's it. 'Everest Anonymous.' "

Meanwhile, over the radio, all the way up the mountain, David Breashears, Dave Carter, and I had to perform the tests that Liesl was using to gauge our mental and physical states. The mental exercises were the more grueling. In fact, as we failed at one or another, we often collapsed in hysterics. For example, we'd be read over the radio a really convoluted sentence that we were supposed to repeat from memory: "On Monday, John went to his cousin Frank's red house and together they bought three blue leather jackets at Joe's store, which had mostly pants for sale." Man, that would be hard enough to repeat at sea level!

Or we'd be handed plastic cards with color names printed on them, except that the word *blue*, for instance, would be printed in red. With a stopwatch clicking, we'd flip through these cards as fast as possible, trying to utter the color of the printed word, not the word itself.

David, who is a competitive perfectionist by nature, was so determined to perform the tests well that if he bollixed one up, he'd blame it on "test anxiety" and ask if he could start over. Dave and I would jeer, "No way, dude, that's it."

We finally got Camp IV established on the South Col on May 22. On the way up to the col, the Sherpa carrying a stuff sack with some of David's personal gear lost his load when he briefly put the sack down, only to watch it tumble thousands of feet down the Lhotse Face. At the South Col, David was missing such crucial items as his mittens, oxygen mask, goggles, and overboots. We found replacements for most of this gear, but no spare overboots, which meant that he'd have to go to the top wearing only his double plastic boots, making his feet far more vulnerable to the cold.

Even before this mishap, David wasn't sure he wanted to go to the top. We all had trepidations about the summit push, as we watched the numbers of climbers camped at the South Col swell. For all of us, weather would likely dictate the timing of summit day, and we feared a repeat of the traffic jam of 1996. My diary recorded David's ambivalence.

April 23
Have to catch up with David @ CIII in 2–3 days. Now he seems to want to perhaps go to the summit with us. . . . David is very down today. . . . Asking himself what he's doing here.

May 22 (on the South Col)
David called me & discussed his doubts about going up. . . . I think he'd lost his motivation cause he'd been here so many times. I told him to give it a shot & see how everything looked @ the South Summit—then he could make a decision. He decided to go.

In the end, at Camp IV, we all resolved to go up. If we started at 10:00 p.m., we ought to get the jump on most of the other teams, whose typical departure times would be two or three hours later. To avoid the predictable bottleneck at the Hillary Step, we'd carry an extra rope to fix there as a "down line," so we wouldn't have to wait our turns to clip on to the single rope in place that served both climbers still heading up and those already descending from the top. David also realized that it would be vital to the *Nova* production to film Dave Carter and me all the way to the top. We set off in the middle of the night of May 22–23, leaving our tents at 10:00 p.m. as planned.

I shared the trail-breaking with two of the Sherpas, Mingma and Dorje. Veikka followed some distance behind as he climbed without bottled oxygen. And David filmed like a pro. Compared with the monster IMAX camera he'd deployed the year before, the video camera he used this year was a piece of cake to operate. There was a full moon in a clear sky, but a bitter wind blew across the southeast ridge. Just before sunrise, however, the wind suddenly dropped. It was turning into one of the most beautiful days I'd ever had on Everest.

I'd been gearing myself up for the ordeal of passing Scott's and Rob's bodies. From a certain distance, I spotted the ledge where Scott had met his end. The trail up the southeast ridge passed farther from that ledge than it had in 1996, maybe out of respect for his dead body. As I had the year before, I saved my visit to my old friend for the descent. Higher, near the South Summit, I was actually relieved not to see Rob's body. The snows of winter had apparently buried it.

At the Hillary Step, however, we were in for a shock. There, hanging head down, one foot tangled in the fixed ropes, was another corpse. It had to be that of Bruce Herrod, the South African who had been the last to reach the summit in May 1996, and who, apparently exhausted, had been unable to down-climb the Hillary Step. We guessed that he had tried to rappel a fixed rope, only to have a foot snag and flip him upside down, from which position he had been too weak to extricate himself. It must have been an agonizing way to die.

We were the first climbers to pass this way since Herrod had perished. We cut him loose from the fixed ropes and watched as his body plunged down the south face. That may seem to nonclimbers a heartless act, but nearly all mountaineers would have done the same—it's customary to drop a dead body found high on an 8,000er into a nearby crevasse. It's literally impossible to carry a body down the mountain from 28,700 feet. And there are worse places to lie for eternity than on the slopes of Everest.

We reached the summit at the remarkably early hour of 6:50 a.m. Dave Carter was in ecstasy, having finally made it to the top of the world, although he was gasping for breath, even with bottled oxygen. I was pretty jazzed myself. With David filming, we spent almost forty minutes on top. I broadcast a live Internet feed to the *Nova* Web page. And we even performed our mental tests on the summit.

It might have seemed like a clockwork ascent, but we were on the verge of a catastrophe. As we started down, Dave Carter's condition rapidly worsened. Guy and I short-roped him to the foot of the ridge where it met the relatively level terrain of the South Col. From that point, he managed under his own steam to stagger several hundred yards over to our tents. There, however, he started to fall apart.

Not surprisingly, my diary ends at the South Col. The drama

that occupied the next two days left me far too exhausted to record the events. In his tent, Dave coughed incessantly and could not catch his breath, no matter how high we cranked the oxygen flow. For some reason he was developing a build-up of phlegm in his trachea that restricted his airflow. No matter how hard he tried to cough it out, the obstruction wouldn't budge. We knew that if we couldn't get Dave lower on the mountain at once, he would die.

The climb to the summit and back had taken fifteen hours. All we wanted to do was collapse in our tents, celebrate our triumph, and get a full night's sleep. Instead, I volunteered to take Dave down the Lhotse Face. He was not only my client, after all, but a good friend of many years' standing.

The descent was a nightmare. Dave would take a few steps, then collapse, gasping for breath. I'd let him rest for a moment, then prod him to move on. Again and again and again . . .

By nightfall, we'd only regained Camp III at 24,000 feet on the Lhotse Face. I had hoped that we could have descended all the way to the comfort of Camp II, but because of Dave's distress, we were moving slower than a snail's pace. Inside one of our tents, I tended to him as a nurse would a baby. Dave simply could not catch his breath. He was fully aware of his predicament.

I got on the radio to base camp, where our expedition doctor, Howard Donner, gave me advice. I was trying to get Dave to relax, but when he felt he couldn't breathe, a kind of panic seized him, which only exacerbated his coughing and gasping. Donner told me that if the mucus plug got worse, I should try the Heimlich maneuver in an attempt to dislodge the obstruction. At last I did, holding Dave in a bear hug from behind, my hands clasped against his chest, as I squeezed with my fist in as forceful a jerk as I could muster.

My efforts succeeded in forcing up only tiny bits of mucus. Unfortunately, they also caused Dave to lose control of his bladder. Eventually he soaked all of his clothing, so he stripped down to his underpants. All through the night, we alternated thrusts and rest. We worked out a system: Dave would point to his throat, then pee out the door, and I'd try yet another violent Heimlich squeeze or two. An outside observer might have been morbidly amused to watch this strangely choreographed dance. To us it was a grim, exhausting fight for survival.

I began to think Dave was going to die. I actually considered performing a tracheotomy, a technique I'd learned in vet school. It would have been a desperate last remedy, but with Donner guiding me over the radio, I might be able to cut a new air passage just below the mucus plug in Dave's throat, saving his life. How we'd get him down from Camp III after that, I didn't even want to contemplate.

At dawn, we decided to try to head down to Camp II. Just before leaving the tent, I gave Dave a last series of Heimlich thrusts, as strong as I could manage. All of a sudden he coughed up the mucus plug. It was slimy green, bloody, and the size of a half dollar. As disgusting as the plug looked, we were overjoyed to see it lying in the snow.

Guy Cotter arrived just as we were starting down from Camp III. Dave's condition had so much improved that he was able to climb down the slopes under his own power, with Guy and me in solicitous attendance. Later, at base camp, he recovered completely.

I'll never know for sure how close a call Dave had, but in the middle of the night it certainly felt like touch-and-go.

Sixteen years later, Dave and I remain good friends. He still climbs and guides a little, but his main focus is on running his family's lumber business in Indiana. That narrow escape from a gruesome fate on Everest, choking to death on his own mucus, seems to have welded a lasting bond between us. And long after 1997, Dave's mother sent me a Christmas card every year, thanking me for saving her son's life.

What's more, Liesl got her film. *Everest: The Death Zone*, with Jodie Foster narrating, ran on PBS in 1998, garnering rave reviews. A decade and a half later, you can still rent the DVD on Netflix, where it's posted with ratings from no fewer than 25,187 viewers. The unscripted climax of the film, of course, turning science into high drama, is Dave's fight for survival as he coughs and gasps his way down the Lhotse Face.

And oh, yes—on October 29, Paula gave birth to our son, after I rushed her to the hospital in the nick of time. We named him Gilbert Edmund Viesturs. Paula and I had started our family, even though I still had six summits to reach to complete my Endeavor 8000. And though I could hardly have imagined it at the time—by the end of 1997, I thought I was done with the mountain for good—two more trips to Everest loomed in my future.

8

▲ ▲ ▲

The Hard Way

Unsoeld and Hornbein's traverse of Everest via the West Ridge in 1963 represented a gigantic breakthrough in Himalayan mountaineering. During the next decade, most of the expeditions that attempted the mountain were content to repeat the two conventional routes, via the South Col and southeast ridge and via the North Col and northeast ridge. But the most ambitious climbers starting scheming up ways to tackle the two most obvious remaining challenges on Everest—the massive east or Kangshung Face, and the equally massive Southwest Face, a daunting triangle of steep snow and ice topped with rugged bands of rock.

The Kangshung Face had first been approached by Mallory and Guy Bullock toward the end of the sprawling 1921 reconnaissance on the first expedition ever sent to Everest. Appraising it as a route to the summit, Mallory declared, "Other men, less wise, might attempt this way if they would, but, emphatically, it was not for us." For six decades thereafter, not a single attempt on the face was launched. The approach to the foot of the wall on the Kangshung

Glacier represented a complex logistical puzzle of its own—as I would find out in 1988, when Andy Politz and I and our colleagues from the state of Georgia got smacked flat by its stern and scary challenge.

The Southwest Face, on the other hand, loomed over every expedition that crossed the Western Cwm on the way to the Lhotse Face. By 1997, I'd stared up at that formidable 7,000-foot-high precipice on five separate expeditions. The most striking aspect of the face was its inescapable danger, for a huge, steep snow slope narrowed to a broad gully a little more than halfway up, and it was obvious that all the avalanches and falling rocks coming down from above would be funneled into that chute. Yet there was no other reasonable line of access to the upper face. What's especially fiendish about the wall is that the technical difficulties are concentrated in the last 2,500 feet below the summit. Getting to those rock bands meant running a gauntlet of falling debris over and over again. Then, even with bottled oxygen, surmounting the final cliff would obviously require climbing of a higher standard than had yet been tackled on Everest, even on the West Ridge.

The first attempt on the Southwest Face was undertaken by a Japanese expedition in the postmonsoon season of 1969. Though the trip was billed as a reconnaissance, several climbers on the team reached the remarkable high point of 26,200 feet. Among the members was Naomi Uemura, who would go on to become famous as the first person to reach the North Pole solo and the first person to climb Mount McKinley solo. Still trying to up his personal ante, Uemura disappeared in 1984 trying to climb McKinley solo in winter.

The Japanese returned in force in the spring of 1970, with a team of no fewer than forty climbers. But they failed to improve on the 1969 high point, instead turning their attention to the standard South Col route.

All this activity stirred the ambition of Norman Dyhrenfurth, still hungry for yet another first on Everest to cap his immensely successful AMEE in 1963. In the spring of 1971, he led an international expedition, with thirty-one members from eleven different countries, to attempt both the West Ridge direct (a straighter line than the Hornbein Couloir) and the Southwest Face. It was a real all-star team, including such paragons as Dougal Haston, Don Whillans, Toni Hiebeler (the German who'd led the first winter ascent of the Eiger *Nordwand*), Naomi Uemura, Pierre Mazeaud (one of the best French mountaineers of his day), and Carlo Mauri (the great Italian who, with Walter Bonatti, had made the first ascent of stunning Gasherbrum IV in 1958).

Dyhrenfurth's avowed goal was to create "an experiment in understanding and cooperation among nations." Alas, the gathering turned into quite the opposite sort of melee, as nationalism reared its ugly head, with each country's representatives jockeying for the leading roles on the two routes. The Australian journalist Murray Sayle, along on assignment for *The Sunday Times*, later wrote a wickedly funny tell-all account of the expedition mess for *Life* magazine, detailing such scenes as the Swiss couple Michel and Yvette Vaucher throwing snowballs at the British tent. Dyhrenfurth later went on record castigating Sayle's "deplorably inaccurate and misleading account."

It may be on this expedition that occurred an exchange that has since become a semiapocryphal legend among mountaineers. During the trip, over the radio, several members heard that a major international soccer match between Germany and England had ended in a German victory. According to the story, the German members of the team walked over to the tent housing Don Whillans, the acerbic and brilliant Brit. "Hey, Don," the Germans crowed, "did you hear that we just beat you at your national pastime?"

"Oh, aye," rejoined Whillans without missing a beat. "But we've beaten you twice at yours, haven't we?"

During the expedition, the sole Indian member, Harsh Bahuguna, died of exhaustion hanging on a fixed rope as he tried futilely to unclip his carabiner to pass an anchor. At the end of two months of sporadic but dedicated effort, Whillans and Haston established a high camp at 27,200 feet. But bad weather defeated any chance of climbing above. Nor did the expedition succeed on the direct West Ridge. Because the venture had basked in such monumental publicity beforehand, the reaction afterward was savage. In *Mountain*, Ken Wilson, the self-styled arbiter of everything to do with climbing, wrote, "For a public and press weaned on mountaineering success, this year's failure on Everest was unacceptable."

At around 26,000 feet, a crux decision faced all the parties trying the Southwest Face. To circumvent the rock band that swept across the upper face, the two Japanese attempts had angled left, hoping to find a passage through a narrow, dangerous gully to reach the highest snowfield of all. Instead, Whillans and Haston had headed right, gradually ascending hundreds of feet of snow ramp as their route angled toward the southeast ridge, first pioneered by Hillary and Tenzing. They were confident that this right-hand ramp would solve the puzzle of the face. But above the high camp, savage cliffs of black rock offered no obvious line, although Haston thought that a snow-choked chimney might go.

At this point Chris Bonington took up the gauntlet. In the autumn of 1972, he led a thirteen-man British team to the Southwest Face. Back was Dougal Haston, abetted by such strong mountaineers as Mick Burke, Hamish MacInnes, Nick Estcourt, and Doug Scott. But the predictable problem of a postmonsoon attempt on Everest took its toll. It was not until early November that the team regained the high camp first pitched by Haston and Whillans in 1971. By then, it was bitterly cold, and the weather stayed fierce day after day. In addition, the snow chimney that Haston had put his hopes on had morphed into "nearly 1000 feet of very difficult rock." Haston tried to reconnoiter an "escape route" rightward toward the southeast ridge, but in 100-m.p.h. winds, he had to turn back.

In the fall of 1973, yet another Japanese expedition tried the face, only to be defeated at the same high point.

Thus the Southwest Face had repelled five major expeditions, including some of the best high-altitude mountaineers in the world. It was indeed becoming a Last Great Problem of the Himalaya.

For Dougal Haston, the Southwest Face had become a personal nemesis. And for Chris Bonington, who was fast establishing himself at age forty-one as the most successful of all expedition leaders in the Himalaya, with triumphs on Annapurna's South Face and Changabang on his résumé, the face was the kind of challenge he loved to sink his teeth into.

In 1975, Bonington put together a team almost as massive and expensive as the AMEE. Haston, Burke, Estcourt, MacInnes, and Scott were back, reinforced by excellent climbers such as Martin Boysen, "Tut" Braithwaite, and Peter Boardman. Only twenty-four, Boardman was signing up for his first Himalayan expedition, but he already had first ascents in the Hindu Kush, the Caucasus, the Alps, and Alaska under his belt. He would go on to become one of the greatest of all high-altitude climbers before his untimely death at age thirty-one, as he attempted an even more difficult route on Everest.

The burgeoning expenses of a team comprising eighteen climbers, forty-one high-altitude Sherpas, forty icefall Sherpas, a BBC team, and a *Sunday Times* reporter were covered by a lavish sponsorship by Barclays Bank. As Dyhrenfurth had in 1963, Bonington in 1975 rationalized that a massive expedition was necessary for so monumental a challenge—no fast-and-light style, however appealing, would win the prize. "On the South West Face of Everest . . ." he wrote in *Everest: The Hard Way*, "there could be no question of such an approach. . . . I found the sheer immensity of the problem fascinating. . . . Perhaps I am a frustrated Field-Marshal, my passion for war games and my early military career providing a clue in this direction." (Bonington was a graduate of Sandhurst, the royal military academy.)

Despite the intensifying cold that had thwarted the first British attempt in 1972, Bonington once again chose to assault the Southwest Face in the postmonsoon autumn. Much of the rock and ice on the face would be covered by monsoon snows, making the climbing slightly less technical and safer from rock fall. But the trade-off was a dramatic increase in avalanche danger. Another consideration was that other teams from other countries already had their eyes on the objective and were wangling for permits for 1976. Bonington had to seize the first opportunity offered by the Nepalese authorities.

On Annapurna's south face in 1970, the strong egos of the principal climbers had sparked some bitter clashes. Mick Burke and the American Tom Frost felt particularly vexed, for while they had led the hardest pitches in the middle section of the face and felt they'd earned the right to go for the top, Bonington passed them over in favor of Don Whillans and Dougal Haston for the summit team. In turn, their teammates felt that Haston and Whillans—particularly the latter—had played a chess game with positions on the mountain, minimizing their own load carries and saving their energy so that they could go into the front from the high camp.

Somehow Bonington held this explosive mixture of strong personalities together. A measure of his teammates' faith in their leader emerged in the official Annapurna expedition book, for which all the members gave Bonington the right to read and quote from their diaries, even when they let fly with accusations against one another. Bonington further won his team's respect by taking on his own share of sharp leads and heavy load carries, while exempting himself from the chance to go to the summit. Unlike Karl Herrligkoffer on Nanga Parbat or Ardito Desio on K2, Bonington was no tyrant who dictated troop movements through a base camp telescope. And in his younger years, Bonington had notched exceptionally bold climbs of his own, the equal of those of any Englishman of his generation, including the first British ascent of the Eiger *Nordwand* and the first ascent of the lethal Central Pillar of Freney on Mont Blanc.

A drama similar to the Annapurna scenario played itself out on the Southwest Face of Everest in 1975. Once again, all the members gave Bonington free rein to quote from their diaries, even when they criticized one another. Of Haston, for instance, Bonington himself wrote in his diary, "Dougal's approach is undoubtedly that of a prima donna; he reckons that he wants to get to the top, that he deserves the top and that he's certainly the best person to go there. I'm inclined to agree with him." Some of the less egotistical (but equally talented) members were disheartened by the jostling for position, with its unequal division of tasks. Thus Martin Boysen wrote in his diary on September 9:

It's such a large expedition. I just don't feel the necessary sense of involvement. It really doesn't matter if I'm here or not. I have done sweet Fanny Adams [i.e., very little] apart from dragging my unwilling body up and down the Ice Fall. Worse, it's dangerous, menaced by avalanches and I just don't feel like sticking my neck out for something I just don't feel wound up with.

With relative efficiency, and huge support from the high-altitude Sherpas, the team built its pyramid of camps and supplies up the fan-shaped lower slopes and through the gully that led to the broad horizontal snowfield below the upper rock bands. There were plenty of near misses by avalanches, one of which destroyed an empty tent at Camp IV while Haston slept alone in the adjoining tent, only a few feet away. All the men confessed to strained nerves and dark apprehensions. But by September 16, the team had established their Camp V at 25,500 feet, on the right edge of the gully-funnel in the middle of the face.

Now, after much consultation with his teammates, Bonington made a crucial decision. Rather than follow the right-rising ramp that had led to the 27,200-foot camp first established by Whillans and Haston in 1971, the team would push up the steep couloir to the left that the Japanese had aimed for on the first two attempts on the face.

The job of leading those pitches, which would turn out to be the hardest on the whole route, fell to Nick Estcourt and Tut Braithwaite. On September 20, that duo surmounted a radically steep series of chimneys and ramps mixed with patches of bare, loose rock. The photos in the lavishly illustrated expedition book make it clear just how "out there" was the climbing Estcourt and Braithwaite tackled above 26,000 feet. Bonington later saluted his two soldiers for "solv[ing] the problem of the Rock Band." Once ropes were fixed through that exposed passage, the team was able to get supplies high enough to build a Camp VI at 27,300 feet at the top of the Rock Band.

From there, someone would be designated to make the first summit bid. The top was only 1,700 feet above Camp VI, but the route was uncertain, and everyone feared the kind of dead end that had stopped the 1971 and 1972 expeditions at 27,200 feet much farther to the right.

In performing their brilliant leads through the Rock Band, Estcourt and Braithwaite had nailed the crux of the whole route. But in doing so, they had exhausted themselves, and, like Burke and Frost on Annapurna, had sacrificed their own chances to go to the summit. The selfless example the two men set was teamwork at its best. Estcourt and Braithwaite reveled in the challenge of climbing at the limits of their skill through the Rock Band, and for them that was reward enough. If only two climbers could get to the top by the Southwest Face, it would be a victory for the whole team.

In the expedition book, Bonington admits that he decided early on who would get the first shot at the summit. "I felt that Doug Scott and Dougal Haston probably were the strongest pair," he wrote. "They seemed to get on well together, were very experienced and determined, and for each this was the third visit to the South West Face." Meanwhile, however, Bonington was trying to position a second party to head for the top after Scott and Haston tried to push the route. (It's worth remembering that Hillary and Tenzing were the second summit party in 1953, after Charles Evans and Tom Bourdillon had made the first try, turning back at the South Summit, only 300 vertical feet short of the top.)

I've always wondered how Bonington pulled off the diplomatic trick of being an absolute leader, in the sense that his orders to his teammates were never countermanded, while still allowing the opinions of members as headstrong as Haston or Whillans to influence his decisions. It's quite a trick. Bonington's own superb climbing on the mountain went a long way toward winning his teammates' loyalty. Among all the expeditions I've been on, the closest comparable leadership model was that of Jim Whittaker on the Peace Climb in 1990, but on that adventure, Jim shared at least nominal leadership with the Soviet and Chinese commanders. And for that matter, the Soviets pretty much ignored what Jim asked them to do. Another comparable model was the one that David Breashears set in 1996 on our IMAX expedition, when he led from the front all the way up Everest. In any event, I'm quite sure that if I'd had the honor to be invited on a climb with the likes of Doug Scott or Peter Boardman, I would have done just what Bonington asked me to do.

Thus Bonington planned to get a second party up to Camp VI with enough supplies to be ready to go for the top a couple of days after Haston and Scott made their attempt. One of the principal climbers, Hamish MacInnes, had been badly spooked by a near-miss in an avalanche, during which he inhaled ice-cold snow that affected his breathing for weeks afterward, so he withdrew his name from the "lottery." And as on Annapurna, Bonington had chosen to exclude himself from any summit attempt. There still remained seven fit and ambitious climbers vying for what they assumed were four places in the two summit teams. In effect, however, there were only three places, since Bonington wanted to follow the example of the British in 1953 and the Americans in 1963 and give one of the summit slots to the best Sherpa. Two of them, Pertemba and Ang Phurba, had carried loads uncomplainingly throughout the trip and were well acclimatized, even though the technical climbing skills of both were minimal.

Although he had already divulged the decision to give Haston and Scott the first shot, Bonington kept his thinking about the second party to himself until September 21, when he announced his plan to his teammates via intercamp radio. Martin Boysen's diary records the high drama of that moment:

> *We waited tense with expectation and ambition. Hamish took the call and Chris came over loud and clear in the warm air of the afternoon.*
>
> *"I've decided after a lot of thought . . ." Wait for it, I listened only for the names not the justifications . . . "Mick, Martin, Pete and Pertemba . . ." Thank God for that. "Tut, Nick, Ang Phurba."*
>
> *The radio stopped and everyone departed quietly with their own hopes, ambitions and disappointments.*

The great surprise in Bonington's announcement was that the second summit party would consist of four climbers, not two: Burke, Boysen, Boardman, and Pertemba. Estcourt, Braithwaite, and Ang Phurba were offered the token hope of a third summit attempt, but everyone on the team knew that was not likely to happen.

The plan for the first summit push demanded an extreme effort from Scott and Haston, for Bonington asked them to string 1,500 feet of fixed rope along the difficult rightward passage of the uppermost snowfield. That would take a whole day in itself, so the duo would have to return to Camp VI and make their summit bid the following day. But a string of fixed ropes would maximize the chances of a second team getting to the summit.

On September 23, Scott and Haston performed their assigned task to a T, even though the terrain was dicey in the extreme, as the men kicked through a thin crust of snow only to feel their crampon points skitter on rock beneath. (I know exactly what that kind of climbing is like, having faced it on the north side of Everest, as well as high on K2 as we traversed out of the Bottleneck Couloir. You're tempted to take your crampons off, because they give such poor purchase on the rock, but boots alone—not to mention Cordura overboots—are no match for snow and ice. Your only hope on such terrain is to make the points of your crampons find tenuous purchase on rock blanketed under powder snow.)

Haston led the crux pitch, a rock step on which he pounded five pitons into manky cracks to use for aid. The rock was so shattered that twice the pitons came loose as he put his weight on them, and he skidded a few feet on the slabs before catching himself. "Nasty stuff, youth," Scott commented admiringly as he seconded the pitch. (Scott called every climbing partner "youth," even though in this case he was a mere year older than Haston.)

Having strung out all 1,500 feet of rope and securing it with decent snow and rock anchors, the two men turned back to Camp VI, well satisfied with their crucial effort. "More to the point," Haston later wrote, "we hadn't exhausted ourselves in doing it."

At 1:00 a.m. on September 24, Scott and Haston woke to the dismaying sound of a rising wind that flung spindrift against the tent walls. It was so cold that both men put on all their clothing and gear, including crampons, harnesses, rucksacks, and oxygen apparatus, inside the tent. They were off by 3:30. Theirs was one of the first pre-dawn starts ever made from a highest camp on Everest. Thanks in part to better clothing and good headlamps, the thinking about summit day had changed a lot since 1963, when Unsoeld and Hornbein felt they couldn't leave their tent until first light at 6:50.

Haston had decided that the two men should carry a stove, a pot, and a bivouac sack. In fact he even contemplated, if the going proved very difficult, bivouacking on the way *to* the summit, rather than as a last-ditch option on the way down. To me, that's unimaginable. I've always felt that bivouacking on an 8,000-meter peak is a desperate resort, something to be avoided at all costs. I heartily endorse the old joke that *bivouac* is a French word meaning "mistake." But once again, it's a matter of each climber's notion of his margin of safety. Mine will always be broader than that of a climber like Haston, who again and again pushed himself to the very limits of survival because a summit meant so much to him.

The going indeed proved slow, and the men's schedule was further hindered when they had to stop for an hour to try to fix Haston's oxygen apparatus, which had stopped working. There at 28,000 feet, with bare hands, they took the whole rig apart piece by piece, finally discovering a lump of ice that had blocked the junction between the tube and the mouthpiece.

The terrain was difficult enough that the men not only roped up but belayed each other, placing the odd piton for protection or anchor. By 1:00 p.m., they had used their last piton, but they now stood at the foot of a diagonal couloir that led to the South Summit. Here, however, they ran into the worst snow conditions they'd found in days: a wind crust below which their feet floundered in soft, loose powder snow. As Haston later described the agony of breaking trail in that couloir, "I'd bang the slope to shatter the crust, push away the debris, move up, sink in. Thigh. Sweep away. Knees.

Gain a metre. Then repeat the process." At that rate, he admitted, he thought that "we'd be lucky to make even the South Summit."

It was not until 3:00, in fact, that Scott and Haston stood on the South Summit. They'd been going steadily for almost twelve hours, and they were very tired. That would have already been an hour beyond my turnaround time, and in their situation, I'm pretty sure I'd have headed down. But those two guys were true hard men, and to be fair, the dictum of a hard-and-fast turnaround time had not come into common practice by 1975. Even today, not everyone adheres to a predetermined turnaround time. Some climbers will retreat in the face of worsening weather or exhaustion, but others simply keep going, no matter what, until they reach the summit. Many first-rate climbers claim their summits only at sunset. The descents they face therafter are usually dicey in the extreme.

It was now that Haston proposed huddling in the bivvy sac until sunset, then going on to the summit when the snow might have frozen up, allowing better purchase. But that's a tactic better suited to the Alps than to Everest. It's so cold and dry at 28,700 feet, I doubt that sunset would have changed the conditions much. Fortunately for both men, Scott nixed the idea of a presummit bivouac. "Look after the rope," he said to his partner. "I'm going to try at least a rope length to sample conditions."

The men moved slowly and carefully up the final ridge. Haston led the Hillary Step, floundering upward in yet more sugary, loose snow. "It gradually dawned on me that we were going to reach the summit of the Big E," he later recalled. As it was, they did not reach the top until 6:00. Despite their fatigue, and the coming on of night, they were overjoyed, "hugging each other and thumping each other's backs." They took photos of each other and stared into the limitless distance on all sides. Those photos, published in

Bonington's expedition book, are amazing and beautiful, with the pale light of the setting sun playing over the tops of clouds well below them. But at the same time, those images seem sinister and foreboding, for they portend the arrival of nightfall, only minutes away. There's no clear statement in the expedition book about how long the men stayed on the summit, but I suspect it was longer than I would have liked. On a summit, time flies, and you're sorely tempted to linger and enjoy the moment, after all the effort that has gone into getting there. By now, Scott and Haston knew that they were committed to a bivouac on the descent.

It was almost pitch dark by the time they regained the South Summit. There, they dug a hole in the snow, crawled into the bivvy sac, and tried to melt a little snow on their stove. No one had ever spent a night out so high on earth. At 8:00, their bottled oxygen ran out.

Haston later called that night out the coldest bivouac of his life. To keep their blood circulating, the men frenziedly attacked the snow hole with their ice axes, until they had crafted a veritable snow cave big enough to lie down in.

Many years later, Scott would remember that night: "I kept thinking about Tom Hornbein. It was obvious we had to keep awake, to keep friction-warming. Then Dougal started talking to Dave Clarke [the team's equpment manager, at that moment way down at Camp II] about the merits of different sleeping bags. I was starting to worry about him, but then I realized I was talking to my feet."

At first light, the men started down. They had had nothing to eat for thirty hours. Now the fixed ropes proved a godsend. At 9:00 a.m., they stumbled back to Camp VI and crawled into their tent. Two of the world's strongest Himalayan climbers had completed an epic journey lasting thirty hours. Anyone of lesser strength and fortitude would not have survived. Inside the tent, they radioed their success to their teammates waiting anxiously below. Cheers erupted from the various camps. So well had the two men taken care of themselves that neither subsequently lost a single digit to frostbite.

On the sixth major attempt, the Southwest Face had finally succumbed. Haston and Scott had indeed climbed Everest "the hard way."

Two days later, on September 26, the second team of four started off from Camp VI. Almost at once, Martin Boysen's oxygen rig malfunctioned and he lost a crampon. There was nothing for him to do but return to the tent. Inside it, as he wrote in his diary, he "howled with anguish, frustration and self pity." Mick Burke, who had become a professional cameraman for the BBC, was determined to film all the way to the summit, so he lagged behind Peter Boardman and Pertemba.

With the route paved by Haston and Scott and the aid of the fixed ropes, Boardman and Pertemba made better progress. They reached the summit at 1:10 p.m., but spent only a few minutes there, as the weather was fast deteriorating. Near the South Summit, they were alarmed to run into Burke, still filming and still bent on getting to the top. Burke asked Boardman to accompany him as he climbed the last 300 vertical feet, so he'd have a partner to film, but Boardman was too tired even to contemplate that extreme and dangerous effort. Instead, Burke shot his two partners trudging in the snow, hoping that footage would pass for the summit. Then he headed up alone.

Boardman and Pertemba agreed to wait at the South Summit for Burke's return, though that delay seemed to endanger their own lives, with the weather getting worse by the minute. Soon they lost sight of their teammate in the blowing spindrift. They waited and waited, anxiety mounting. Pertemba was especially eager to head down at once. "Ten more minutes," Boardman said.

When the time limit expired, the men started down. Pertemba got off route, and Boardman had to guide his partner's shaky steps back to the upper end of the fixed ropes. As the storm intensified, the two endured a grim retreat, regaining Camp VI in darkness only at 7:30. A pillar of strength all day, as he had shepherded Pertemba back to safety, Boardman took half an hour to crawl the final hundred feet to camp. He collapsed inside his tent and wept. Then he radioed the terrible news about Burke to his teammates scattered below.

No trace of Mick Burke has ever been found. He was so myopic that he wore virtual Coke-bottle glasses, and his teammates speculated that in the blowing snow, unable to clear his vision, Burke might have stepped off the summit ridge and fallen all the way down the Kangshung Face.

It would be easy to fault Burke's judgment for going on solo to the top of Everest in the teeth of a mounting storm, but I'm not willing to do so. Once again, each climber has to decide where his own margin of safety lies. It's a very private matter.

The great success on Annapurna's south face in 1970 had been bitterly undercut by Ian Clough's death in an avalanche at the beginning of the retreat from base camp. Now the first ascent of the Southwest Face was likewise marred by the loss of one of the team's most popular members.

Many years later, Bonington said, "I'm almost certain Mick

made the summit." If so, he would have been the first person ever to reach the top solo.

"Did Mick make a mistake?" Bonington added. "Sure. But I would have done the same. Lots of people have done the same."

The problem posed by the other great unclimbed wall on Everest, the Kangshung Face, was the mirror image of the challenge of the Southwest Face. On the Kangshung, all the technical difficulties lie in the first 4,000 feet. But those difficulties are fierce indeed. From a huge crevasse-riddled field of snow and ice crowning the mountain, a series of buttresses plunge toward the Kangshung Glacier. Not only are those buttresses alarmingly steep—they're threatened by every avalanche and collapsing serac coming down from above.

It was not until 1980, fifty-nine years after Mallory and Bullock's reconnaissance, that any Westerner returned to the Kangshung Glacier. That year, Andy Harvard inspected the face from up close, took lots of pictures, and came back reporting that he thought there were two relatively safe routes through that ominous 4,000-foot wall.

The following year, a very strong team came to Everest from the Tibetan side to attempt the Kangshung Face. The leader was Lou Reichardt, who three years before had been one of the four climbers to make the first American ascent of K2. Along with Reichardt came his buddy John Roskelley, who had also gotten up K2 in 1978. With his partner, Rick Ridgeway, Roskelley had reached the top without supplemental oxygen, the first two climbers to pull off such a feat on K2. The day before, Reichardt had finished the climb oxygenless himself, after his rig had broken down and he had simply discarded it. Their triumph, and the shining example of Reinhold

Messner and Peter Habeler, who that same year had become the first men to climb Everest without bottled oxygen, convinced the Kangshung party in 1981 not to bring the cumbersome apparatus.

All but three members of the nineteen-man team were Americans. Besides Roskelley and Reichardt, they included such all-stars as George Lowe, famed for his cutting-edge climbs in the Tetons, Canada, Alaska, and Pakistan; David Breashears, who had been a legendary rock climber in Colorado (nicknamed the "Kloberdanz Kid" after one of his finest routes), and who would later become the first American to get to the summit of Everest twice; Gary Bocarde, who had put up some of the hardest new routes in Alaska; and Sue Giller, the only woman on the team, who at the time was probably America's strongest female mountaineer.

Rounding out the entourage were Chris Jones, an Englishman transplanted to the States, who with George Lowe in 1974 had climbed the north face of North Twin, the hardest route then forged anywhere in the Canadian Rockies; and the Austrian Kurt Diemberger, a legend in his own right, who had made the first ascent of Broad Peak in 1957, the only one of the fourteen 8,000ers to be knocked off alpine-style. Diemberger and Breashears were ostensibly along as filmmakers, though David would do his share of leading on the climb.

As an added bonus, the team persuaded Sir Edmund Hillary to come along to base camp, where he would end up playing a crucial role in shoring up the team's morale when it had reached a low ebb.

As Andy Politz and I with our Georgia teammates would in 1988, the 1981 Kangshung team decided to tackle the face in the postmonsoon season. That meant that the lowland approach, like ours, would be an ordeal by soggy, washed-out trails and nearly incessant rain. Still, the party reached base camp by the early date of August 28, and four days later they chose their route—the central and most massive of all the buttresses. It's a magnificent line, leading straight as an arrow up the headwall of mixed rock and ice, through the billowing snow mushrooms and serac towers above, and on to the final snowfield directly beneath the summit. I think that in 1988 we might have chosen that very route ourselves, had it not already been climbed. But that central buttress is so massive and technically difficult that it probably would have been too much for our smaller and less experienced team. Instead, we focused our energies on the next buttress left, or south, of the central pillar.

Rotating leaders, the 1981 team got 2,000 feet of fixed rope strung up the buttress in only three days. The crux pitches, harder than anything yet climbed on Everest, were led by George Lowe, with Sue Giller belaying. Some of the climbing required direct aid to surmount overhangs, and the rock was so rotten it scarcely took pitons.

"We were right on the edge of control," Giller remembered decades later. "Every time George would move his feet, he'd knock a rock off, and I was right in the line of fire. I was terrified he'd fall off and get hurt. How could I lower him? What if he had to come to my rescue?"

Congenitally modest, almost self-effacing, Lowe recalls, "It didn't seem unreasonable. It was hard; the rock was pretty bad. But I could get in some pretty good protection every thirty feet or so. . . . Sometimes, though, I could reach down and just pull out the previous piton with the sling [attached to it]."

Optimism was running high at advance base camp under the buttress, but the team could not ignore the dangers of the route. The names they bestowed on the features along the way reflected that edge of fear. The approach gully became the Bowling Alley, because of the rocks careening down it; the camp at the top of it, nestled on a small snow ledge under an overhanging cliff, was named Pinsetter Camp.

On September 5, Kim Momb (Roskelley's partner on Makalu the year before) and George Lowe tried to push the route through the mushroom towers above the buttress. They found hideous conditions, breaking through snow crust up to their thighs. A single pitch took two hours to lead. Momb led another pitch by crawling on all fours. He came back down with the malediction "We're screwed."

John Roskelley was probably the strongest climber of all on the team. Besides K2, he'd previously notched landmark new routes on Dhaulagiri, Makalu, Nanda Devi, Great Trango Tower, and Gaurishankar. But from the start in 1981, Roskelley hadn't liked the looks of the Kangshung Face, and he'd played no part in leading pitches on the buttress. Now he declared unequivocally that the route was too dangerous to attempt.

That judgment might not have swayed the rest of the party, but Roskelley exhorted the whole team to abandon the Kangshung Face, hike back out and around to the north, and salvage the expedition with a routine ascent of Everest via the northeast ridge. Even though the Chinese had granted the team an alternate permit for the conventional north-side route, such a shift in goals would have been a logistical nightmare.

But Roskelley wouldn't let it go. "He was like this little black cloud that ran around base camp," Sue Giller remembers. And despite their close bond on K2, Reichardt weighed in years later: "John's idea was ridiculous. By the time we could have ferried all our gear over there, the climbing season would have been over."

In 1989 on Kangchenjunga, I was teamed up with Roskelley.

He's eleven years older than I am, and knowing about his extraordinary record, I was in awe of the guy and considered it an honor to share an expedition with him. On Kangchenjunga, we got along fine. But there I also saw how strong-willed and inflexible John could be.

That said, I've always admired John's willingness to voice his opinion and his refusal to be swayed by others. If he thought a route wasn't safe, he'd stand his ground, even if it meant walking away from a climb. His example had a strong influence on me, helping me to stand my own ground in similar situations.

On Kangchenjunga, I also saw what happens when John decides a certain "project" isn't to his liking. After brilliantly leading most of our route, John felt that his heart simply wasn't into the rest of the climb. His closest partner, Jim Wickwire, was suffering from the early stages of pneumonia and was having a hard time contributing to the effort. John also disapproved of our hiring Sherpas to carry loads up the face, as he thought the terrain was too risky for them. Using Sherpas for support also simply wasn't John's style. For these reasons, and to accompany Wickwire on the way out, he left the expedition early. I was surprised by John's decision, but respected the fact that he walked his talk.

At base camp in September 1981, the team was torn with uncertainty and dissension. Then, of all people, Sir Edmund Hillary leaped into the fray. He gathered the team together and urged them to stick with the Kangshung Face. "You have a chance to make history," he said. "A chance to explore an unexplored face on the highest mountain on earth."

In the end, only Roskelley and one other climber voted against the Kangshung Face. Roskelley promptly packed up his gear and left the expedition. Sadly, shortly thereafter, Hillary developed cerebral edema and had to be evacuated to the lowland village of Kharta.

With George Lowe, Sue Giller, Dan Reid, Kim Momb, Chris Jones, and David Breashears in the vanguard, the team redoubled its efforts. On September 26, the team established its Helmet Camp at 22,000 feet above the central buttress. Yet already other climbers were coming down with physical ailments, while several began to agree with Roskelley that the route was too dangerous. On October 5, Lou Reichardt led up the jumbled slopes above Helmet Camp. Gary Bocarde had predicted that it would take two weeks to find a way through the crisscrossing crevasses there. That day, Reichardt solved the passage in only two hours.

Nevertheless, the team had reached an altitude just shy of 23,000 feet. A full 6,000 feet of unknown terrain yawned above. The able and willing manpower had been reduced to five climbers. Reluctantly, Reichardt called an end to the assault. It took five more days to evacuate the mountain and begin the hike out.

As David Breashears wrote in his memoir, *High Exposure*, "The climbers had made a splendid effort but we all knew we'd reached the end. It was a defeated team that left the mountain, vowing to return another year and finish the route."

Two years later, once again in the postmonsoon autumn, a new American team arrived. Back from the 1981 effort were Reichardt, Momb, Lowe, Reid, Jim Morrissey, and Geoff Tabin. Among the other eight climbers was Andy Harvard, whose 1980 reconnaissance had sprung the Kangshung effort into being. This time,

Reichardt ceded leadership to Morrissey, a forty-seven-year-old heart surgeon and excellent climber who had been with Roskelley on Great Trango Tower in 1977.

The 1983 team made fast progress up the 4,000-foot buttress that had been pioneered two years earlier. Many of the fixed ropes were still in place, and though the climbers were leery about their condition, they found that most of them were still safe to ascend with jumars. On other pitches, the climbers reled the rock and ice, but kept an ascender clipped to the old fixed rope as a backup.

The great innovation of the 1983 team was a pulley system designed by John Boyle and modified day after day to fit the job. Once the pulley became fully operational, huge quantities of gear and food were easily hoisted up the buttress, toil that would otherwise have required dozens of load carries, every one exposed to falling rocks and avalanches. Many years later, Reichardt reflected, "The winch up the wall made a huge difference."

By late September, the team had ferried 2,000 pounds of supplies up to the Helmet Camp, with thirteen climbers installed there. In the *American Alpine Journal*, Morrissey later joked about the party's remarkable physical condition: "The good health may be attributed to the fact that none of the physicians (we were three) wanted to get stuck evacuating the ill and infirm. The frequency of maladies was inversely proportional to the number of practicing physicians."

Unfortunately, several members soon came down with ailments that would preclude any chance for the summit. Andy Harvard cracked several ribs and contracted pleurisy during a coughing fit. Two of the very strongest technical climbers, Dave Cheesmond and Carl Tobin, succumbed to pulmonary edema and frostbite, respectively.

The healthy members pushed on up the surprisingly easy slopes above Helmet Camp, establishing a Camp II at 25,000 feet, then a Camp III at 25,800 feet. That still left a climb of 3,200 feet to the summit, but the team felt they could go for the top without another intermediate camp. This year, all the climbers were using supplemental oxygen.

On October 8, Kim Momb, Lou Reichardt, and Carlos Buhler set off at 4:30 a.m. Once again, they found the going easy. As Reichardt later claimed about the upper Kangshung Face, "It's actually the gentlest ridge on the mountain." Buhler would later be touted by the mountaineering press as my chief rival to become the first American to climb all fourteen 8,000ers, but that was a pure media fiction. Neither of us sensed any such rivalry, and after 1991 Carlos turned his ambitions toward lower, more technical peaks such as Changabang.

When I think about that trio heading toward the summit on October 8, 1983, I can't suppress a feeling of envy. In 1988, Andy Politz and I flirted with the idea of going for the summit alpine-style in a single push, once we got to the top of our buttress. It would have been a balls-out effort, an ascent of 6,000 feet on unknown terrain, but for weeks I dreamed about it as a kind of ultimate Himalayan coup. As this was only my second Himalayan expedition, I probably overestimated our abilities and underestimated the immense effort such a push would have required. As it turned out, the dream was shattered when we turned back on our own buttress in the face of appalling risks from falling rock and collapsing seracs.

In 1983, only in the last thousand feet did the Kangshung steepen, reaching an incline of 45 degrees. The snow conditions were ideal, however, for step-kicking with crampons, and the three men made steady progress. Shortly after noon, they intersected the standard route at the South Summit. The Hillary Step went smoothly, and at 2:45 the men stood on the summit. The Kangshung Face had been climbed at last. Momb radioed down to his teammates that the air was so still on top, they could have lighted a candle. Reichardt was wearing only polypro underwear and a wind suit.

On the descent, at the Hillary Step, the three men met a Japanese team still heading up the standard route. The Japanese were utterly astounded to learn what the Americans had accomplished and where they had come from. In turn, Reichardt and his partners tried to convince the Japanese that they should turn around, as it was too late in the day to push on to the top. The Japanese refused. To Reichardt's horror, as he descended the ridge leading to the South Summit, a Sherpa from the Japanese team moving just a few steps behind him slipped and fell, without uttering a word, 5,000 feet to his death in the Western Cwm. And that night, two Japanese climbers, who were apparently trying to bivouac near the summit, must have also fallen to their deaths. All that was later found of them were a body and a single boot on the upper edge of the cwm.

The next day, October 9, George Lowe, Jay Cassell, and Dan Reid repeated the march to the summit without incident. If anyone deserved the triumph, it was Lowe, whose brilliant climbing on the buttress in 1981 had paved the way for success two years later.

A third trio, including a rejuvenated Dave Cheesmond, prepared for yet another summit push on October 10, but that day a storm descended on the mountain. By the time it ended, three feet of new snow had treacherously loaded the upper slopes. The only prudent course was retreat.

On the way down, Lowe and Cheesmond performed a deed that few Everest climbers had carried out before 1983. To leave the mountain in as pristine a state as possible, they spent hours chopping the fixed ropes that had been strung up the buttress.

The joint effort by two American expeditions in tackling the Kangshung Face remains one of the greatest deeds in Everest history. Lou Reichardt later said that the climb was much harder than K2. Not the least of the accomplishments of the two teams was the fact that on such a dangerous wall, no climber suffered a major injury, let alone a loss of life.

Had the expedition been led by someone such as Chris Bonington or Reinhold Messner, an official book chronicling the adventure would have soon been published. Whether or not the Kangshung team tried to interest an American press in such a book, I don't know. Unlike Bonington, none of the fourteen men on the 1983 expedition had any track record as an author. Jim Morrissey's article for the *AAJ* is a masterpiece of understatement, a mere five pages long. Unless you know the mountain, you might think, reading that lighthearted piece, that the first ascent of the Kangshung Face was a lark.

The British climbing historian Peter Gillman put the climb in better perspective. "It was a stunning achievement," he said two decades after the ascent. "Yet today, it's so underrated. It's virtually unrecognized—even by Americans."

9

▲ ▲ ▲

A Little Bit of Will

With the British success on the Southwest Face and the American on the Kangshung, all the major walls of the great pyramid of Everest had been climbed. There were, to be sure, new routes that no one had yet attempted. But some of the greatest breakthroughs of the 1980s on the world's highest mountain involved radical new styles rather than new lines. It's a pattern in mountaineering that has generally held true since the first ascents in the Alps, beginning with Mont Blanc in 1786. As the great Victorian climber Albert Mummery once quipped, "It has frequently been noticed that all mountains appear doomed to pass through the three stages: An inaccessible peak—The most difficult ascent in the Alps—An easy day for a lady."

Mummery was exaggerating for comic effect, but the truth of his aphorism holds good today. The ultimate challenge of the 1950s—getting to the top of Everest by any means possible—has been transformed into a fairly routine (albeit extreme) guided outing in 2013. Thus climbers must constantly reinvent the rules by which they play the game to keep it fresh. Often this dictates limiting the resources with which they're willing to attack an objective. Everywhere in the great ranges, for example, alpine-style assaults—going light in a single push for the summit, without fixed ropes or well-stocked camps—has succeeded and, in aesthetic terms, improved on the slow-going logistical pyramid of the traditional expedition-style approach.

This kind of progress does not necessarily take place in other fields of exploration. For instance, on Shackleton's second Antarctic expedition, in 1908–09, three men—Douglas Mawson, Alistair Mackay, and Edgeworth David—man-hauled a pair of sledges across 1,260 miles of polar ice during 122 days, as they tried to discover the South Magnetic Pole. That record would not be matched for another seventy-five years.

From the first Everest expedition in 1921 through the end of the 1970s, nearly every team that tackled the mountain did so in the spring or autumn seasons. The summer monsoon could be counted on to shut down Everest under a relentless smother of falling snow. Most of the climbers who got high up on the mountain or reached its summit did so in the months of May or October. Even during those prime months, mountaineers found the upper reaches of Everest appallingly cold. Frostbite was a routine occurrence, while there were a number of deaths from hypothermia or altitude sickness.

No one seemed to have even contemplated the idea of trying to climb Everest in the winter, until a tight-knit band of Polish hard men (and a few women) began toying with the notion in the mid-1970s. If temperatures of minus 30 occurred routinely in May or October, how much colder must the mountain be in January or February? Attempting the first winter ascent of Everest was a truly visionary scheme for that era, and many experts in other countries thought the mission foolhardy. Yet it had the same logic as the inevitable progress in mountaineering lampooned by Mummery. In the Alps, first winter ascents came into vogue early on. In 1882, a plucky band of Italians made the first winter ascent of the Matterhorn. The ultimate prize came in 1961, when Toni Hiebeler led a team of four Germans making the first winter ascent of the Eiger *Nordwand*, the most dangerous face in the Alps. Climbers around the world gasped with admiration at the German achievement, but nowadays not a winter goes by without numerous ascents of that wall. (The first *solo* winter ascent of the *Nordwand* took place in 1983, by a Slovak climber, Pavel Pochylý, whom most of us have never heard of.)

My co-author, David Roberts, was invited on the expedition that made the first winter ascent of Mount McKinley in 1967. Even though David had participated in the first direct ascent of the Wickersham Wall, McKinley's biggest face, four years earlier, he declined the invitation for two reasons. One, he thought the expedition would be the most miserable ordeal by cold he could imagine, and two, he thought the team didn't stand a chance in hell of succeeding. He was right on the first count, as Dave Johnston, Art Davidson, and Ray Genet (good friends of David's) nearly died during a forced six-day bivouac at Denali Pass.

When word got out in the late 1970s that a group of Poles was gearing up for a winter ascent of Everest, much of the climbing world was aghast, and few of their contemporaries outside Poland gave them much chance of succeeding. But that band of cold-weather masochists had been gearing up for such a project for more than half a decade. In 1973, two of them, Andrzej Zawada and Tadeusz Piotrowski, got to the summit of Noshaq in the

Hindu Kush in winter—the first 7,000-meter peak ever climbed in the coldest season. The next year, Zawada and Andrzej Heinrich reached 27,000 feet on Lhotse in the winter but had to turn back short of the summit.

Why would it happen to be Poles who became the unmatched pioneers of winter ascents on the world's highest mountains? In her superb book *Freedom Climbers*, Bernadette McDonald gives some cogent answers. World War II had squeezed Poland between brutal invasions on either side—Germans from the west, Soviets from the east. And postwar life under Communist oppression became an ordeal by poverty, hunger, and imprisonment for the slightest acts of rebellion. In this milieu, Polish climbers found an avenue of escape. As McDonald writes, "Ironically, the system that stifled them at home provided their ticket to freedom. The centralized government was happy to grant them permits to climb abroad, for their international successes brought glory to Poland."

For Polish mountaineers, an expedition to the Himalaya loomed as almost prohibitively expensive. And their gear was far inferior to the equipment that Americans, Brits, and Western Europeans brought to the great ranges. Much of it was homemade, or had been designed for purposes different from mountaineering. For climbing in storms the Poles used welding goggles. Their currency had no value outside Poland, and this made it even harder for them to buy gear manufactured outside their country, so they improvised or traded with Westerners. Even buying plane tickets to Nepal or Pakistan was a near impossibility for the Poles, so they loaded up cargo trucks and drove to the Himalaya!

Yet the very hardships of normal life in Poland bred a toughness in its climbers that mountaineers leading relatively cushy lives in Seattle or Chamonix could scarcely comprehend. And no Himalayan challenge posed a more stirring test of endurance under extreme conditions than a winter attempt on Everest.

The leader of the expedition was Andrzej Zawada. By the fall of 1979, he was fifty-one years old, but an inborn spirit of rebellious iconoclasm still burned in his soul. As a teenager, he had joined the partisans undermining the puppet dictatorship that ran Poland under the thumb of Moscow. At seventeen, he landed in prison, where he heard the screams of some of his best friends as they were tortured and even executed. Later, as the star climber of the Warsaw Mountain Club, he managed to run afoul of his own organization, when he planned and carried out a winter traverse of the Tatras, the alpine range that straddles the border between Poland and Slovakia. (The club had forbidden the traverse as too dangerous.).

Zawada had been one of the pair who made the first winter ascent of Noshaq in 1973, as well as one of the two who reached a high point on Lhotse of 27,000 feet in 1974. Everest was the next logical step.

To train for the Himalaya, the most committed Polish climbers deliberately bivouacked in the Tatras in winter. Their attitude toward the practice was the complete opposite of mine. As mentioned in chapter eight, I've always done everything I could to avoid bivouacking. But among the Poles, according to McDonald,

Bivouacking became so commonplace (and popular) in the 1970s that top climbers began to compete with each other to see who could do it most often. Specific rules developed: bivouacs inside tents didn't count; using a bivouac sack subtracted one point; sticking one's legs in a backpack scored the highest points. The eventual leader of the "bivy competition" was Andrzej Heinrich, a notoriously tough Himalayan climber who boasted hundreds of bivouacs.

Geez, that's a good definition of *hard man*!

In 1977, Zawada first applied to the Nepalese authorities for an Everest permit in winter, but he had to wait two years before it came through, And when it did, only on November 22, 1979, Zawada had to scramble frantically to put a team together and raise funds for the venture. In Nepal, the "official" winter climbing season ends on February 15. In order to try to meet that rather arbitrary deadline, the Polish team had hoped to be at base camp by December 1. That proved impossible now, and in the end, the Poles established their camp below the Khumbu Icefall only on January 5. This meant that they had considerably less time to work out a route up the mountain than a conventional spring expedition such as the ones I would be part of from 1991 through 1997, when we got to base camp by the end of March in order to go for the top in middle to late May.

Among the thirteen members of the team, two of the strongest were Krzysztof Wielicki and Leszek Cichy. Twenty-nine years old at the time of the expedition, Wielicki had trained as an electrical engineer. He had a reputation as something of a climbing daredevil, and he had already survived two bad accidents, one in a fall on a Polish cliff where he broke three vertebrae, the other in the Dolomites when he was hit on the head by a falling rock. The stone crushed his helmet and knocked Wielicki unsconscious, but after he woke up, he finished the route and bivouacked just below the summit. According to McDonald, "The next day a local doctor stitched up his head and warned him not to climb—good advice that Krzysztof promptly ignored."

Wielicki would go on to become the driving force in a whole series of Polish winter expeditions to the high Himalaya. He deserves, in fact, to be regarded as the all-time pioneer of winter climbing in the great ranges. And in 1996, Wielicki became only the fifth person to reach the top of all fourteen 8,000ers. The year before, in 1995, I had the privilege of pairing up with Krzysztof on Gasherbrum I, as he closed in on his lifelong goal. Although he was forty-five years old that summer, he performed spectacularly. I was thirty-six at the time, and I was truly impressed with Krzysztof's strength, patience, and confidence. (Little did I know that I, too would be forty-five when I finally climbed Annapurna, my fourteenth 8,000er, in 2005.) There's something to be said for being older and wiser when climbing in the Himalaya. Experience plays a key role in knowing how to temper your pace for an endurance event, and how to climb with maximum efficiency and minimum waste of energy. Patience is also crucial, and with age we get better at waiting.

Getting up both Gasherbrum I and Gasherbrum II that summer, Krzysztof notched his eleventh and twelfth 8,000ers. The next summer he would finish his own equivalent of Endeavor 8000 by succeeding on two of the hardest, K2 and Nanga Parbat.

Amazingly, in the winter of 2012–2013, at the age of sixty-two, Krzysztof led a team to Pakistan to attempt the first winter ascent of Broad Peak, one of only five 8,000ers (all in the Karakoram) that had still not seen a winter ascent. Four members of the team reached the summit, but two died on the descent. Even so, Krzysztof told me recently that he feels a mandate for the Poles to climb all of the 8,000-meter peaks in winter, and that he will be the spearhead leading this charge. His duty, he feels, is not necessarily to reach the summit himself, but to organize and lead the expeditions.

Leszek Cichy, twenty-eight years old in the fall of 1979, was a rising star in Polish alpinism, but had far less experience than Wielicki. He was not expected to be a member of the summit team, but his performance on Everest that winter dazzled his teammates.

In only ten days after reaching base camp on January 5, 1980, the Poles got three camps established above the Khumbu Icefall. But now conditions turned brutal. In the brief note in the *American Alpine Journal* covering the expedition, Marek Brniak evoked the nightmare of those days in late January:

> *In the Western Cwm the temperature averaged −25° C. and on the higher reaches −45° C was recorded. Wind speeds reached well over 100 mph. As the days went by the color of the surrounding mountains changed. The peaks grew dark. Wind stripped the snow cover off the slopes, exposing rock and bare ice. Moving on the ice-covered stretches required double attention, extra belaying and fixed ropes on otherwise easy sections. Deep breathing with the mouth wide open to get enough oxygen caused throats, chilled by the icy, thin air, to become swollen and inflamed.*

Andrzej Zawada pulled off several tricks to keep the team's morale from plummeting. Among them was a big aluminum basin the team bought in Kathmandu and lugged into base camp, where it served as a bathtub, filled with kettles of water heated on the kitchen stove, so that the members could take turns escaping the cold in their portable hot spring.

Even so, by the end of January, only four of the thirteen members were still fit and eager enough to contemplate the final assault.

They were Zawada himself, Walenty Fiut, Cichy, and Wielicki. The latter two also happened to be the youngest members of the team, both along on their first Himalayan expedition. On February 11, Fiut, Cichy, and Wielicki finally got to the South Col, but the wind was so fierce there that they pitched their Camp IV just below its crest on the west side. The American-made tent had a pole arrangement too complex to assemble in the gale, so the climbers spent a sleepless night holding the roof up with a single pole. Over the radio, Zawada and others exhorted them to hang on and survive.

The next morning, all three stumbled back down to Camp III. Wielicki had frostbitten feet, so he kept going all the way down to Camp II. Fiut, spooked by the night at the South Col, retreated all the way to base camp. The expedition was on the verge of collapse, so Zawada tried to rally its members. "How powerless is any leader at moments like these?" he later reflected. "If I wanted to save the expedition, there was only one thing to do, and that was to attempt the climb myself."

On February 13, Zawada and Ryszard Szafirski reoccupied Camp IV on the South Col. The next day they set out at dawn for the summit, but the bitter cold and the ceaseless wind turned them back only 750 feet above camp. They limped back down to Camp III. Still, it had been a gutsy effort by the fifty-one-year-old leader.

As if the mountain itself were not a formidable enough obstacle, a bureaucratic snafu now raised its ugly head. According to McDonald, the Nepalese permit explicitly forbade any movement upward on Everest after February 15. The *AAJ* report, however, claims that only now did the team learn by radio at base camp of the February 15 deadline, and that it came as a shock to all the Poles. In desperation, on the fifteenth Zawada sent a porter out to the lowlands to contact the Ministry of Tourism and plead for an extension. Again according to McDonald (who got her story in 2009 from the surviving expedition members), "What [Zawada] didn't know was that the porter was fed up with the whole expedition: the cold, the wind and the endless effort. Unbeknownst to Andrzey, the porter's request was for just two more days. . . . Two days is all they got."

In other words, the team must reach the summit by February 17 or else pack up and start the homeward journey. It seemed an impossible ultimatum.

But now the two youngsters, Wielicki (despite his frostbite) and Cichy, sprang into action. They got back to the South Col on February 16. The temperature that night was minus 42 degrees Celsius, and the wind continued to roar.

Nevertheless, the two men set out the next morning, carrying only a single oxygen bottle apiece. They moved almost wordlessly. Wielicki had no feeling in his feet, but he wasn't ready to turn back. At base camp, the rest of the team waited with mounting anxiety. At 2:10 p.m., Zawada tried to radio the summit duo, but got no answer. With gallows humor, the teammates joked about each cutting off one or two of their own fingers as a good-luck token for their friends.

At 2:25, the radio sparked into life. "Guess where we are!" Cichy's voice boomed over the wind.

"Where are you? Over."

"At the summit. At the summit." Base camp broke out in a frenzy of jubilation, while, 11,000 feet above, Wielicki and Cichy hugged each other.

The descent turned into an extreme ordeal. The two men ran out of bottled oxygen before they regained the South Summit. The wind continued unabated, flinging snow in their faces, and the welding goggles they wore were all but useless. It grew dark very early, and then both men's headlamps failed. They groped on downward in pitch darkness, crawling part of the way. At last they found their tent at Camp IV. Inside it, Wielicki spent most of the night trying to thaw his frozen feet over the camp stove. Two days later, the men regained base camp.

The first winter ascent of Everest by the Poles remains one of the greatest of all Himalayan deeds. I can only imagine the courage and perseverance it must have taken for Wielicki and Cichy to push on in such dreadful conditions. The coldest I've ever been in the Himalaya was when I climbed to the summit of Annapurna in 2005. On the north face, Veikka Gustafsson and I were in shade for most of the day. The wind kept sucking heat out of our bodies. Stopping for a break in that bitter cold was not an option, and with every step I took, I had to scrunch my toes to keep frostbite at bay. I cannot fathom what it would be like high on Everest in winter, with equipment barely suited for the conditions.

That the first winter ascent of any of the fourteen 8,000ers should have come on the highest one of all is itself astounding. That the team succeeded in getting to the top in only forty-three days after establishing their base camp serves as a striking testimony to their drive and courage. That, despite the shortness of the February day, Wielicki and Cichy got to the top by the quite reasonable time of 2:25 p.m. is proof of their superb efficiency as climbers.

Moreover, that the first winter ascent came on the first attempt is also remarkable. And that the Poles observed the arbitrary Nepalese deadline of February 17 and still pulled off the climb gives further proof of their competence and hardihood.

The men became heroes at once in Poland, but the deed was barely recognized outside their native country. And in that recognition, a sour note threatened to tarnish the great accomplishment. By 1980, Reinhold Messner was starting to be hailed as the best high-altitude climber alive. But out of some bizarre streak of envy, perhaps, he now announced that the Polish climb was not a true winter ascent, since the Nepalese calendar officially deemed the end of winter to occur on February 15. Giving the Poles their due in her official Himalayan record, Elizabeth Hawley dismissed this specious canard, haughtily vowing, "I am not amongst these quibblers."

Gradually other climbers started saluting the Polish achievement, so Messner came partway around. Now he granted that it was indeed a winter ascent, but he declared that the Poles had carried it out illegally. Only after the Nepalese Ministry of Tourism certified the ascent as occuring within the "official winter window" did Messner finally back down.

Thirty-three years after this great leap forward in Everest annals, the first winter ascent remains hugely undervalued. None of the team members, not even Zawada, wrote a book about the expedition. And not until 2011, when Bernadette McDonald published *Freedom Climbers*, based on many months of interviews with Polish climbers and commissioned translations of their journal articles, did anything like a coherent account of this extraordinary expedition appear in English.

When I met Wielicki on Gasherbrum I in 1995, I was only hazily aware of his great deed on Everest fifteen years earlier. On our expedition, we chatted about each other's past climbs as well as future plans. His winter ascent of Everest was simply one of many hard climbs he had done, and he wasn't the least bit boastful about his track record. Now, having read McDonald's account of the climb, I'm more in awe of it than ever. Hats off to the Poles, to the vision it took even to conceive of a winter ascent of Everest that early, and to the courage it took to pull it off.

Speaking of Messner, the great climber from the German-speaking South Tyrol region of Italy, had first made a name for himself in the 1960s, with very hard alpine routes in very fast times in his native Dolomites. In the Andes in 1969, he paired up with the Austrian climber Peter Habeler at the beginning of one of the legendary partnerships in mountaineering history. In 1974, the two men astonished the climbing world by dashing up the Eiger *Nordwand* in only ten hours, halving the previous record. The next year, they climbed Gasherbrum I in the Karakoram in the purest of alpine styles—three days, with no porters or teammate support and no bottled oxygen, solving technical difficulties without even bothering to rope up.

Since the days of Mallory, climbers had argued about whether it was possible to climb Everest without the aid of oxygen. Although on the 1924 expedition Teddy Norton had reached 28,150 feet without it, in the next fifty years no one had gone higher without breathing bottled gas. In 1978, Habeler and Messner determined to try. Allying themselves loosely with an Austrian expedition, they went for the top unsupported on May 8. Many in the climbing world had predicted that anyone trying such a feat would die in the attempt, or at least suffer irreversible brain damage. Some members of their own party were skeptical about the wisdom of the effort.

But Messner and Habeler pulled off the first oxygenless ascent of Everest in blithe style, though on the way down Messner contracted snow blindness that turned the further descent from the South Col into an ordeal. I was eighteen years old when the two men accomplished that feat, and the news of their triumph electrified me. The photos of those two men climbing "naked"—wearing only down suits, carrying no rucksacks, with only a handful of snacks and a liter of water each in their pockets—were mesmerizing, as I tried to imagine myself in their shoes. In the end, that ascent of Everest in 1978 profoundly influenced my own decision to try to get up all fourteen 8,000ers without supplemental oxygen. Messner set the standard in Himalayan climbing. A true visionary, years ahead of his time, he broke physical and psychological barriers that no one else had dared to test.

Along with being a great mountaineer, Messner was a purist and an idealist. A book he wrote in 1981, called *Siebter Grad*, translated into English as *The Seventh Grade*, has become one of the most influential polemics in the history of our pastime. In it, Messner argues for climbing mountains only "by fair means," by which he implies not relying too heavily on artificial aids and safety hatches. Some of his phrases have become catchwords in mountaineering, such as the aspersion against climbers "who carry their courage in their rucksack." A kindred essay, called "The Murder of the Impossible," excoriated Cesare Maestri for desecrating Cerro Torre in Patagonia by wielding a gasoline-powered compressor to drill a four-hundred-bolt ladder up the beautiful peak in 1970.

Because he is so strong-willed, even dogmatic, Messner has found himself at the center of many a controversy during his long career. In 1970, on his first expedition to an 8,000-meter peak, Messner and his brother Günther made the first ascent of the huge and daunting Rupal Face, but in a desperate traverse over the mountain and down its opposite face, Günther vanished. Decades later, Mess-

ner publicly blamed his teammates for his brother's death, reignit-
ing the firestorm of acrimony that the expedition had kindled.

And in 1978, after what should have been their greatest triumph, Messner and Habeler had a bitter falling out, in part because
Habeler wrote his own book about the Everest climb, which told a
version of the story slightly less flattering to Messner than Messner's own. It would take decades for the men to repair the breach.

With that great climb, however, Messner was only beginning
his Everest campaign. In 2003, he told my co-author, David Roberts, "The idea to climb Everest without oxygen was not what I
really wanted. It was always to climb Everest alpine-style." So he
concocted an even more "out there" project for 1980. He would
climb Everest by a harder line than the South Col route, again
without bottled oxygen. He would do it solo. And just to up the
ante, he would tackle the mountain in the monsoon season of summer, when virtually all climbers deemed Everest too choked with
snowstorms to attempt.

Messner jumped on the new openness on the part of the Chinese authorities to approaching Everest from the north, snagging
the first permit after a thirty-year closure to climbers from the
West. Initially, he planned to follow the north face and northeast
ridge route pioneered by Mallory in 1924. To emphasize the pur-
ism of his approach, he intended to bring along only a single companion, his then girlfriend Nena Holguin. He would do without
porters or Sherpas. The Chinese demanded that he also hire a liai-
son officer and a translator. They would not go beyond base camp
on the Rongbuk Glacier, however, while Holguin would go only
to advance base. Her company was psychologically important to
Messner. As he explained in 2003, "It is much easier to speak and
divide the worry. It is important to be able to say, 'I don't feel well,

maybe I should not go.' I could do this maybe with a friend, but it is better with a woman."

The four-man party set up camp on the Rongbuk in late June. During the next several weeks, Messner made several forays up the East Rongbuk Glacier, having to rebreak the trail in deep, soft snow each time. On his last effort, he reached the North Col, but decided the conditions were too dangerous to push higher. Rather than give up his attempt, he put it on hold, while he spent several weeks exploring in the vicinity of Shishapangma.

When he returned in mid-August, Messner seized upon a window of relatively good weather, with the temperatures dropping and the snow freezing hard enough for good step-kicking. On August 17, he and Holguin reached advance base camp again. The next day he set out to climb the mountain. Holguin later wrote about that parting, "Yes, he has gone! A tender kiss on the lips was all."

Before dawn on the eighteenth, just short of the North Col, Messner suddenly broke through a snow bridge and fell into a hidden crevasse. As he later wrote, "It felt like eternity in slow motion, rebounding back and forth off the walls of ice, although it was in reality only eight meters deep." A small snow bridge inside the crevasse stopped his fall, but he had no idea how stable it was. And at that moment, his headlamp died. "I see a twinkle from a lone star through a small hole somewhere up above," he later recalled.

It's bad enough to fall into a crevasse anywhere on a mountain, even when roped to a partner. It's really serious on a solo climb. That was my greatest fear on my only solo expedition, when I attempted the Great Couloir on Everest in 1993. In all my years of Himalayan mountaineering, I've never fallen into a crevasse. A few times I've broken through a snow bridge but managed to catch myself with my arms and crawl out. I'm sure good luck has played its part in my escaping from crevasse falls, but I also think that my ultracautious approach has kept me safe. Experience teaches you to see faint markings on the snow's surface that indicate a hidden crevasse, but some are truly invisible and undetectable. Some of the best climbers in the world have broken through snow bridges and fallen to their deaths.

Even though he had fallen only 25 feet into the crevasse, Messner was in a real predicament, in the dark with a useless headlamp. In that moment, he promised himself that if he got out of the crevasse alive, he'd give up the expedition and go home. (Ever since 2006, when my friend and partner Jean-Christophe Lafaille vanished on a solo winter attempt on Makalu, I've thought that the most likely fate to which he succumbed was falling into a crevasse. The fall itself might have killed him, or he could have found himself in a trap from which he could not escape. If so, a terrible way to die.)

Now, however, Messner kept his wits about him. After an hour of gingerly feeling his way, he discovered a snow ramp that led him to the surface. And as he emerged, the impulse to abandon the expedition dissolved. Instead, as the rosy glow of dawn gathered in the east, he pushed on to the North Col. He climbed so efficiently that by the end of the day, he had covered almost 5,000 vertical feet—an amazing performance. He pitched his one-man tent on a small platform of snow, fixed a dinner of tea and cold meat, and managed to sleep well.

Messner has always been prone to hallucinations on high peaks. It's a phenomenon I just don't understand. I've always said that if I started hallucinating on an 8,000er, I'd know it was time to go down. But during that evening as he camped on his small niche, Messner became convinced that a second climber was there with him. He knew somehow that that teammate was not real, but he welcomed its company as "the partner within myself."

He set out the next day at sunrise but soon had an instinct that the northeast ridge, with its notorious Second Step, would not go. Instead, he started angling right across the face below the ridge, just as Norton and Somervell had in 1924, four days before Mallory and Irvine set out on the attempt from which they would never return.

That evening Messner camped on a snow mushroom that he thought should protect him from any avalanches coming down from above, but he was discouraged to realize that in a full day of arduous effort, he had gained only 1,300 feet. He was at 26,900 feet, with more than 2,000 vertical feet to climb to reach the summit. The invisible companion had stayed with him all day, and that evening it was so real that Messner felt his partner cramping his own space inside the tent.

In 2003, Messner reflected on that hallucination. "Being alone in such bad conditions, we become schizophrenic," he claimed. "I didn't know who the other one was. But this is easier—for a few days schizophrenia was my answer. It is the only solution to survive—to have another with whom to divide the fear and the joy."

On the morning of August 20, Messner was alarmed to find light snow falling, with clouds thickening and lowering on the mountain. Others might have turned back, but Messner was too invested in his solo quest to give up now. Carrying only a camera and his ice axe, he started up the Great Couloir. At the Yellow Band, he left the couloir and struck out to the right toward the north pillar, where bare rocks seemed to give better purchase than the soft snow. As visibility shrank to about fifty yards, he felt disoriented, unsure where he was on the mountain. On top of this, he began seeing double. The urge to give up was powerful. As he later wrote, "No despair, no happiness, no anxiety.... There are actually no more feelings, I consist only of will."

His progress had slowed to taking a few steps, then leaning on his axe as he gasped for breath. But suddenly, out of the mist, he spotted the Chinese tripod on the summit. He covered the last stretch crawling on his hands and knees. It was 3:00 p.m.

As he later wrote, "I have never in my whole life been so tired as on the summit of Mount Everest that day. I just sat and sat there, oblivious to everything. For a long time I could not go down, nor did I want to." In Messner's situation, I'd like to think that I would have felt an urgency to descend at once. It was getting late. I doubt that I would have spent more than fifteen minutes on top. In 1991, when I reached the summit alone in marginal weather, I lingered for a mere three anxious minutes on top before heading down. Messner, however, spent a precious hour on the summit. What he felt there was not the rapture that caused Maurice Herzog to linger on the summit of Annapurna in 1950. It was sheer stupefaction.

As it was, Messner barely regained his tent at 26,900 feet just as darkness enveloped the mountain. Too tired to eat or drink, he spent a sleepless night. The next morning, he abandoned everything but his camera and ice axe and headed down. In a masterpiece of understatement, he later described that descent: "Soft snow gave me a lot of trouble; I slid and fell more than I climbed down. It was not all that dangerous, because I fell like a cat. Luckily, I have good coordination and am able to dodge stones and crevasses quite neatly."

Peering through a telephoto lens from advance base camp, Nena Holguin caught sight of her lover as he reached the North Col.

"Seems as if a drunken man is descending from the col," she wrote in her diary, "not the same man who went away four days ago."

Messner's solo, oxygenless ascent of Everest in monsoon season is one of the greatest deeds in the history of Himalayan mountaineering. And Messner himself might well win a poll of experts convened to vote on the greatest climber of all time. What's hard for me to fathom, though, is how his mystical side, with all the hallucinations, seems to enhance his ability, rather than sabotage it. Whatever makes Messner tick is the diametrical opposite of the rational clarity that I strive for on every attempt on a big mountain. But it works for him, and he's still alive, at sixty-nine, as so many of his most gifted peers are not.

Nena Holguin started up the glacier to meet Messner as he stumbled down. In her diary, she wrote, "He glances at me, comes on with sunken head, is no longer consciously there. Going up to him I say: 'Reinhold, how are you?' A few sobs are the answer. . . . 'Where are all my friends?' is his first question. 'I'm your friend, Reinhold. Don't worry . . . ' "

Messner's Everest solo was an achievement that in some ways can never again be matched. Yet only six years later, two Swiss climbers, Jean Troillet and Erhard Loretan, surged up another route on the north side of the mountain in a style that was every bit as audacious as Messner's.

By 1986, Loretan had climbed eight of the 8,000-meter peaks. He would soon find himself in a head-to-head race with the Frenchman Benoît Chamoux to become the third climber to claim all fourteen (after Messner and the Pole Jerzy Kukuczka)—a race that both tried to downplay, but that ended in truly dramatic fashion in

1995, as the men worked their way side-by-side up the fourteenth 8,000er for each of them, Kangchenjunga. The race ended with Loretan topping out on October 5 only hours before Chamoux disappeared near the summit.

In 1986, there were three principal climbers on the north side of Everest in the summer monsoon season. Besides Troillet and Loretan, the ace French mountaineer Pierre Béghin had his sights set on a bold project on the mountain. Originally Troillet hoped to solo a route on the pillar between the Great and Hornbein couloirs. Troillet and Loretan had climbed well together before, notably on very fast ascents of K2 and Dhaulagiri. But Béghin and Loretan had only recently met at a trade festival in Annecy, France. There, Béghin asked Loretan to join him on some Himalayan project, and Loretan agreed. In the end, Troillet invited the other two to make a three-man team. Their goal was to link the Japanese Couloir lower on the north face with the Hornbein Couloir above 26,000 feet. They wanted to climb the route as fast as possible, alpine-style, with an absolute minimum of gear.

The only detailed account of the climb appears in Loretan's memoir, *Les 8000 Rugissants* (*The Roaring 8,000ers*). As I prepared for the east ridge of Annapurna in 2002, I had the stunning first ascent of that route, by Loretan and Norbert Joos in 1984, before my eyes. Those two, rather than descend their route, had cut themselves off from retreat on the way up and had ended up traversing the mountain via a blind descent of the Dutch Rib on the north face. It had turned into an all-out ordeal.

Loretan's book, published in 1996 by a small Swiss press, had never been translated into English, and I don't read French. In terms of a "route description" in 2002, therefore, I had to rely on J.-C. Lafaille's chats with Loretan before our expedition. It was only when I wrote *The Will to Climb*, my book about Annapurna, published in 2011, that my co-author, David Roberts, translated many of the passages from the Annapurna chapter in *Les 8000 Rugissants*, giving me a far richer understanding of just what Loretan and Joos had pulled off on that epic traverse.

David believes that *Les 8000 Rugissants* is one of the very finest climbing memoirs ever written, and that, in its mixture of verbal wit and a kind of absurdist sensibility, it's utterly unique in the genre. What a shame it's not yet appeared in an English edition! Today, in fact, the memoir is out of print even in Switzerland. On Bookfinder.com, the world's leading resource for used and obscure books, I dug up a single copy, for sale through a French dealer for $63.50. If only I could read French, I'd snatch it up.

The Everest chapter in Loretan's book, according to David, is every bit as droll, slyly self-deprecating, and downright funny as "Tell Me Why," the chapter that narrates the Annapurna traverse. Loretan has a way of getting his digs in at climbers more media-hungry than himself, and Béghin turned out to be just such a guy. As Loretan puts it,

> *Pierre Béghin let us know that he was duty-bound to his sponsors. He was thus obliged to take along a camera team, as well as a doctor. His wife would also come, and also the son of his wife. . . . In my whole life, I've participated in only two expeditions with lots of people—those were K2 [in 1985] and Everest. Both were horror shows.*

The team ended up comprising eleven members. Loretan invited Nicole Niquille, the first woman to be certified as a Swiss guide. With Annie Béghin, Niquille hoped to make the first female ascent of Everest without bottled oxygen, but neither woman acclimatized well. They got no higher than the foot of the north face, and both left the expedition early.

On the subject of being part of a team of eleven, Loretan spins a characteristic riff:

> *Suppose that you have to put together a jigsaw puzzle of eleven pieces, and suppose that you have eleven pieces in your hands. . . . If the eleven pieces come from two or three different puzzles, you indeed have to fit them together by force, round off their corners, amputate their rough edges—and you will never end up with the harmony of a whole picture.*

While insisting, tongue-in-cheek, that he is unwilling "to wash my dirty laundry in public," he lets Niquille do it for him. Once back in Switzerland, she wrote a piece for a magazine that Loretan quotes, in which she deplored how a civilized group had degenerated into a "hysterical eruption," and how money and fame had "choked in their tentacles friendship, the pleasure of going to the mountains, and the appetite for a common effort." At base camp, some kind of wholesale collapse of teamwork had clearly occurred. Without naming names, both Niquille and Loretan evidently point the finger at Béghin, with his family, his sponsors, and his film crew.

Like Messner, Loretan, Troillet, and Béghin had decided to attempt Everest in the monsoon season, though none of them specifies why. Loretan has fun with the miseries of the season: "The monsoon—that's when the earth gets caught up in yearning for the time when everything was made of liquid." On the sodden approach to the Rongbuk, "The ground was greasy, the trucks often got stuck in the mud many times, and the men had to give a hand to the short-winded motors." At base camp, a "broken-down team gathered. . . . Because of the trucks, we had climbed much too fast. Nausea, headaches, insomnia, vertigo. All the warning lights on the control panels of our depressurized bodies turned on."

The monsoon made the carrying of loads up to advance base camp on the backs of the yaks another ordeal. At one point, the men strung a Tirolean traverse across a glacial torrent. Loretan muses, "Yaks have many advantages over humans, but they are pretty clumsy at rope work, and instead of using the Tirolean traverse, they had to climb another hour to find a ford." In that ford, "We managed to reduce the salinity of the Indian Ocean by dissolving several kilos of sugar in the coffee-colored water of the stream."

Along with getting in sly digs at Béghin and the "horror show" of an eleven-person team, Loretan could make fun of himself. He had brought along a *parapente*, a collapsible device that fits in a backpack. Once unfurled, the *parapente*, part wing, part parachute, allows an expert to sail off a cliff to the valley below. Loretan was nursing what he calls "the slighty crazy idea" of using the device to paraglide off the summit of Everest. (That startling deed would actually be accomplished only two years later by Jean-Marc Boivin, who got a running start from just below the top of Everest and sailed down to Camp II in only twelve minutes!) But, writes Loretan, "In 1986 the *parapente* was still in its early stages. In fact, it was really an umbrella [the play on words here is between *parapente* and *parapluie*], but less convenient, because it didn't even have a handle."

Loretan decided to make a practice run from a cliff at 19,700 feet above advance base camp. He narrates the attempt as a comedy of errors.

I unpacked my sail. The wind was pretty violent. So much the better! The violence would compensate for the lack of lift characteristic of these altitudes. I struggled with myself for an hour and a half to get up the nerve to take off. . . . Finally, with the sky streaked with a rainbow, the cloth inflated, and I took off!

Between a flight and a fall, the only difference has to do with its duration. If you fall for a long time, it's a flight. If you fly only briefly, it's a fall. The spectators watching my flight unanimously declared it a fall.

The doc confirmed the general impression with his diagnosis: "Severe sprain of the ankle, 'soccer heel,' violent blow to the bones with instep and heel damaged. . . . I hope that there are no broken or cracked bones. Complete immobilization for eight to ten days, then you can try to lace up your boots and see how it goes."

The *parapente* accident could well have been fatal. But in this whimsical passage, Loretan treats it like a joke. At the time, he must have wondered whether the damage he had done to his body would cancel any chance of climbing the mountain. Did he contemplate throwing in the towel and going home? Not according to his memoir. Instead, he rested at base camp for a full fifteen days, while the others acclimatized on lower peaks. At last, Loretan couldn't stand it anymore.

He decided he had to try simply to walk. In running shoes, the pain in his bad foot was unbearable, but with climbing boots he could barely manage. Two days later, with Nicole Niquille, he climbed a minor summit near base camp. He actually brought his *parapente* with him in hopes of making another "flight," but thought better of it.

The next day, with the whole team, Loretan headed up toward the Lho La, the pass that overlooks the Khumbu Glacier on Everest's west shoulder. But now he suffered another accident, when he fell into a snow hole and in the process gashed his arm badly with the pick of his ice axe. Once again, in his memoir Loretan treats this mishap as comedy:

> *Somewhere I had read that Trotsky was killed with the blow of an ice axe to his head. I can well understand why he didn't survive the caress of metal: just above the elbow, my arm was cut across seven or eight centimeters [about three inches] with a beautiful slash. Blood flowed in abundance.*

Alerted by radio, the team doctor climbed up to the snow hole, bandaged up Loretan's arm, and helped him down to advance base camp. "The blade of the ice axe," Loretan wrote, "had transformed my arm into an anatomy lesson: you could see the artery pulsing amid the tatters of carved-up flesh." At advance base camp, the doctor turned the dining tent into an "operating room," as he disinfected the wound, cut off loose pieces of flesh, and sewed up others. Fortunately, neither Loretan's biceps or tendons had been cut, but now the doctor ordered another week of complete rest before his patient could try to climb. Loretan mused, "The sky was bound up with my inactivity: it snowed every day, as if to mitigate the weight of my convalescence."

By now, Loretan must have felt like a virtual cripple. Yet on August 29, six weeks after the team had first reached base camp, he headed up the north face with Béghin and Troillet. "We crouched at the foot of the wall, waiting for the *mâchicoulis* to stop vomiting its torrents of snow." (The *mâchicoulis* was a gap in the floor of the battlement of a medieval castle, through which the defenders could drop stones on the invaders.)

The men had agreed that speed meant safety, so they carried less gear and food than anyone had ever assaulted Everest with. They took neither a tent nor sleeping bags, but only sleeping-bag covers to use like bivouac sacks; a snow shovel "to bury ourselves in the cloak of the mountain as we sought out the illusion of warmth"; no climbing gear (not even a rope!); no bottled oxygen; a single stove and pot; and a mere half pound of food apiece, mainly Ovo-Sport, a Swiss energy bar.

They started up the Japanese Couloir at midnight on August 29. The snow was so deep and loose that the men sank in to their knees, and it seemed so unstable that at any moment they expected a slide to carry them down into the bergschrund. They traded leads every fifteen minutes. Despite his injuries and the enforced rest prescribed by the doctor, Loretan somehow felt himself "in Olympic form." He guessed that having spent six weeks at an altitude of 18,000 feet had allowed him to acclimatize perfectly. Perhaps resting at this altitude combined with Loretan's natural strength made an ideal recipe for preparing to climb at an extreme level.

The three men uttered not a word to one another, but they moved as efficiently as climbers ever have, gaining 6,600 feet of altitude in ten hours. That's an unbelievable pace. The best I've ever managed at comparable altitudes on an 8,000er was when I climbed 7,500 feet on K2 from base camp to Camp III in ten hours. But I was not dealing with thigh-deep snow, I was on a route that I'd already traveled numerous times, and I had the benefit of fixed lines on most of the critical passages. At 11:00 a.m. on August 30, approaching 26,000 feet, the three men found themselves just below the Hornbein Couloir. They used their snow shovel to dig a cave (Loretan calls it an "igloo"), in which they rested for several hours. In his ironic way, Loretan jokes about the tight confines of their snow hole: "To be comfortable there, you had to be fond of elevators, spaceships, bathyspheres, squash courts, and everything that is packed into tin cans."

Setting out at 8:00 p.m. on August 30, the men stripped down their belongings even more radically, leaving behind their sleeping-bag covers, their stove and pot, and their shovel. In fanny packs they carried only a water bottle and an energy bar each, as well as a single camera. In one hand, each climber clutched his ice axe, in the other, a ski pole.

The three men moved with steady, mechanical, wordless efficiency as they climbed the Hornbein Couloir. But Béghin started to lag behind. Not far above the snow hole, Troillet and Loretan heard their partner call out, "I'm going back to the igloo!" In his own brief note in the *American Alpine Journal*, Béghin explained his turnaround:

> *At 8000 meters I was so sleepy that I decided to go back to the snow cave to have another try in the daylight. But I could not find it! I sat in the snow to bivouac without any equipment. . . . There was no wind and I passed the night without frostbite.*

This setback underlines the unbelievable performance of Troillet and Loretan. At the time, Pierre Béghin was one of the strongest climbers in the world, but he could not keep up with his Swiss partners.

Around midnight, the two men hit a rock band. In his memoir, Loretan boasts about how, on all his attempts on 8,000ers, he never studied route topos or the accounts of other climbers beforehand. Instead, he relied on his "adaptation to the terrain." Almost mystically, he claims, "I know where the summit is, and I know where the starting point is. Outside of that, as in life itself, I improvise."

Indeed, on his blind descent of Annapurna in 1984, Loretan had carried in his pocket only a postcard showing the mountain from the north as a route guide.

To me, this attitude is extraordinary. I do just the opposite when I prepare for a climb: read everything I can about the route, study photos and topos till I've got them memorized. Loretan must have been a different breed of climber. Yet there's a certain logic to his approach, trusting his own well-trained instincts over outside information. There's more mystery in Loretan's style of climbing, but also a bit more risk.

Finding their way through the rock band with only the cones of light from their headlamps, however, proved an "abominable" challenge. Later Loretan realized that that passage was the crux pitch that for Hornbein and Unsoeld had sealed their point of no return. Working their way up a chimney toward the right, the two men heard rather than saw a big avalanche tear across the gully they had just vacated.

Two or three hours after parting from Béghin, Loretan was seized with the "third man" hallucination—the conviction that he and Troillet were climbing upward with a shadowy companion right beside them, whom they could never quite confront. It was the first time such a phenomenon had ever worked its way into his mind, and Loretan was mildly disturbed by it. At 27,500 feet, they took another rest stop, sitting on their packs and huddling against each other, but cold soon drove them on.

The moon rose, and then the sun. At last, the two men reached the point where the West Ridge and the north face join. Loretan's account of the final push to the top is uncharacteristically straight: "We continued for fifty meters, our heads bowed as a sign of obstinacy. And then suddenly there was nothing above us except the sky. I felt a lump in my throat, tears in my eyes. It was 2:30 p.m. I was on the summit of Mount Everest, the summit of the world. Joy, weeping with joy."

It was a perfect day. The two men spent an hour and a half on top. "That was the only time," Loretan later wrote, "that neither Jean nor I were obsessed with thoughts about the descent."

But then Troillet had his own hallucination, as he saw an electric transformer take shape in a distant cloud. "I was quite sure that there were no electric transformers in the vicinity of Everest . . ." Loretan later wrote. "It was time to descend."

That descent was probably the most astounding part of the whole climb. Sitting on their rear ends, using their axes as brakes, Loretan and Troillet glissaded the whole of the Hornbein and Japanese couloirs! Picking up Béghin on the way, they regained the foot of the north face in the unthinkably short span of three and a half hours. The whole climb to the summit and back had taken only forty-three hours.

News of the astonishing deed quickly traveled around the world, where it was greeted with admiration and incredulity. During the twenty-seven years since that landmark ascent, Everest has been climbed more quickly than Loretan and Troillet's time, but only by the well-worn standard South Col and North Col routes. Given the difficulties of the route the Swiss pair chose, it's fair to say that their deed has still not been matched. Even the otherwise stolid Walt Unsworth, in his definitive history of Everest, was moved to pronounce the deed "one of the greatest mountain climbs of all time. Just think of it—the highest mountain in the world climbed in less than two days!" Unsworth might well have added, "and in the purest and simplest of styles."

I'm in awe of Loretan in particular because he climbed so many of the 8,000ers in spectacular fashion by difficult routes. By 1986, if he had simply wanted to bag his ninth 8,000er, he could have climbed Everest in conventional fashion, via the South Col route. Instead, he wanted to make a statement about the boundaries of alpinism.

Closing his Everest chapter in *Les 8000 Rugissants*, Loretan lets pride trump his penchant for the absurd.

This meteoric ascent made a certain impact on the climbing world. And on the medical world as well. I knew that certain experts in high-altitude physiology expressed their doubts in the face of such a record time. Some of them asked me if we were shooting amphetamines. I answered, "No!" They told me that the limits of human medicine had previously been met and that there was no scientific explanation for such a feat. I answered: "It's pretty simple. All it takes is a little bit of will."

Twenty-seven years after their great deed on Everest, Troillet continues to lead expeditions to the Himalaya. After finishing his pursuit of all fourteen 8,000ers in 1995, however, Loretan retreated into an almost reclusive privacy in his small hometown in Switzerland. On our way to Annapurna in 2002, I met the man very briefly in a restaurant in Kathmandu. Loretan was leading a trekking group. J.-C. Lafaille introduced me to him, but we had no time to chat, and the language barrier stood between us as well.

Among all the great mountaineers around the world whom I wish I'd gotten to know better, Erhard Loretan ranks right at the top of the list. The combination of the boldness of his climbs and the quirky, understated brilliance of his writing fascinates and awes me. As I was researching *The Will to Climb*, I exchanged a couple of cursory e-mails with Loretan, as I asked for further details about his Annapurna traverse.

Perhaps that exchange might have opened the way to a friendship. If I'd found myself in Switzerland, I'm sure I'd have looked Loretan up. But on April 28, 2011, on his fifty-second birthday, as he was leading his girlfriend up an easy climb in the Alps, she slipped and fell off a high snow ridge, and the rope pulled Loretan off as well. She survived the fall; Loretan did not.

It's the classic irony—a great adventurer, who has survived all the close calls his boldest deeds subjected him to, ends up getting killed in a silly accident on a routine outing. But it never ceases to shock. Loretan's great climbs survive him, as does his reputation. But he deserved to live longer than fifty-two years, and to savor his accomplishments in his old age—as I hope to in mine.

Epilogue

▲ ▲ ▲

The Future of Everest . . . and a Fond Farewell

Well, after 1997, I *really* didn't expect to return to Everest again. Instead, I focused on finishing Endeavor 8000, my campaign to climb the fourteen highest peaks in the world. In 1999, I got to the top of Manaslu and Dhaulagiri only twelve days apart, pulling off one of the best twofers of my career. Two years later, I summitted on Shishapangma, removing the annoying little asterisk that turning back 100 yards from the summit in 1993 had tacked onto my résumé. Then, with my good buddy J.-C. Lafaille, another twofer in 2003, summitting on Nanga Parbat and Broad Peak.

By the end of that summer, I'd climbed thirteen of the fourteen 8,000ers. But I'd failed twice on Annapurna, turning back in 2000 in the face of horrendous avalanches on the north face, and in 2002 because I couldn't justify to myself the risk on steep, unstable snow slopes high on the east ridge. I'd come to think of that mountain as my personal nemesis, and I spent many sleepless hours wondering whether I could ever find a reasonably safe way to get to its summit. When Greg Child interviewed me for *Rock and Ice* in 2002, just after my second defeat on Annapurna, I told him that if I had to stop at thirteen and never finish Endeavor 8000, I'd be okay with that. (Greg titled the piece "Unlucky Thirteen.") I'd be disappointed, to be sure—but I wouldn't second-guess that decision for the rest of my life. The risks on Annapurna seemed off the scale.

Meanwhile, Paula and I were building our family. After Gil came along in 1997, in the summer of 2000 Paula had given birth to a daughter whom we named Ella. When we'd first gotten married, we'd had a friendly disagreement about how many kids we should have. I'd always envisioned two as the right number, while Paula hankered after four. Now she convinced me that three wouldn't be a bad number, so by January 2004, Paula was pregnant again.

Despite what I told Greg Child about being willing to close the book with thirteeen 8,000ers, I'm congenitally unable to leave a project unfinished. I often liken it to a household chore, such as building a patio deck. Until I've hammered the last nail into the last board, the incompleteness of something I've started nags away at me. (I'm sure there are deep-seated psychological reasons for my perfectionism, but I don't think I need a shrink to figure them out, as I believe that my drive to finish a project has done me far more good than harm.)

So I planned to give Annapurna another shot in the spring of 2004, once more approaching from the north, and in all likelihood following the route by which the French had made the first ascent in 1950. I actually secured places for Veikka Gustafsson and myself on an Annapurna permit held by the husband-and-wife team of Gerlinde Kaltenbrunner and Ralf Dujmovits (both of whom have by now climbed all fourteen 8,000ers). Veikka had become my partner of choice on 8,000-meter peaks, and there was no one with whom I would have felt more comfortable tackling a difficult and dangerous mountain.

But that very danger unsettled both Paula and me, and with her just beginning a pregnancy, the spring of 2004 seemed an unpropitious time to do battle with my nemesis. At that point, an escape hatch presented itself, in the form of yet another film project David Breashears was putting together. Stephen Daldry, the British director acclaimed for such films as *Billy Elliott* and *The Hours*, had become fascinated with the 1996 tragedy on Everest, even though he'd never climbed a peak in his life. Having read *Into Thin Air*, he intended to craft a scripted movie with professional actors, not around the whole disaster but around the three characters whose personalities and fates he found most intriguing: Scott Fischer, Rob Hall, and Beck Weathers.

Most of the film would be shot near sea level in settings that would stand in for Everest, but Daldry wanted real Everest footage as well, and he wanted to travel to the mountain. He hired Breashears to do the filming, and David immediately invited me to help organize the food and equipment and to run the logistics of the expedition. We rounded out the team with Veikka, Robert Schauer (the great Austrian climber who'd backed up David's IMAX filming in 1996), Jimmy Chin (a very strong climber and up-and-coming photographer and filmmaker), and a Teton guide named Amy Bullard. I looked forward to being back on Everest again with such trusted friends as David and Veikka. I hadn't seen Robert since we'd parted ways after our IMAX expedition. As we hugged good-bye at the end of that tragic season, he had said, "Next time, let's have some fun."

I rationalized the Everest project by planning it as the first half of a twofer: on Everest, I'd get acclimatized for a second expedition, and once we were done filming, Veikka and I would zip over to Annapurna and try to climb it fast.

It didn't quite work out that way. Daldry was a good sport and an interesting guy to hang out with. Despite being slightly out of shape, having just kicked a two-and-a-half-pack-a-day smoking habit, he was keen to go not only to base camp below the Khumbu but to probe partway through the icefall. On April 7, I roped up with him and started through the labyrinth. That evening I wrote in my diary, "Played in icefall w/ SD. Even though he was convinced he wouldn't cross the ladders, he did."

It turned into an odd expedition. Much of David's filmmaking consisted of shooting scenics with a high-resolution film camera. I never quite understood how Daldry would integrate these panoramas into his action film, but David explained it rather cryptically as "like painting the inside of a Ping-Pong ball." With a camera mounted on a tripod, which he rotated through a set number of degrees, David would film the inside of a spatial sphere. Then the footage would be digitally spliced together. Eventually, a professional actor in a comfortable studio in England would be "painted," thanks to David, into a scene in the Western Cwm or up on the Lhotse Face.

We had good weather, and despite the by-now normal hordes on the south side of Everest (that spring no fewer than sixty-four expedition teams tackled the mountain), we decided to go for the summit in mid-May. We avoided the traffic jam by leaving the South Col at 10:00 p.m. on May 16, and at sunrise I stood on the summit. All five of my teammates also summitted without incident. In some ways, it was the smoothest and easiest of all my Everest expeditions, in large part because each of us was hired to do a job with well-defined responsibilities. Everybody got along well, and we were all experienced climbers who took care of ourselves while we looked out for one another. At age forty-four, I'd climbed as well as I ever had, and now I'd stood on the highest point on earth a total of six times. Being there with great friends was icing on the cake.

In the end, Daldry got sidetracked by other projects. Nine years later, there's a real possibility that the film he cared so much about will never get made. (That's showbiz, as many folks have told me.) It seems a pity if David's stellar work ends up in the cinematic trash bin, but all of us had a good time on Everest that year, I met some memorable characters in the world of moviemaking, and I got paid well to revisit what had become one of my favorite places on earth.

Unfortunately, we spent so much time on Everest that the twofer with Annapurna went out the window. I'd have to put it on hold. That May several of the team on our Annapurna permit reached the summit without incident. I wondered if I had missed my golden opportunity. During the next year, my nemesis would keep me awake long into the night on too many occasions. But on October 12, Paula gave birth to another beautiful baby. We named her Anabel.

Ever since 1996 and *Into Thin Air,* the focus of media attention on Everest has been negative. The hordes, the traffic jams, the incompetent clients paying big bucks to get dragged up the mountain, the indifference to dying climbers as others clump past them toward their selfish personal goals—these have become the stock clichés of the Everest soap opera.

It's not that there isn't some truth to those stereotypes. Everest has indeed become far too popular for its own good—especially on the two standard routes on the north and the south. Accurate statistics are hard to come by, but according to the respected Everest chronicler Alan Arnette, in the spring of 2012 something like 548 climbers reached the top of Everest, 150 of them on May 25 and 26 alone. The experienced German mountaineer Ralf Dujmovits, who in 2009 became the sixteenth person to climb all fourteen 8,000ers, took a photo high on the Lhotse Face that spring that instantly "went viral." When I saw the photo, my jaw hit the floor. It shows a line of something like 150 climbers treading on one another's heels as they slide their ascenders up the fixed ropes—a "human snake," as some have called it. And that photo cut off the head and tail of the snake, as even more plodders formed at either end of the procession. In disgust, Dujmovits gave up his own attempt to go to the top without bottled oxygen. As he kicked steps down the Lhotse Face just above the human snake—Dujmovits being far too good a climber to need a fixed rope there—some of the folks in the line screamed at him, for fear he would fall and knock them off their own feet.

Had I been on Everest that spring, somewhere in the middle of that human conga line, I would also probably have turned back. I can hardly bear to drive down the highway behind another car going well under the speed limit, let alone put up with being on a mountain, attached to a single strand of rope, stuck among a hundred or more people, going only as fast as the slowest person somewhere at the front of the line. Crowded slopes are the reality of Everest these days, and my view is jaded by the fact that I've been there when there were very few other climbers around.

In the spring of 2012, ten men and women died on Everest. It's one measure of the dehumanization of the place that that toll seems to have been accepted as business as usual, rather than mourned as tragedy. On the Hillary Step on May 25 and 26, it was reported that climbers had to stand in place waiting for their turns on the fixed ropes for as long as two and a half hours. It's a wonder more of them didn't come to grief.

Many folks have suggested that China and Nepal ought to limit the number of expeditions to which they grant Everest permits. But it's not up to us Westerners to tell those nations—especially Nepal, one of the poorest countries on earth—how to run their tourism industry. Meanwhile, the number of outfitters offering guided trips on Everest keeps burgeoning, and the top-end companies now charge as much as $75,000 per client. Despite that astronomical fee, there are plenty of customers willing to fork over a good hunk of their life savings to have a chance to reach the top of the world.

As I said at the outset of this book, however, the Everest soap opera fails to mirror my own experience on Everest. Yes, in the latter years, I've had to figure out strategies to avoid getting stuck in the traffic jam above the South Col, and I've seen my share of follies carried out on the mountain—but not among my own teams. The clients I've guided to the top were competent climbers to begin with, and it's been immensely gratifying to help them realize lifelong dreams.

In this book, I've emphasized the great deeds in Everest history, of which there have been many. Although I've ended my accounts of those deeds with Loretan and Troillet's dazzling climb up the Japanese and Hornbein couloirs in 1986, it's not because great things weren't done during the subsequent twenty-seven years. Perhaps inevitably, however, the more recent "firsts" have focused not on new routes, but on bold new ways of upping the Everest ante. They aren't stunts, exactly, but they tend to be records defined by somewhat arbitrary parameters.

The most heartening trend during the last quarter century is the emergence of Sherpas as some of the best climbers on Everest. The record for summiting the most times is twenty-one, first accomplished by the mild-mannered, unaffected Apa Sherpa, who topped out most recently in 2011, at the age of fifty. The speed record for an ascent from base camp on the south to the summit—11,335 feet of climbing—is held by Pemba Dorje Sherpa, who made the climb in 2004 in the stunning time of eight hours and ten minutes. Pemba's record was questioned at first, most vocally by the Sherpa who held the previous record, but a thorough investigation by the Nepal Ministry of Culture and Tourism certified the deed.

In May 1999, Babu Chiri Sherpa spent twenty-one straight hours without supplemental oxygen on the summit, some of it asleep, without suffering any ill effects. No one else has even tried to duplicate that feat. Sadly, Babu Chiri died on Everest in 2001 when, at an altitude of only 21,300 feet, as he casually photographed the surroundings of Camp II, he slipped and fell into a crevasse.

Some of the most dazzling performances on Everest have been performed on the way down. In the previous chapter, I mentioned Jean-Marc Boivin, who in 1988 parasailed from the summit to Camp II in only twelve minutes. In 2001, at age twenty-two, the French wunderkind Marco Siffredi performed the astounding feat of descending the Great Couloir on the north side of Everest by snowboard. Tragically, that bold accomplishment was not enough to satisfy Siffredi, who disappeared the following year trying to snowboard the far more treacherous Hornbein Couloir.

Casual observers have sometimes lamented the state of Everest as "climbed out"—meaning that there are no significant new routes left to pioneer on the mountain. But they're wrong. The Fantasy Ridge on the east face of Everest remains virtually untouched. It's an immensely long ridge festooned with double cornices on the far right-hand edge of the Kangshung Face, angling up to its intersection with the northeast ridge well below the point at which climbers heading up from the North Col strike that ridge.

Though the route was named by Mallory way back in 1921, it was not attempted until 1991. At least four parties have tried to tackle the route, but gotten nowhere on it. In 2003, the strong South African husband-and-wife team of Ian Woodall and Cathy O'Dowd, with a single Sherpa, started up a snow ramp on the south side of the Fantasy Ridge. After, in their words, "an avalanche nearly wiped out the entire route including base camp," they gave up the effort at only 19,000 feet. And in 2006, an American team announced its intention of going after the Fantasy Ridge. After much preexpedition media hype, the team came home with its collective tail between its legs. Thanks to a lack of snow leaving gaping crevasses on the approach and ominously teetering seracs along the ridge, according to team member Dave Watson, "At first sight, it was obvious: if we tried it we would disappear."

The Fantasy Ridge, then, is a project for the next generation. So, too, is the Horseshoe Traverse, an enchainment whose name (if not concept) seems to have been bestowed by the longtime Everest chronicler Elizabeth Hawley. The idea is to make a continuous alpine-style traverse starting on the southwest side of Nuptse, over that summit and along the tortuous ridge to Lhotse, over *that* summit and down Lhotse's north ridge to the South Col, up Everest by the Hillary-Tenzing route, then down the West Ridge.

No one so far has even launched an attempt on the Horseshoe

Traverse. To me, it's an immensely appealing idea, a natural challenge that strikes your eye every time you enter the Western Cwm and are surrounded on three sides by Everest, Lhotse, and Nuptse. But it would be so committed, with so many places along the way from which retreat in a storm might be impossible, that I'm not sure even the best climbers of today could be up for it. As Greg Child, who has climbed both Everest and K2, says, "I can't think of anything more difficult to do than the Horseshoe Traverse. It's beyond the pale."

I finally reached the summit of Annapurna with Veikka Gustafsson on May 12, 2005. It was 2:00 p.m. when we topped out. For months beforehand, my emotions had been strung as tight as a piano wire. I expected that if I reached the summit, I would break down in tears, but it didn't turn out that way. On top, Veikka and I hugged each other as we cheered, and I sent a message down to base camp by two-way radio. "This is one of the happiest days of my life," I said, "and one of the hardest." On the summit, I felt overwhelmed with joy, but it didn't provoke tears. They would come later, after I reached base camp. On top, my emotions were kept in check by my eternal vigilance: *The summit is only the halfway point.* And indeed, the descent would throw all the obstacles in our way that the mountain could manage to scheme up.

When I returned to Seattle later that month, my predominant feelings were relief to be finished and pride in what I had accomplished. An eighteen-year campaign that had dominated my life and defined me as a public figure had finally come to a close. I'd climbed all fourteen 8,000ers without even a minor injury. It would take many months before relief shaded into restlessness, but at some point, the nagging question crept into my thoughts: *Now what can I find to replace this amazing and time-consuming campaign?* Endeavor 8000 had been the vital fabric of my life for almost two decades, and now that it was over, I felt a void.

At first, finding other avenues of adventure came easily to me, with abundant rewards. I ran the New York marathon with Paula. I undertook two sledging trips on Baffin Island, one with dogs, the other man-hauling just as Scott and Shackleton had done. It was hard work, to be sure, but throughout both trips, I kept having the giddy realization, *Boy, the air is pretty thick down here near sea level!*

I also got to climb beautiful mountains on continents other than Asia, including Aconcagua in South America for my second time, and the Vinson Massif, the highest point in Antarctica, for my first. I kept climbing Rainier two or three times every year, including guiding Commissioner Roger Goodell of the NFL to the summit in 2009. He later called that climb "one of the greatest experiences of my life." And I went back to guide on Denali, where I had last climbed in 1985.

Although in general after 2005 I was done with 8,000-meter peaks, I'd always kept on my personal back burner the possibility of returning to Everest. I had no immediate plans or any particular desire to go, but if the right opportunity came along, I might be tempted. Another film project or something equally unique would be the only reason to go back. Annapurna and K2 had presented the sternest challenges during my Endeavor 8000, but I'd had an incomparable range of experiences on my ten expeditions to Everest.

Then, in 2009, the opportunity presented itself. Two years earlier, Eddie Bauer, the Seattle-based equipment company, had become one of my chief sponsors. The company hired me as one of several mountain guides to help design and test a new line of high-tech clothing and gear called First Ascent. (My first sleeping bag, at age fourteen, had been a classic green Eddie Bauer mummy bag.)

We spent two years creating and testing a product line that included everything from base layers to fleece jackets, wind shells, down jackets, gloves, tents, and packs. As a final test of our products, and to mark the official launch of First Ascent, the folks at Eddie Bauer asked us to use what we had developed on Everest in 2009. We would also be photographed and filmed "in action," for use in promotions and advertising. The hope was to rejuvenate the Eddie Bauer brand by bringing the company back to its roots of expedition outfitting, a function it had not served since the late 1970s.

Tempting though the proposal was, I did not immediately say yes. It was a tough decision to make. By early 2009, Paula was pregnant again. Our brood would consist of four kids, each with his or her own passion for the outdoors. In fact, on August 15 that year, Paula would give birth to our third daughter, whom we named Nina.

By now, of course, Paula knew just how dangerous any trip to an 8,000er, no matter how well organized, would be. There was a constant reminder of that fact in the doleful roster of former partners of mine who had died on such expeditions, including Rob Hall, Scott Fischer, Chantal Mauduit, and J.-C. Lafaille. When a woman is pregnant, moreover, she's emotionally more vulnerable. We were also in the midst of a move to Sun Valley, Idaho, and that made everything more complicated. Paula's doubts and fears in January and February couldn't help reinforcing mine.

For weeks, we deliberated long and hard. In the end, I felt that this new expedition had more upside than downside. I could help launch a brand of clothing and gear that I had a hand in designing, I would be paid well for my efforts, and I would have one more chance to visit a mountain that had come to feel like a close friend. At last, Paula agreed with my logic, and she supported me as whole-heartedly as she had always done. Still, this separation would prove to be the toughest we had ever undergone.

Another reason I wanted to go back to Everest was that, on the verge of turning fifty, I hoped to find out if I could still climb above 26,000 feet as well as I had in my early thirties. Even after climbing Annapurna, I'd kept up the rigorous daily workouts with which I'd always trained for expeditions. As a guide and professional climber, I felt that it was my job to be fit and ready at a moment's notice to go on a climb. At forty-nine, I felt as fit as ever, but Everest would be the real test.

The rest of the team was made up of first-rate mountaineers who were both RMI guides and members of the First Ascent design team. The overall leader would be Peter Whittaker, the son of my former RMI boss Lou Whittaker and the nephew of Jim Whittaker, the leader on our 1990 Peace Climb. Peter had tried Everest twice before but had yet to reach the summit. He would lead our small group of professional climbers.

A second team, with bona fide clients along, would be led by Dave Hahn, who now holds the record for most ascents of Everest by a non-Sherpa, with fourteen. Our teams would share base camp but climb on separate schedules.

On April 8, we reached that base camp below the Khumbu Ice-fall. We had built into our expedition a steady stream of Internet dispatches with stunning high-def video to be sent to folks back home, so they could follow our progress day-by-day. This meant that all the way up the mountain, we had to shoot video and pho-tos. The photos would later be used for catalogues and advertising. The video would be shown on large flat screens in all of the Eddie

Bauer stores to captivate customers and demonstrate that Eddie Bauer was back on the cutting edge of adventure.

I got a bit impatient with the rigid and pokey schedule that all this production dictated for our team. I guess I just wanted to get up the mountain as quickly and safely as I could. The bells and whistles of the media effort seemed like a distraction, but in the end I reminded myself that that was the reason we were on Everest, and that production took precedence over our schedule.

As for my conditioning—it turned out that I moved faster through the icefall and up to the lower camps than any other member of the team. The others kept scolding me for my pace, and telling me to slow down. For me, climbing fast was a way not only to acclimatize, but to build strength for later on during the expedition. I had also made a pact with Paula that since I was not guiding, I would climb through the icefall as fast as I could on each of my passages and not wait around for anyone else. But on April 14 I wrote in my diary, "I seem to be the topic of many discussions because my speed is causing folks to try to keep up & I'm causing team separation. So, I guess I need to chill out & put on my 'guide hat' for a day." In the end, my speediness became a running joke. Whenever someone got sick, something went wrong, or something broke, the standard line was "It's Ed's fault!"

We were thus a pretty harmonious group. There were more tensions around how we presented our climb over the Internet than there were about the climbing itself. Privately, I really missed Paula and the kids, as my diary frequently attested. And I was upset by knowing that as she watched our day-by-day progress, with the production team sometimes overdramatizing just how dangerous Everest was, she might buy the hype and get angry with me for taking unnecessary risks. By e-mail or sat phone, I reassured Paula that everything was fine, and urged her to take the dispatches with a grain of salt.

We got Camp I established on the edge of the Western Cwm on April 14, Camp II on the nineteenth, and Camp III on the Lhotse Face on the twenty-seventh. There was a predictable crowd of climbers on the South Col route that spring, with the usual scrambling for the best tent platforms, especially at Camp III, where good sites are hard to find. The newest tactic was for Sherpas from each team to race to these small, precious campsites and stake a claim by roping off an area. It was like a land grab, and it created a lot of tension among expedition teams. The Everest chronicler Alan Arnette counted up thirty-six different parties on the mountain that spring. As we got higher, I began calculating just how to avoid getting stuck in the traffic jam on summit day, a nuisance we had managed to evade in 1997 and 2004.

In early May, we took a prolonged rest break at base camp—too long for my liking—before heading up on our summit attempt. Then the weather turned bad, and we were further delayed. I hate sitting around, and feeling extremely fidgety, I took hikes down the valley every day just to stay fit and kill time. Finally, on May 14, having received a good forecast, we started up the mountain. We hoped to snatch the first relatively good day, May 18, to go to the summit. Most of the other teams were planning on the better day being the nineteenth, so they would be a day behind us. In this way we might trade slightly worse weather for fewer people on the summit ridge. The disaster of 1996 was still fresh in my mind, and the lessons that I learned from the events of May 10–11 that year underpinned my planning on Everest in 2009. On May 16, we slept at Camp III, then climbed to the South Col the next day, where our Sherpas had already established our highest camp.

We had planned to get up and start climbing that very night at 11:00. But an ominous cloud cap formed on top of Everest, and the winds battered our tents all night. There was nothing to do but wait it out for another day. In our tent, Peter and I tried to keep each other entertained with jokes, books read aloud, music, and conversations about what we'd do once we got back down to thicker air, hot showers, and refrigerators full of beer.

The biggest drawback of the enforced delay was that throughout the eighteenth, other climbers arrived at the South Col, all with plans to go for the top on the nineteenth. Now we would need a plan to escape the traffic jam.

Originally, I'd planned to climb Everest without supplemental oxygen, but now, realizing how debilitating an extra twenty-four hours at 26,000 feet would be, and also to keep the team harmonious and give myself some margin to help out others if they got into trouble, I agreed to breathe bottled O's on summit day.

It was a calm night, but I didn't sleep well at all. I'd developed a bit of a sore throat from breathing the cold, dry air, and just as I'd doze off, my own coughing would wake me up. With all the climbers on the South Col poised for an ascent the next day, I'm sure my anxiety about this one last stab at Everest played its part as well. I could never be sure I'd be up to the challenge of those last 3,000 feet of climbing, no matter how well I'd trained. Not only did I not want to let myself down, I wanted to succeed for the team.

We got up to leave our tents at 11:00 p.m. It was colder than usual for mid-May, around minus 30 Fahrenheit when we left camp. I'd hoped that an early departure would once again put us ahead of the mob, but by now other teams had learned the trick. Some climbers from other teams actually got off as early as 8:30.

I carried two quarts of warm sweetened tea and several energy gels in my pack, along with my camera, sunglasses, and spare mittens. As it turned out, however, I took only one sip of tea all day and ate nothing. Peter Whittaker stayed in the lead of our team the whole way, making frequent radio calls to base camp to report our progress. He was on a kind of manic high, in part because of his failures on his two previous attempts. Now he could feel the summit in his grasp.

At the bottom of the feature sometimes called the Triangular Face, our team caught up with a massive line of other climbers who were hardly moving. As I later learned, a single Korean was creating the roadblock. At the head of that line, refusing to step aside, he took one excruciatingly slow step after another, as a Sherpa unclipped his ascender from one fixed rope and clipped it to the next one for him.

The only resort for us was to get off the fixed line and leap-frog past people. In the dark, that was potentially dangerous, but after all, when I'd first climbed Everest in 1990, there were no fixed ropes strung to the summit. All of us were competent mountaineers, so throughout the day, we passed climbers from other teams, including a whole gaggle taking a rest break between the South Summit and the Hillary Step.

I reached the top at 8:30 a.m., half an hour after Peter. I felt slightly choked up as I radioed news of my own success down to base camp, but it was very cold on top, and with so many other folks hanging around there, the summit was not the transcendent experience I'd tasted in 1990, when I had the highest place on earth to myself. As I later wrote in my diary, "No real time to savor the moment nor even to just take a look around. . . . Just glad to be on top & to have pulled it off."

On the way down, nearing the South Col, Peter almost collapsed. The manic fervor of his first triumph on Everest had sapped all his energy, and now he crashed. I stayed just behind him as he stumbled and staggered back to camp, so he could count on me for backup. Still, I was really happy for my friend to have succeeded in a personal challenge that meant so much to him.

For me, the highlight of May 19, 2009, was calling Paula via sat phone from my tent on the South Col. She was overjoyed, not only because I'd gotten to the top, but because now I was headed down the mountain and back toward home. Both of us knew, though, that I still needed to keep up my guard as I descended the Lhoste Face and Khumbu Icefall one final time. *Climbing a mountain has to be a round-trip.*

It was inevitable that reaching the summit of Everest for my seventh time would not be a life-changing event of the sort that finally getting up Annapurna had been. According to Alan Arnette, at least 281 men and women climbed the South Col route to the summit in the spring of 2009, and a sizable chunk of them did so on the same day I did, May 19.

It was gratifying that despite being on the cusp of fifty years old, I had felt as fit and climbed as well as I ever had. I could even take a certain satisfaction in the notion that within our Eddie Bauer team, I was not only the oldest climber, but could pull my weight as well as all of my partners.

Yet as I descended the mountain during the next several days, I felt a poignancy that surprised me. By the end of 2009, I recently calculated, I'd spent the equivalent of two and a half years on Mount Everest. Except for Mount Rainier, no piece of mountain topography had come to be as familiar to me as Everest. And no terrain anywhere in the world had been the arena for so many profound moments in my life, ranging from the wonderful to the heartbreaking, from getting to the top alone in 1990 to climbing past the bodies of Rob and Scott in 1996.

As I made my way down Everest, starting on May 20, it was like a farewell journey. I was quite sure that I would never again sleep on the South Col, or traverse the Lhotse Face, or hike across the Western Cwm, or wend my way, heart in throat, through the Khumbu Icefall. That descent was like saying good-bye to an old friend.

All the way down, however, I stayed vigilant. And only when I got through the icefall for the last time did I give way to full-on celebration. "Yahoo!!" I wrote in my diary. "All done, safe & sound!! Done and going home."

In devoting so much of my life to Everest, I had become part of a ninety-year-long pageant of adventure dating back to Mallory. I had joined an elite fraternity. And any brotherhood that contained the likes of George Mallory, Eric Shipton, Sir Edmund Hillary, Tenzing Norgay, Reinhold Messner, Doug Scott, Peter Boardman, Krzysztof Wielicki, and Erhard Loretan, among others, was a society to which it was a great honor to belong.

I learned a lot about life and about myself during my twenty-three-year span of campaigns on Everest. They aren't the kinds of neatly phrased slogans you can pin up in your kitchen like refrigerator magnets. They're subtler and harder to put into words. One of them, however, has everything to do with Paula and our four children.

I went to Everest six times when I was single, five more times after Paula and I met, and four times after we married. The last two of my Everest expeditions came after I'd become a father. The stories are legion of great climbers whose marriages have fallen apart because the mountains were more important to them than the loved one waiting at home. Conversely, there are scores of first-rate mountaineers who, concluding that risk and family were incompatible, gave up serious climbing after they had children.

I'm proud to believe that I've managed to integrate the two. It was really rough on my kids (and on me) to say good-bye to them as I headed off to the airport for another expedition to an 8,000er. No matter how many times I tried to placate Gil or Ella with the claim that when I was home, I spent more quality time with them than fathers who worked nine-to-five office jobs, they'd dissolve in tears and beg me not to go.

After Paula and I started having children, it became much more emotionally stressful for me to go on expeditions. Yet once on the mountain, I never let the tug of home undercut my resolve to give the climb my best effort. In the face of weeks of storms, I never opted for the escape route of an early departure. I like to think that in the Himalaya and the Karakoram I climbed as well as I ever could, and that the rest of the year I was a good and loving father.

All the credit really should go to Paula, Gil, Ella, Anabel, and Nina. As I wrote in my 2009 diary on April 8, "I love & miss Paula & kids already. How could I be so fortunate to have them?"

The cumulative impact of my experiences on the highest mountain in the world amounts to a fund of memories and achievements that I believe will enrich the rest of my life. In old age, I'd like to be able to say, as Maurice Herzog wrote of the first ascent of Annapurna, that Everest was "a treasure on which we should live the rest of our days."

Acknowledgments

For me to look back and see that Everest was the objective of my first Hima-layan expedition in 1987, and that Everest, as of 2009, remains the most recent objective among my thirty-one Himalayan expedi-tions, strikes me as quite extraordinary. If I've truly reached the end of my campaign on 8,000-meter peaks, then I could not ask for a more fitting conclusion than having Mount Everest serve as the bookends of my climbing career on the 8,000ers.

My experiences on Everest have been life-changing, and the friendships formed there everlasting. I can attest that the "Everest experience" is one of the unique events in anyone's life, whether it's the magical trek though the Khumbu, or helping to manage base camp, or the climb itself. To take part in the collaborative effort of an Everest ascent turns one into a different person. Everyone revels in the excitement and shares in the journey. I've seen through my own eyes how important teamwork is for these expeditions, and I never take for granted the contributions made by my teammates. I thank everyone who has helped me along the way to take part in eleven safe expeditions.

In my dedication to this book, I've saluted some, but certainly not all of the partners, teammates, Sherpas, staff, and friends with whom I've been on the highest mountain on earth. As for those others—I thank you as well. Several of those to whom I feel a special debt of gratitude are Eric Simonson, for believing enough in me to invite me on my first Everest expedition; Jim Whittaker, for including me in his International Peace Climb; Hall Wendel, for trusting my judgment and not giving up; Rob Hall, for asking me to partner with him on two of his commercial expeditions; and David Breashears for entrusting me with organizing and co-leading three of his expeditions. The memories we share enrich our lives and can be recalled instantly with a simple look, or a "remember when." No matter how many times you've been to Everest, the experience never leaves you.

I also want to thank my loving wife, Paula. Her emotional support and belief in me during these last nineteen years have given me strength beyond measure. As the Everest expeditions went by, our family grew. The love, cards, letters, and drawings given to me by my four children as I departed from home brought joy and tears to my eyes, as I knew that part of them was with me as I climbed Everest's slopes. I thank them for accepting my absences so that I could "do-what-I-do."

Once again, piecing together the events of all my expeditions and organizing my thoughts in an orderly and readable fashion have been the handiwork of David Roberts. Our fourth collaboration was as enjoyable and smooth as the first. I've often said that I supply the building materials and David builds the house. David has a gift with words that I'll never have, and I thank him for once again finding my voice as he crafted this book. His historical knowledge and enthusiasm for recounting some of the greatest Everest expeditions of years past made this book richer in many ways. Writing a book together is like climbing a mountain. Finding the right partner and enjoying the process have always been paramount for me, and I feel we've succeeded in this.

Thanks to Stacy Creamer, my editor at Touchstone Books, for once again wanting to bring my stories to the world. Having her at the editorial helm for *No Shortcuts to the Top* helped that book reach heights that I never expected. To have her working with us again is a delight. Stacy's assistant, Miya Kumangai, skillfully managed the many details that go into making a published book. And Gypsy da Silva superintended the copyediting with her matchless aplomb.

Stuart Krichevsky, my literary agent, helped make this book possible and ironed out the lumps and bumps so that David and I could have a smooth ride. Stuart's colleagues, Shana Cohen and Ross Harris, also performed many a vital task.

Emily Burke spent invaluable time and energy researching, acquiring, and gaining permission for the beautiful historical photos published in this book. Anne-Laure Treny gave us much-needed assistance in translating the witty prose of Erhard Loretan's memoir.

Last but not least, thanks to Tom Hornbein, not only for writing the introduction to the book, but also for showing all of us what's humanly possible in the example of his amazing ascent of Everest's West Ridge with Willi Unsoeld in 1963. We can all learn from Tom's humility and thoughtfulness. I thank him for his contribution and friendship.

Bibliography

Anker, Conrad, and David Roberts. *The Lost Explorer: Finding Mallory on Mount Everest.* New York, 1999.

Béghin, Pierre. "Everest, The Hornbein Couloir Direct from Tibet," *The American Alpine Journal,* vol. 29, 1987.

Bonington, Chris. *Everest the Hard Way.* London, 1976.

Boukreev, Anatoli. *Above the Clouds.* New York, 2001.

Boukreev, Anatoli, with G. Weston DeWalt. *The Climb.* New York, 1998.

Breashears, David. *High Exposure.* New York, 1999.

Brniak, Marek, and Józef Nyka. "Two Polish Ascents of Everest," *The American Alpine Journal,* vol. 23, 1981.

Carter, H. Adams. "Mount Everest from the North," *The American Alpine Journal,* vol. XII, 1961.

Douglas, Ed. *Tenzing: Hero of Everest.* Washington, DC, 2003.

Dyhrenfurth, Norman G., and William F. Unsoeld. "Mount Everest, 1963," *The American Alpine Journal,* vol. XIV, 1964.

Gillman, Peter, and Leni Gillman. *The Wildest Dream: Mallory: His Life and Conflicting Passions.* London, 2000.

Haston, Dougal. *In High Places.* London, 1972.

Hillary, Sir Edmund. *High Adventure.* London, 1955.

Hornbein, Thomas. *Everest: The West Ridge.* San Francisco, 1965.

Hunt, Sir John. *The Ascent of Everest.* London, 1953.

Krakauer, Jon. *Into Thin Air.* New York, 1997.

Loretan, Erhard, with Jean Amman. *Les 8000 Rugissants.* Fribourg, Switzerland, 1996.

McDonald, Bernadette. *Freedom Climbers.* Victoria, British Columbia, 2011.

Messner, Reinhold. *The Crystal Horizon: Everest—The First Solo Ascent.* Seattle, 1989.

Morris, James. *Coronation Everest.* London, 1958.

Morrissey, James D. "Kangshung Face of Everest," *The American Alpine Journal,* vol. 26, 1984.

Norton, Colonel Edward F., et al. *The Fight for Everest: 1924.* London, 1925.

Noyce, Wilfrid. *South Col.* London, 1954.

Roberts, David. "50 Years on Everest," *National Geographic Adventure,* April 2003.

Shipton, Eric. *That Untravelled World.* London, 1969.

Simonson, Eric. "Everest Attempt Via the Great Couloir," *The American Alpine Journal,* vol. 30, 1988.

Tabin, Geoffrey. "The Kangshung Face of Everest," *The American Alpine Journal,* vol. 24, 1982.

Tilman, H. W. *Mount Everest: 1938.* Cambridge, U. K., 1948.

———. *The Ascent of Nanda Devi.* Cambridge, U. K., 1937.

Ullman, James Ramsey. *Americans on Everest.* Philadelphia, 1964.

Unsworth, Walt. *Everest: The Mountaineering History.* Seattle, 2000 (third edition).

Viesturs, Ed. "Everest Attempt," *The American Alpine Journal,* vol. 36, 1994.

Viesturs, Ed, with David Roberts. *K2: Life and Death on the World's Most Dangerous Mountain.* New York, 2009.

———. *No Shortcuts to the Top: Climbing the World's 14 Highest Peaks.* New York, 2006.

———. *The Will to Climb: Obsession and Commitment and the Quest to Climb Annapurna—the World's Deadliest Peak.* New York, 2011.

Whittaker, Jim. *A Life on the Edge.* Seattle, 2000.

———. "Everest International Peace Climb," *The American Alpine Journal,* vol. 33, 1991.

Wielicki, Krzysztof. *Crown of the Himalaya: 14 x 8000.* Kraków, Poland, 1997.

Index